Postcard History Series

Fayette County

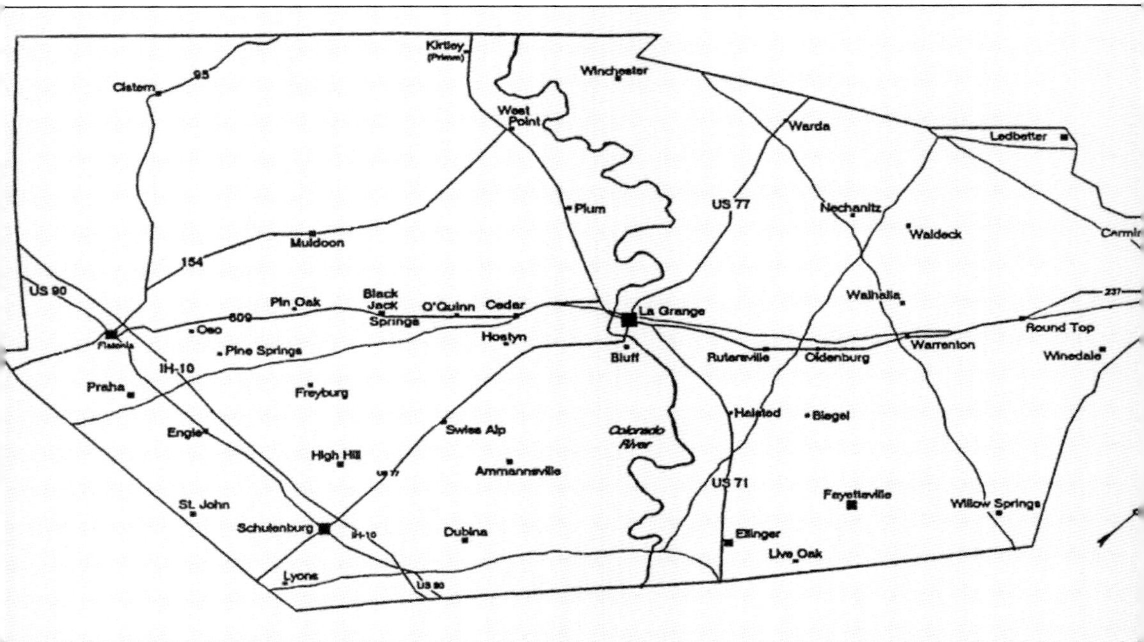

Map of Fayette County, Texas. This map of Fayette County, Texas, shows major towns, minor communities, and primary roads. (Gary E. McKee.)

On the Front Cover: High School La Grange, Texas. Here is the Casino Building, also known as La Grange High School and La Grange City Hall. Completed in 1881, this building served La Grange as its first high school, where the mascot was the wildcat and the school colors were orange and black. This structure can be seen in an 1880 bird's-eye view map by Augustus Koch. The building still stands on the corner of North Fannin and East La Fayette Streets. (Gary E. McKee.)

On the Back Cover: Greetings from Bluff, Texas. Bluff was a community of German and Czech settlers, inhabiting the area from the outcrop overlooking the Colorado River, south to Williams Creek and west to Hostyn. Bluff's borders often included nearby Cedar, O'Quinn, and Black Jack Springs. Early settlers included the Willrich and Kreische families, who lived on the Bluff itself, and the Fietsam, Laux, Albrecht, Lueders, Hausmann, Otto, Ganzer, Merrem, and Munke families, who lived on the prairie south of the Bluff, many of which are buried in Bluff Cemetery, now known as Williams Creek Cemetery. (Gary E. McKee.)

POSTCARD HISTORY SERIES

Fayette County

Jon Todd "JT" Koenig

ARCADIA
PUBLISHING

ISBN 978-0-7385-8486-7

Published by Arcadia Publishing
Charleston, South Carolina

Printed in the United States of America

Library of Congress Control Number: 2011923772

For all general information contact Arcadia Publishing at:
Telephone 843-853-2070
Fax 843-853-0044
E-mail sales@arcadiapublishing.com
For customer service and orders:
Toll-Free 1-888-313-2665

Visit us on the Internet at www.arcadiapublishing.com

This book is dedicated to three women, without whom this volume would not have come about: Elva Oeding Koenig (1912–2003), Margaret Munke Oeding (1890–1971), and Sophie Struve Pohl (1872–1952), the author's grandmother, great-grandmother, and great-grandaunt, respectively. Their postcard collections were the genesis of this book.

Contents

ACKNOWLEDGMENTS

As with any significant effort such as was expended with this book, the writer cannot take all of the credit. There have been many who assisted me, not the least of which are those who graciously allowed me to use their postcards. These persons' names are noted throughout, and I want to express my humblest gratitude for their generosity. In addition to these individual contributors, I also wish to credit those institutions whose collections are included herein and which have collaborated with me on this project.

The images of the von Rosenberg family of Texas collection have enhanced many of this book's chapters. Kathy Carter and the Fayette Heritage Museum & Archives was of immense help, as were archivists Donna Green and Sherie Knape. The Texas Czech Heritage and Cultural Center's library in La Grange was a wealth of information. Finally, the E.A. Arnim Archives and Museum of Flatonia catapulted my efforts beyond what I had imagined I could accomplish, and I wish to single out the generous collaboration provided to me by its board of directors, and especially Judy Pate.

In addition to the above, I want to acknowledge the support I have received from Michael Speck, who willingly joined me in postcard hunts and research trips; from my grandmother Mildred Willmann Todd, who hosted my frequent visits to La Grange; and from my parents, Rodney and Rebeca Koenig, who foster my passion for history and are the reason why I am here to enjoy it. My sincerest thanks go to all of the above.

INTRODUCTION

I was born in Austin and grew up in Houston. Despite this, Fayette County is my touchstone. I have lived in numerous Texas cities, as well as overseas, and I currently live in Poulsbo, Washington. In the end, however, I consider Fayette County my true home. Why is this? The answer is, in a word, family.

I was blessed with the best of both worlds growing up. My father's parents, John and Elva Koenig, lived in the country on a farm near O'Quinn. My mother's father and stepmother, B.E. and Mildred Todd, lived in La Grange. Often on weekends, holidays, and summers, my brother and I were with our grandparents in Fayette County. Through their influence, we were exposed to the culture that still pervades Fayette County today. We visited with friends and family in Fayetteville and Schulenburg. We enjoyed feasts in Ammansville and High Hill and attended church in Swiss Alp and La Grange. We took part in reunions, weddings, funerals, bible schools, and county fairs. In the country, I picked dewberries and mustang grapes along the roadside, fished in tanks, and took cattle to auction. In town, we frequented the old library and learned how to swim in the La Grange pool. All of these memories were treasures.

As I grew older, I lost interest, focusing only on the here and now. It was not until my older relatives began to pass away, that I wondered again about all those people I had heard about, whose names I could not remember. This was the impetus for me to start searching. I visited my relatives again. I strolled through cemeteries and searched the county clerk's office, and slowly, I began to put the picture back together.

My Grandmother Koenig once admonished me to be careful what I said in public because you never knew who was listening. She said if you threw a rock, chances are you would hit a relative. Through 10 years of genealogical research, I now know she was right, as the families of Fayette County are intricately linked through blood, marriage, and shared experience. In seeking to understand who my family was, I have learned much about how they lived and how their lives impacted the history of Fayette County and Texas. Whether they were "old-time Americans" or German or Czech immigrants, the people of Fayette County overcame many struggles as strangers in a new world. In this volume, I have attempted to show snippets of those pioneers' lives.

Assuredly, I have missed opportunities to speak to certain aspects of Fayette County's history; however, this volume is not intended to be a definitive history book. I have let the postcards guide me, and where they opened a window, I have taken a snapshot and relayed that image as best I can. Undoubtedly, there will be mistakes, and for these I ask the reader's forgiveness. My hope is that through piquing the reader's interest, they will be encouraged to explore their own ancestry, and Fayette County's collective history will be cherished and preserved.

One

Monument Hill
The Spirit of Fayette County

The shell-stone cenotaph with its colored plaster mural, atop the Bluff, was created in 1936 by Pierre Bourdelle. Its Art Deco bronze angel, by Raoul Josset, pays tribute to the Fayette County men who were lost in the Dawson Massacre and the Mier Expedition.

Following Texas's independence at the Battle of San Jacinto in 1836, in which many Fayette County men participated, Mexico continued to lay claim to its former territory, resulting in numerous incursions into Texas by the Mexican Army. On September 11, 1842, under the command of Gen. Adrian Woll, the Mexican Army attacked San Antonio and captured what were deemed rebellious traitors but who were, in fact, patriots of the sovereign Republic of Texas. Hearing this, many local men mustered under the Historic Oak in the La Grange town square. On September 16, 1842, under the leadership of Nicholas Mosby Dawson, they left to aid San Antonio's plight.

Traveling over 100 miles in less than two days, and collecting volunteers along the way, the company met Woll's forces at Salado Creek on September 18, 1842. Woll's cavalry mercilessly fired upon Dawson, killing 36 of his men, including Dawson, before retreating to the Rio Grande. Capt. William Mosby Eastland, Dawson's cousin and a Fayette volunteer, arrived at the massacre site too late to save the victims. He buried the dead on the banks of Salado Creek where they fell.

Later that year on Christmas Day, retribution-seeking Texans crossed over the Rio Grande into Mexico and occupied the border town of Mier. A larger and stronger Mexican force, under the command of Gen. Pedro de Ampudia, surrounded these Texans and forced their surrender on December 26, 1842. After being held in Matamoros, they were marched to Monterrey, then Saltillo, and then farther south toward Mexico City. Pres. Santa Anna, shamed by his defeat at San Jacinto, ordered a lottery be held to decimate one-tenth of the prisoners. The prisoners chose beans from a clay jar, and those who drew the black bean were executed and buried in the village of Cedral.

Despite the passage of many years, the men of the Mier Expedition were not forgotten. Taking advantage of the US Army's presence near Cedral during the waning days of the Mexican-American War, Mier Expedition survivor Capt. John Dusenberry gathered the bones of the executed men and brought them back to Texas. The remains were brought to La Grange, the home of the only officer who drew a black bean, Capt. William Mosby Eastland. The residents of La Grange were so moved by this that the remains of the Dawson Massacre victims were also retrieved from their grave at Salado Creek and brought home to Fayette County. So on September 18, 1848, the people of La Grange laid their heroes to rest once again in sacred ground atop the sandstone bluff overlooking their city.

The original vault, built in 1848 by Heinrich Kreische, was simple in design and constructed of sandstone. A more permanent mausoleum was pursued through various efforts, however, these efforts came to naught. Thus, the heroes slumbered in their modest crypt for many years with little notice or care, except that of the Kreische family, who acquired the land the tomb was located on. In 1904, after maintenance funds were not regularly provided to them, the Kreische family catalyzed the purchase of the tomb by the State of Texas.

In the 1930s, the state became involved again and decided the tomb should be moved to Austin's State Cemetery to be better looked after. This decision motivated La Grange's populace again. In 1933, sufficient funds were collected to repair the tomb and to provide a new granite enclosure. In 1936, the tomb was joined by the 48-foot shaft, which now draws so many to the site. This is an example of what sacrifice and bravery brings, and the continuing efforts of the people of La Grange—periodic though they may have been—show that while heroism may not always be praised on a daily basis, it is remembered, and shall forever be, in the tributes that places like Monument Hill represent.

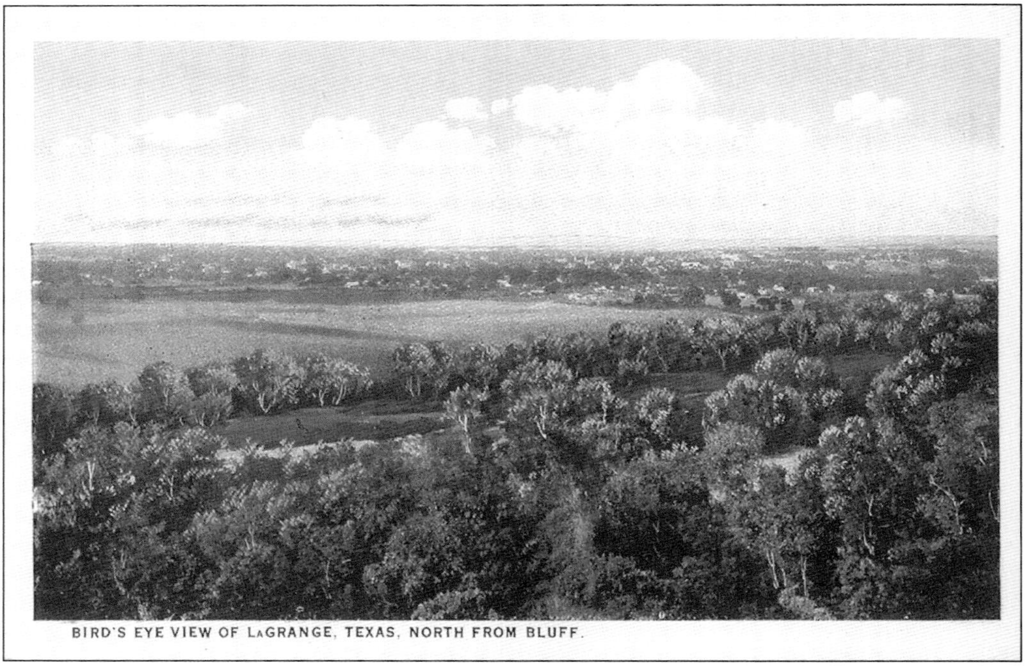

Bird's Eye View of La Grange, Texas, North from Bluff. The Bluff, a sandstone outcropping forming the northern end of the geologic feature known as the Oakville Escarpment, sits at the Colorado River's bend where La Grange has nestled since its founding in 1837. (Author's collection.)

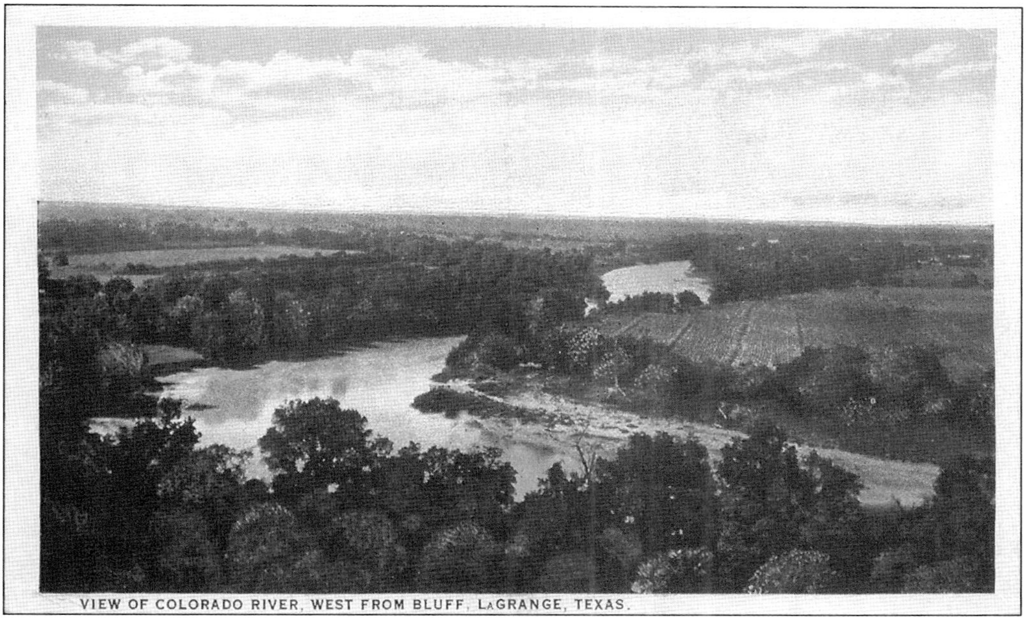

View of Colorado River, West from Bluff, La Grange, Texas. Here is a view from the Bluff looking north towards the area of Dancy's Bluff, alongside the Colorado River to La Grange's west. (Author's collection.)

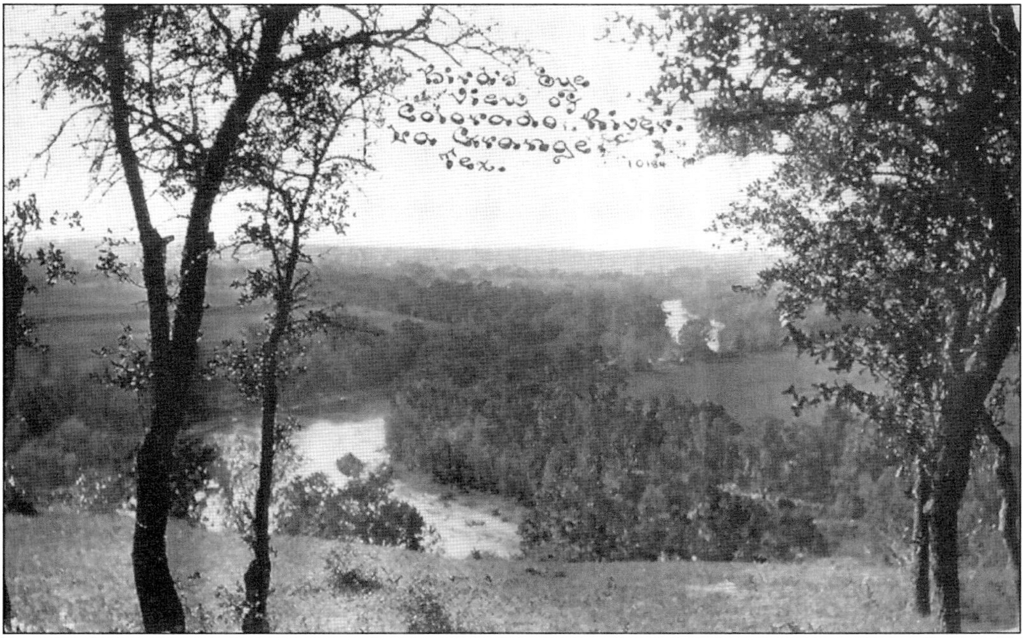

Bird's-Eye View of Colorado River, La Grange, Tex. This is another view from atop the Bluff of the Colorado River valley, some 200 feet below. (Author's collection.)

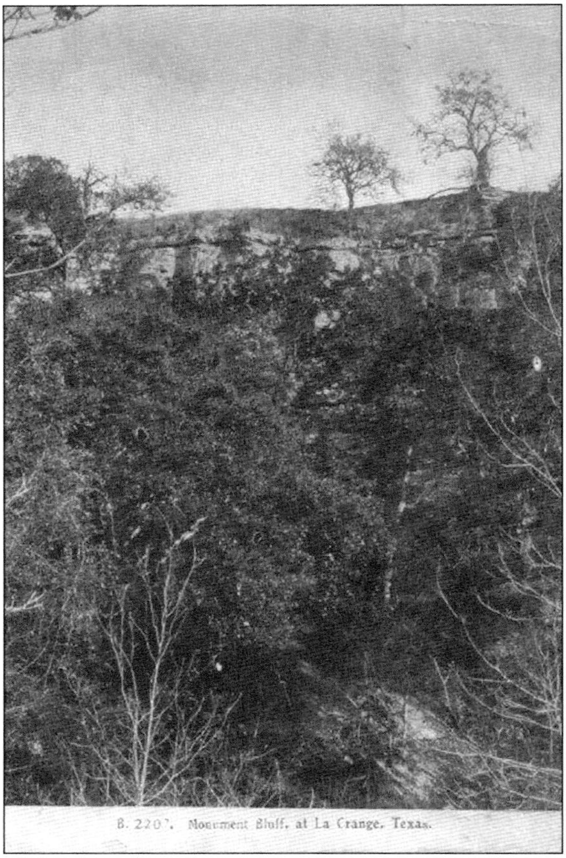

Monument Bluff, at La Grange, Texas. Here is a view of Monument Hill from the vantage point of looking up from the banks of the Colorado River. (A. Neale Rabensburg.)

Highway 72, Showing Colorado River Bridge in Distance, La Grange, Texas. Shown is Highway 77 as it makes its way up the Bluff. This road was built in 1926, as was the bridge in the background. Prior to 1926, the path to the river was a gravel road through what are today the Monument Hill and Kreische Brewery State Historic Sites. This prior road was built in part by Heinrich Kreische, whose home and brewery business were located atop the Bluff. (Fayette Heritage Museum & Archives.)

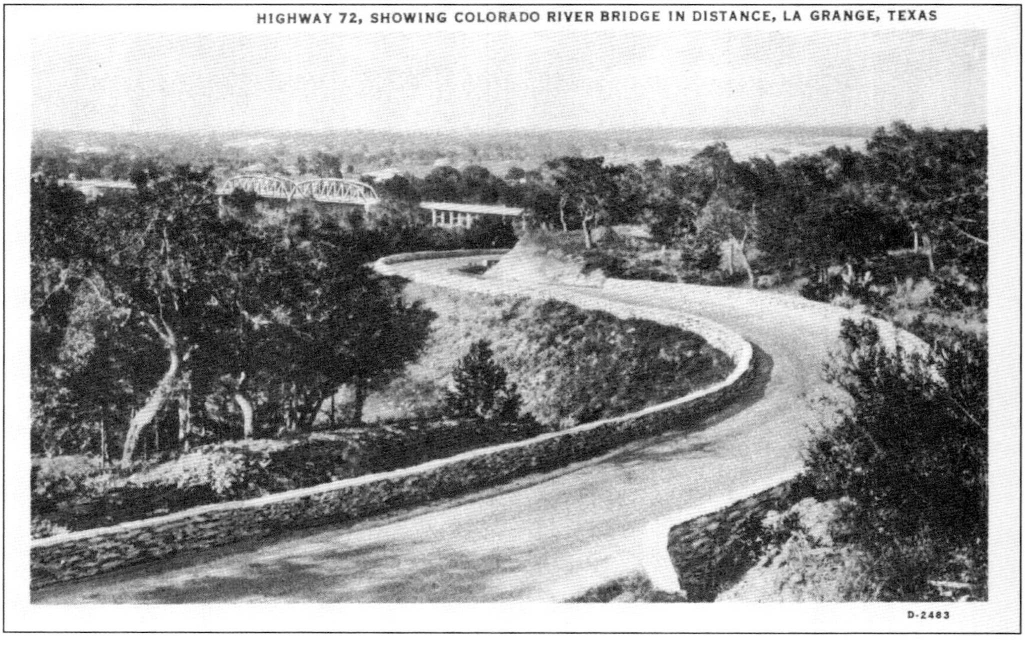

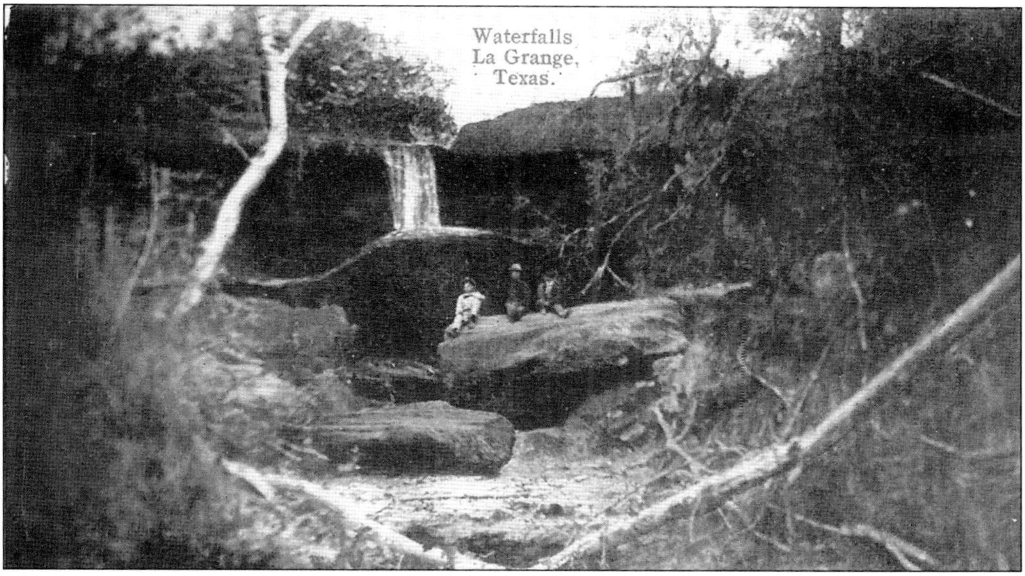

WATERFALLS, LA GRANGE, TEXAS. The sandstone of the Bluff soaks in a great deal of liquid, however, during heavy rains, streams, such as Buckner's Creek just west of the Bluff, can often become filled with roiling waters. The waterfall pictured here is likely in the area of the Colorado River's bend southwest of La Grange and is similar to the artesians water sources Heinrich Kreische harnessed in his brewing operations in the 1870s and 1880s. (Carolyn Heinsohn.)

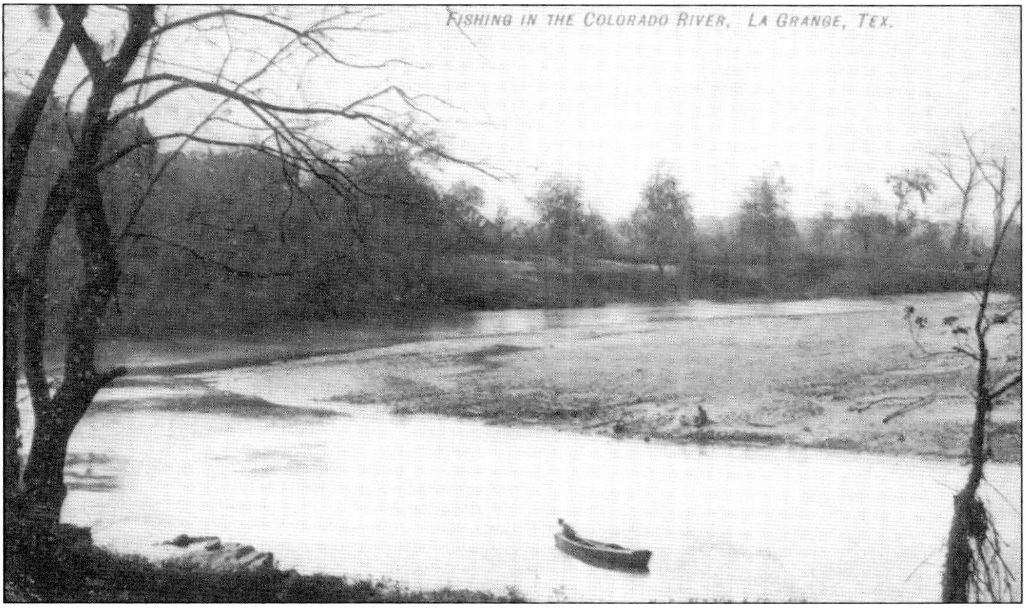

FISHING IN COLORADO RIVER, LA GRANGE, TEXAS. A fishermen appears along the riverbank just below the Bluff. In addition to catfish, bass is found there. The Colorado's origins lie in West Texas, near Lamesa and Big Spring, and at its confluence with the Concho, San Saba, Llano, and Pedernales Rivers in the Hill Country. The river has flooded several times, most notably in 1869, 1913, and 1938. The 1913 flood was so great that the river merged with the Brazos River, creating a lake 65 miles wide. (Gary E. McKee.)

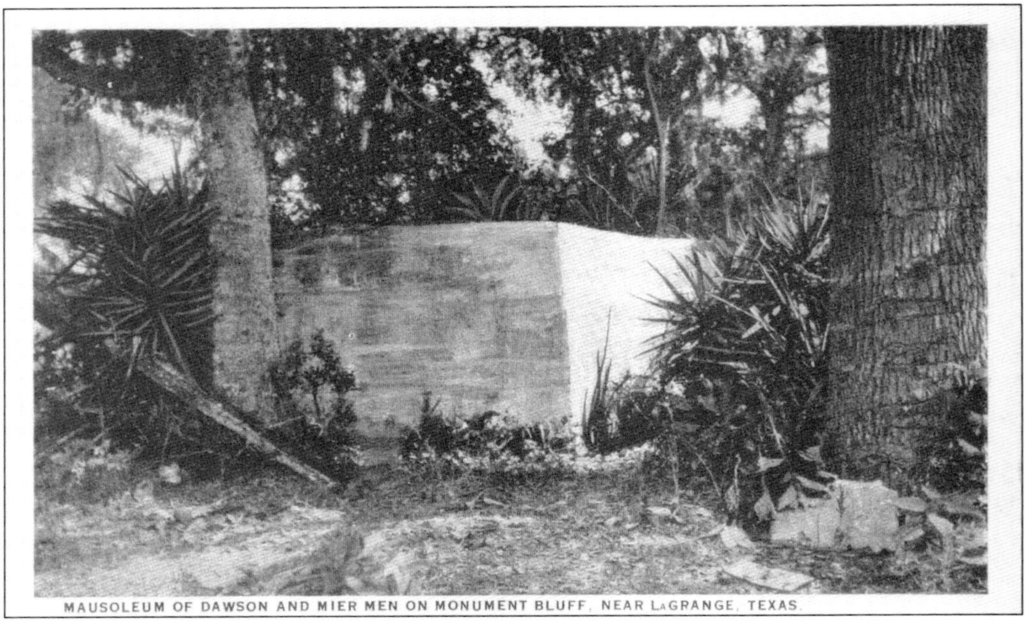

MAUSOLEUM OF DAWSON AND MIER MEN ON MONUMENT BLUFF, NEAR LA GRANGE, TEXAS. Following the massacres of the Dawson and Mier Expeditions, attempts to collect the remains of those who perished were thwarted until the Mexican-American War (1846–1848) allowed for the heroes' bones to be collected from their graves in the cemetery at Cedral, Mexico (where the Mier Expedition men who drew the black beans were buried), and the banks of Salado Creek (where Dawson and his men had been hastily buried). (Gary E. McKee.)

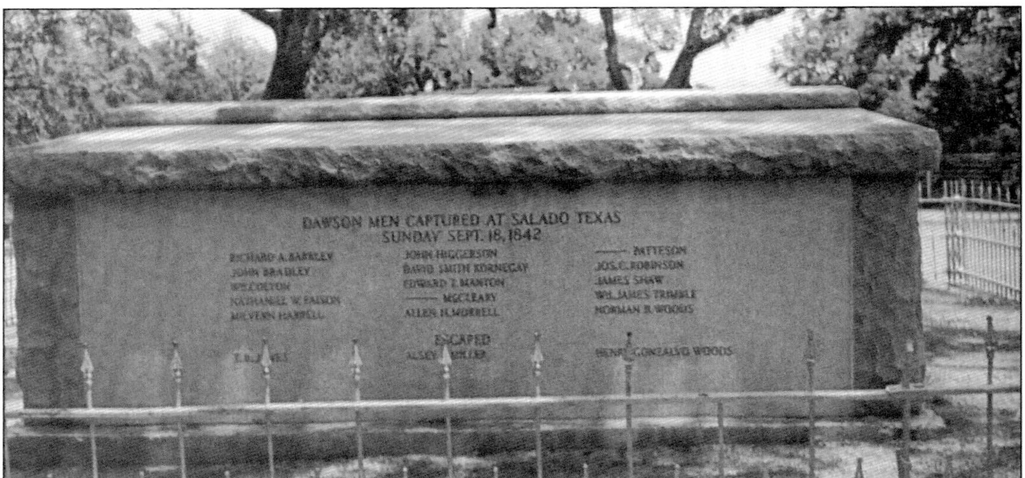

TOMB OF DAWSON MEN. After the initial sandstone tomb was built in 1848, the Monumental Committee was formed to raise funds for a permanent structure, and the *Texas Monument* newspaper was created to aid the cause. In 1856, these efforts morphed into a college called the Texas Monumental and Military Institute, which took over Rutersville College, north of La Grange. Because the funds raised were used for the college instead of a new tomb, the original tomb suffered until 1933, when the Daughters of the Republic of Texas helped erect the current granite enclosure. (Gary E. McKee.)

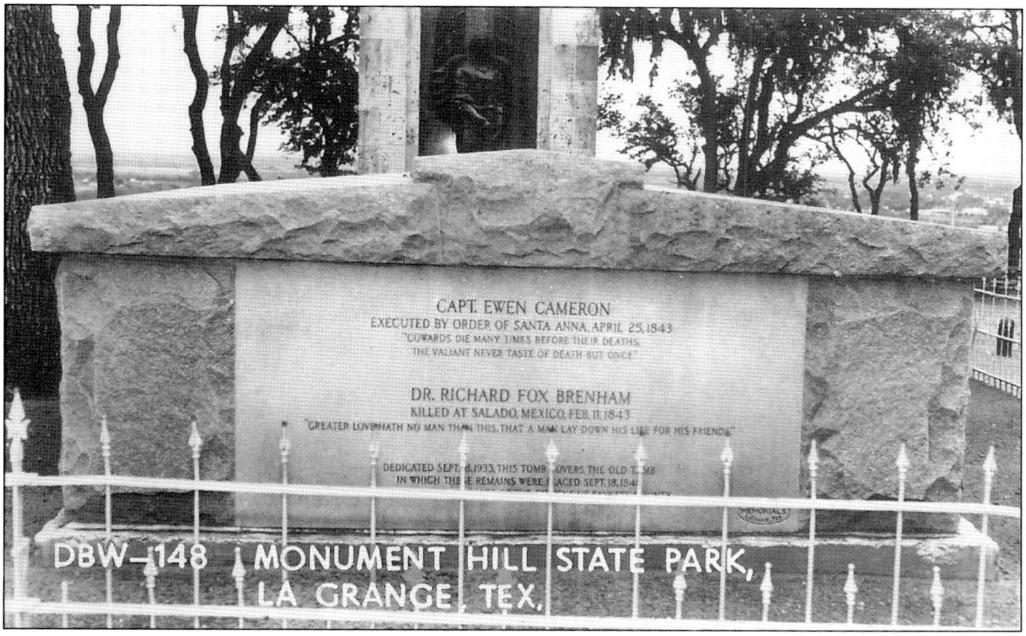

Monument Hill State Park, La Grange, Tex. Capt. Ewen Cameron (1811–1843) was executed by order of then Mexican president Antonio Lopez de Santa Anna (1794–1876). Cameron drew a white bean during the infamous black bean episode, in which those who drew such were doomed to death by firing squad, but Cameron had angered his Mexican captors for his role in prior escape attempts. He was shot by firing squad at Perote Prison near Vera Cruz on April 26, 1843. (Author's collection.)

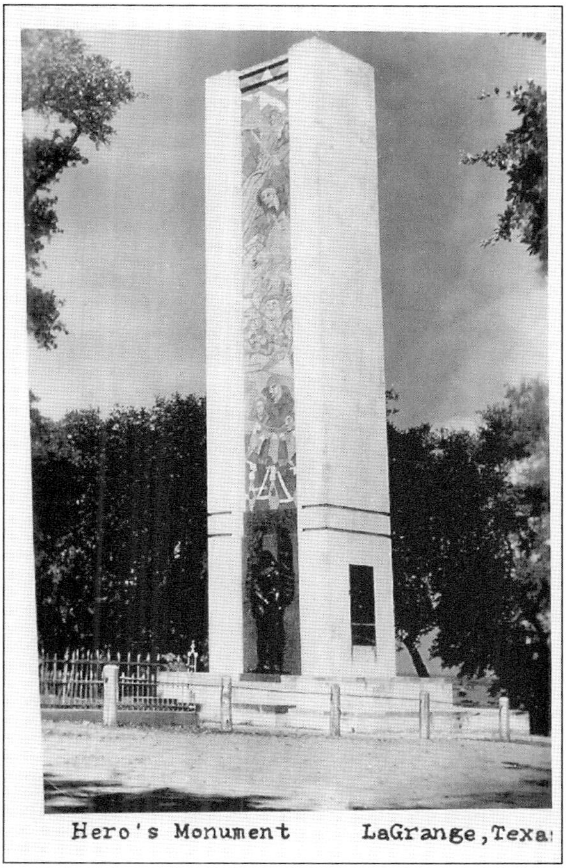

Hero's Monument La Grange, Texas. During Texas's centennial in 1936, the residents of Fayette County erected a 48-feet-tall shell-stone cenotaph adjacent to the tomb of the Dawson and Mier heroes. The shaft was an Art Deco design with a mural depicting the events that led up to the deaths of those interred in the tomb. The mural was created by Pierre van Parys Bourdelle (1901–1966), and the bronze angel was created by Raoul Jean Josset (1899–1957). (Author's collection.)

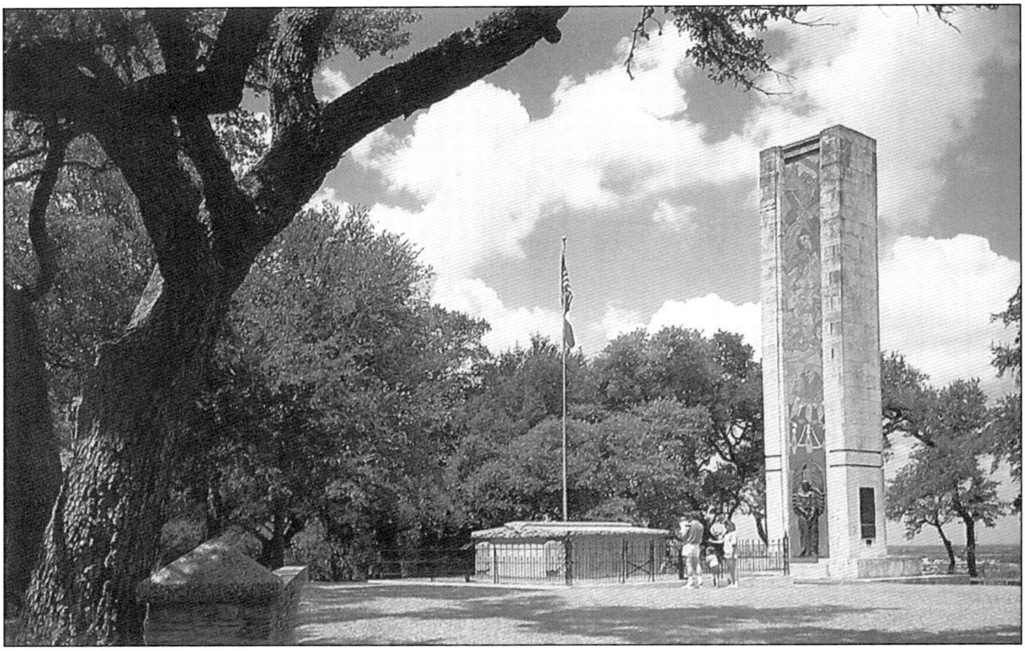

MONUMENT HILL MONUMENT AND TOMB IN SPRING. Depicted is a uniquely Texas view from about 1975, encompassing both the tomb and the 1936 monument, which Fayette County takes great pride in. (Author's collection.)

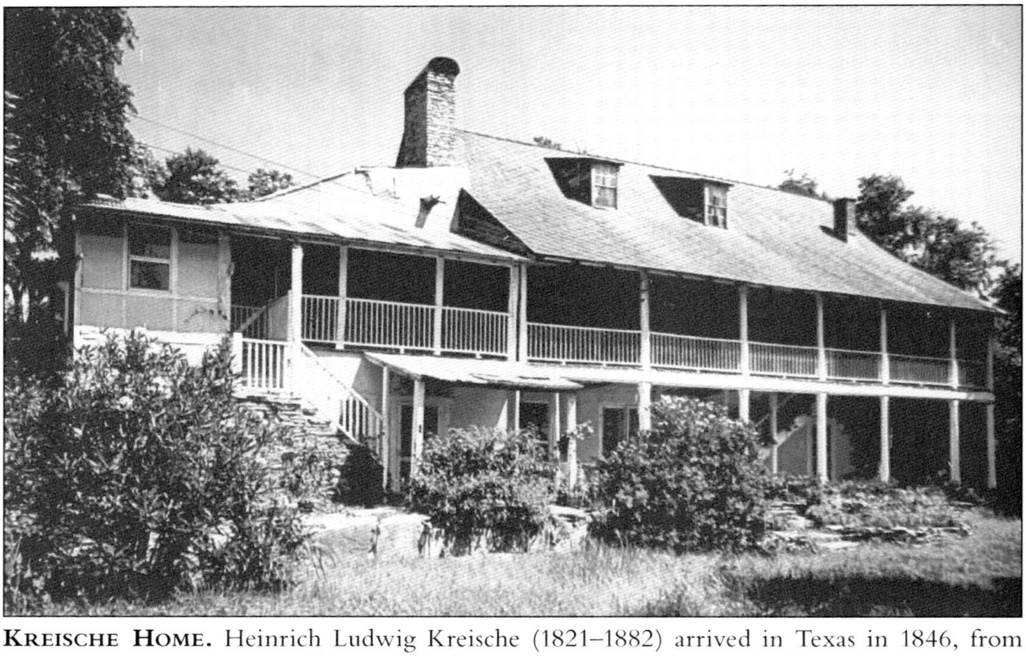

KREISCHE HOME. Heinrich Ludwig Kreische (1821–1882) arrived in Texas in 1846, from Saxony, Germany. In 1849, Kreische purchased 172 acres of land on the Bluff from Georg Carl Willrich (1798–1876), including the land on which the Martyrs' Tomb was located. There, Kreische settled and built the home shown here in stages, after his 1855 marriage to Josefa Appelt (1833–1906). (Fayette Heritage Museum & Archives.)

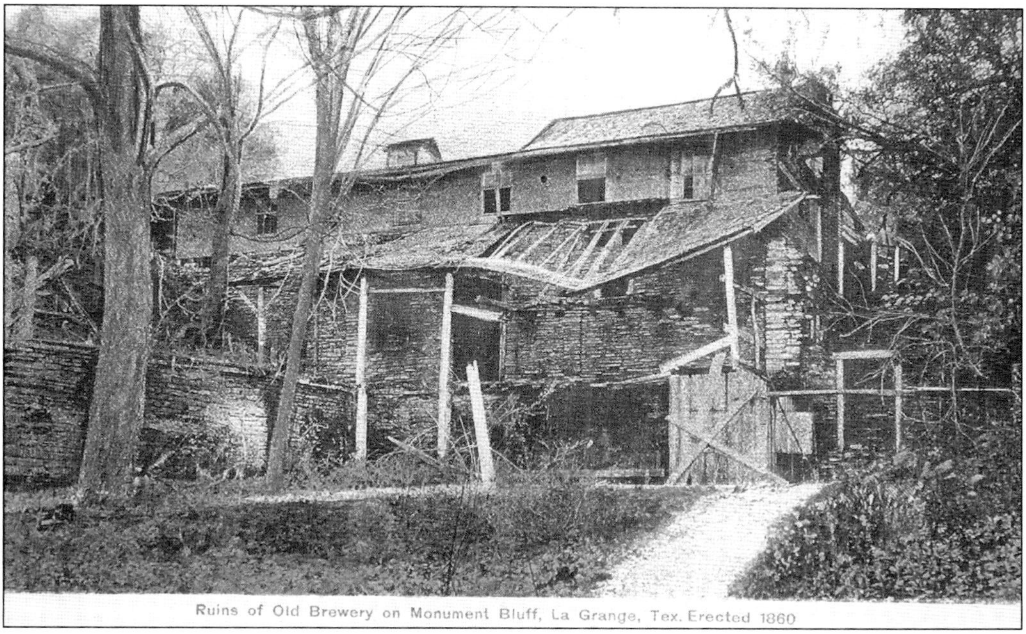

RUINS OF OLD BREWERY ON MONUMENT BLUFF, LA GRANGE, TEX. ERECTED 1860. In the late 1860s, Kreische began operating a brewery on additional acreage he purchased in 1866. The brewery's design used local topography, allowing gravity to assist the brewing process using the area's natural artesian water. The brewery was ranked third in Texas in output, with 774 barrels of beer produced in 1878. Operations continued until 1884, when competition from national brewers, coupled with Kreische's death in 1882, caused the brewery to close. (Author's collection.)

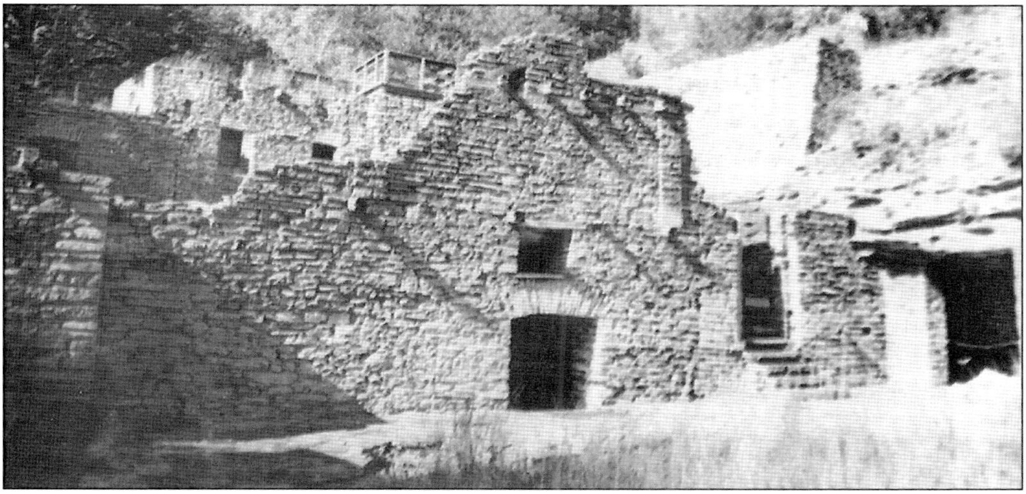

KREISCHE BREWERY RUINS. Shown is a current picture of the Kreische brewery ruins. The Kreisches lived in their home located up the ravine from the brewery until Julia Kreische's death on September 21, 1952. Thereafter, the home, brewery, and land upon which they stood were gifted to the nearby Queen of the Holy Rosary Catholic Parish of Hostyn. The property on which the Kreische home and brewery stood was transferred to the Texas Parks and Wildlife Department in 1977. (Author's collection.)

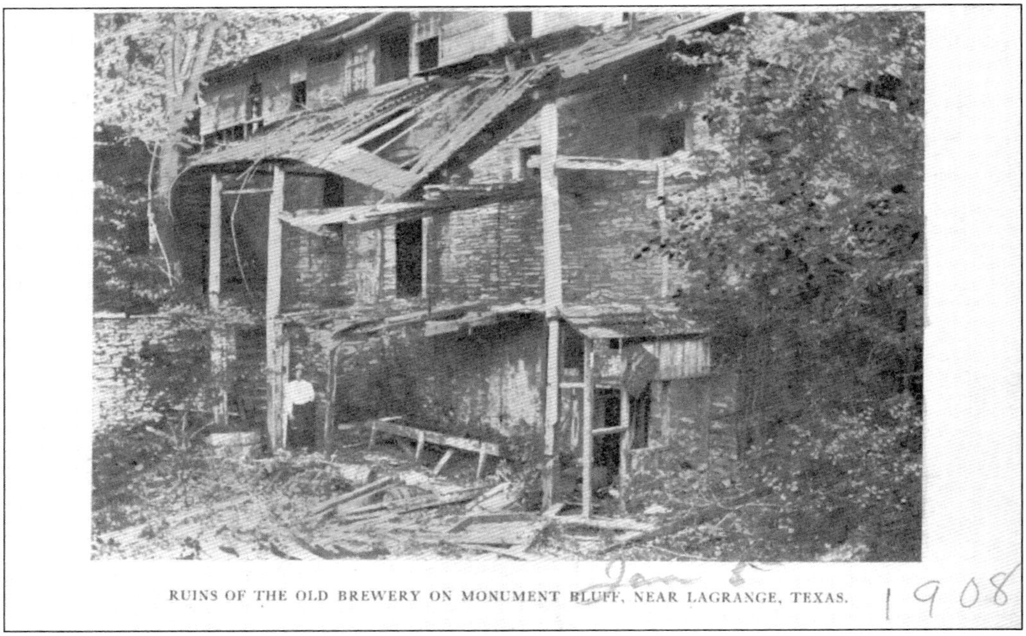

RUINS OF THE OLD BREWERY ON MONUMENT BLUFF, NEAR LA GRANGE, TEXAS. Yet another view is pictured of the dilapidated brewery ruins, which deteriorated rapidly following Heinrich Kreische's death. (Gary E. McKee.)

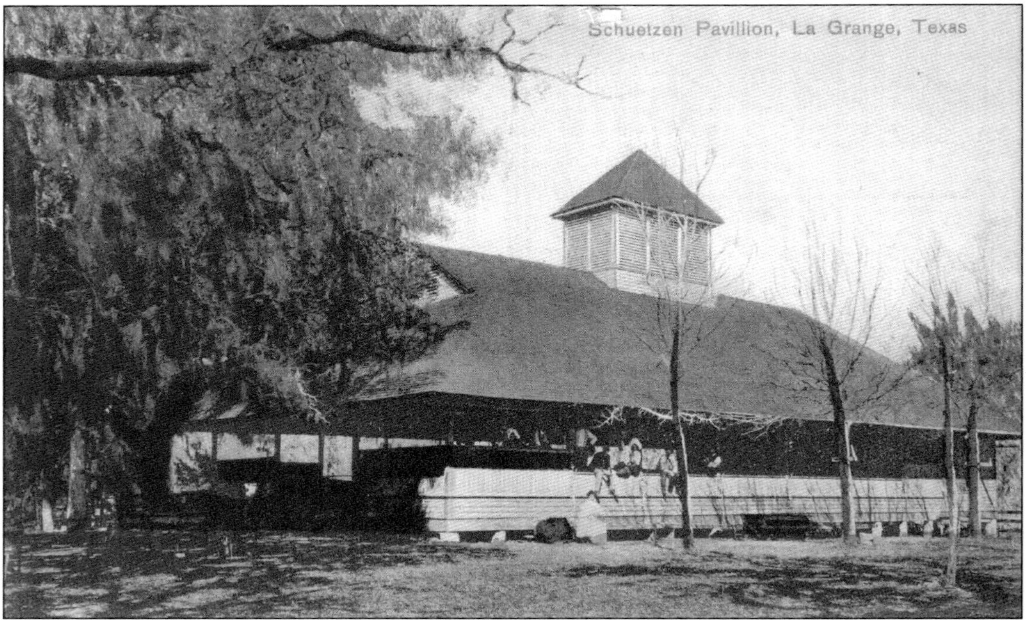

SCHUETZEN PAVILION, LA GRANGE, TEXAS. The Bluff Schuetzen Verein (shooting club), pictured here, was built and operated by Heinrich Kreische, on whose land it was situated. The building attracted people to Kreische's nearby brewery. The structure was used for dances, shooting club meetings, and other entertainments. (Gary E. McKee.)

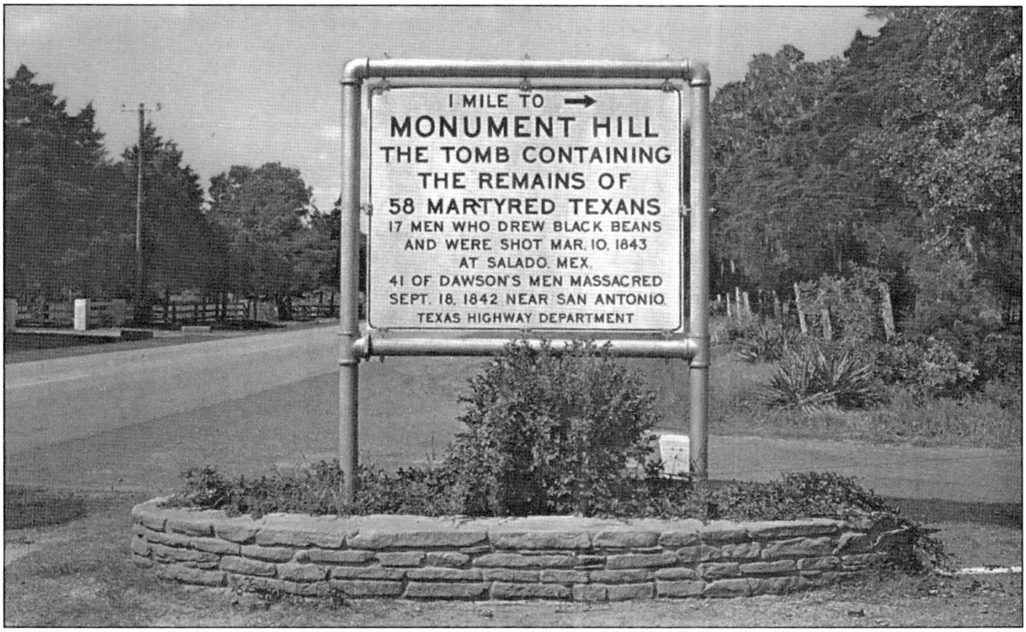

TEXAS HIGHWAY DEPARTMENT SIGN. Shown is the old sign leading the way to Monument Hill and the Martyrs' Tomb. (Gary E. McKee.)

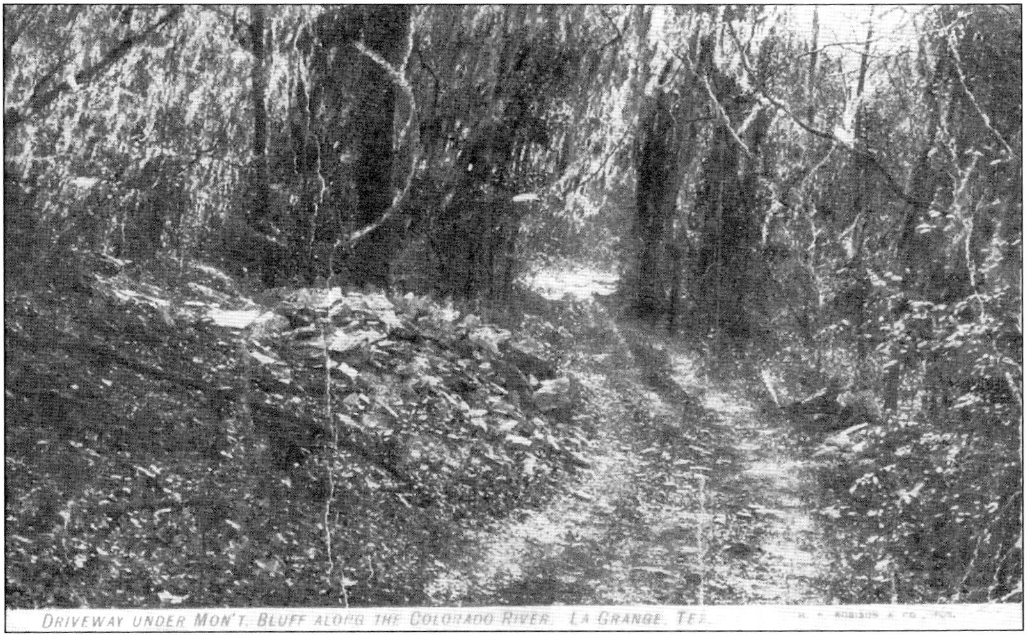

DRIVEWAY UNDER MON'T. BLUFF ALONG THE COLORADO RIVER, LA GRANGE, TEX. In addition to his home, brewery, and other buildings in and around La Grange, including the third courthouse, Kreische constructed road improvements on his property atop the Bluff, which are visible here. The original Bluff road crossed through Kreische's property, went past the brewery, and down to the river, where Kreische ran a ferry to allow travelers passage across the Colorado River to La Grange. (Gary E. McKee.)

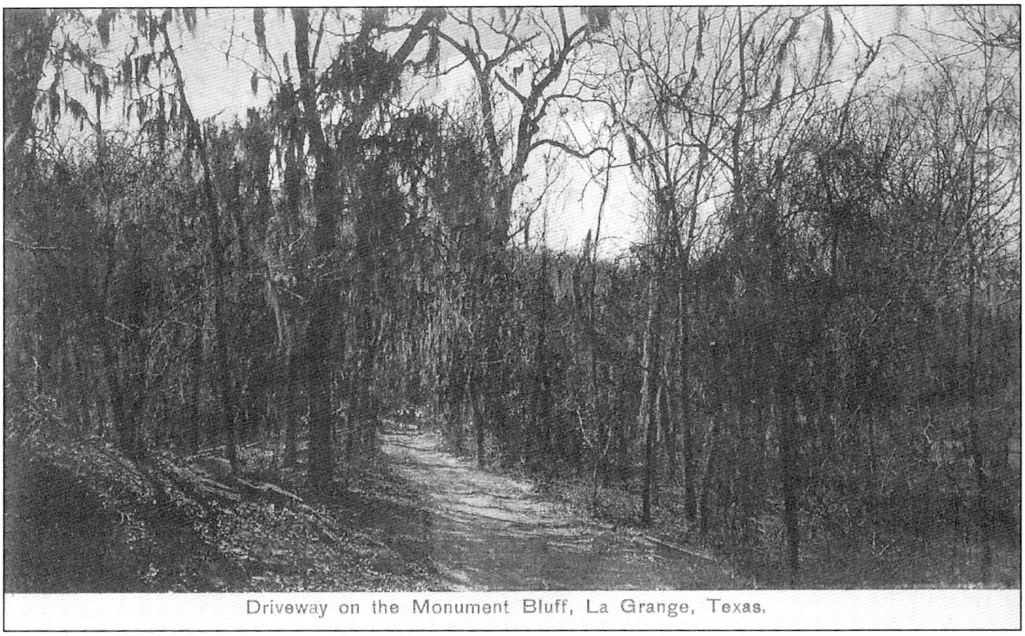

DRIVEWAY ON THE MONUMENT BLUFF, LA GRANGE, TEXAS. Kreische used this road to deliver his "Bluff Beer" to the river. Along his road, Kreische built culverts, small bridges, and water diversion devices, which can still be seen today. Part of the road has been cleared and can again be enjoyed as an interpretive trail in the Kreische Brewery State Historic Site. (Author's collection.)

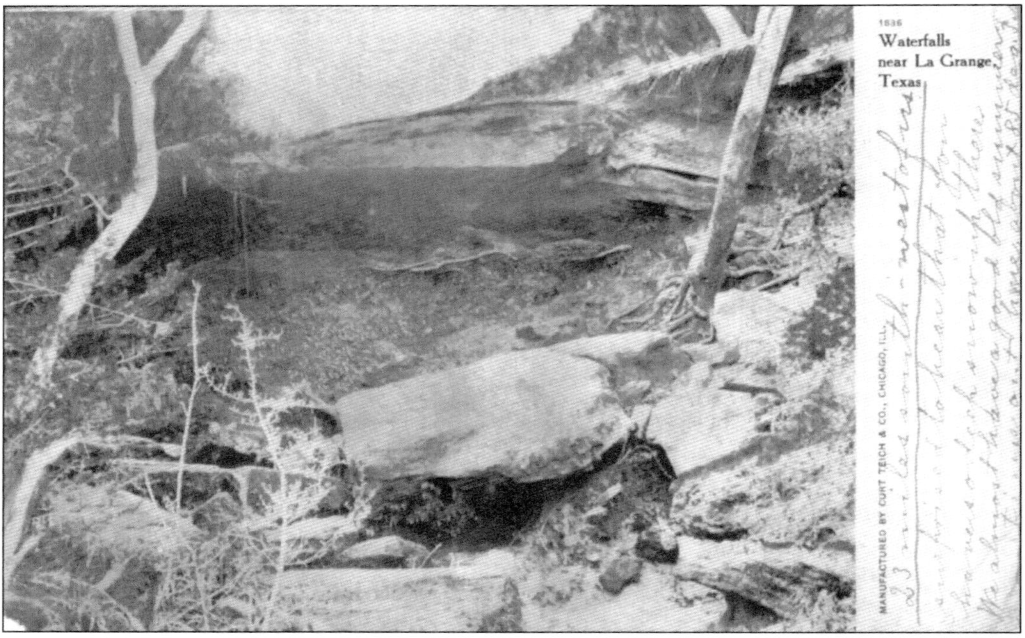

WATERFALLS NEAR LA GRANGE, TEXAS. A view of a dry creek bed on the Bluff, similar to those which were used by the Kreisches and other Bluff inhabitants for their water supply, is pictured above. (Gary E. McKee.)

Two

La Grange
The County Seat

As late as the 1820s, the area of La Grange was home to the Native American Tonkawa tribe. The Tonkawa were skilled horsemen and hunters. Tonkawan men were fierce warriors, and the women were known for their physical strength and invincible spirit. In short, those who settled Fayette County found themselves neighbors to an outwardly friendly but often volatile native populace. Despite early camaraderie, by 1859, the Tonkawa were deemed a "nuisance" and were removed.

During this early period, more and more Americans settled in Fayette County. Among the first was Col. John Henry Moore (1800–1880), who founded the county's primary settlement in 1831 after purchasing the land on the Colorado River, across from Buckner's Creek (which is named after Aylett "Strap" Buckner). The homestead called Moore's Fort, comprised of a single-room cabin and a twin blockhouse, would later become La Grange. A small community grew up around Moore's Fort, and in 1837, a town site was platted opposite the picturesque sandstone bluff.

The actual creation of a formal political entity did not happen until after Texas's independence. On December 14, 1837, the Congress of the Republic of Texas created Fayette County, naming it after the Revolutionary War hero Gilbert du Motier, the Marquis de la Fayette (1757–1834). The new town site was designated the county seat and was named La Grange, after the Chateau de la Grange-Bleneau, the ancestral home of the marquis's wife, Adrienne de Noailles de la Fayette (1759–1807); du Motier spent his last years there. So influential were La Grange's early residents that the new city was chosen as the site of the Republic of Texas's capital city. However, because of Pres. Sam Houston's veto, that honor went to a town then called Waterloo, later named Austin. La Grange was officially incorporated in 1850.

Initially, a homogenous society of Anglo settlers, mainly from the American South, inhabited La Grange. However, the city's cultural make-up changed in the 1840s and 1850s with the arrival of immigrants from the various German states that were undergoing significant changes of their own as a result of the Revolutions of 1848. This trend of diversity increased when Czech immigrants joined their German counterparts in the 1850s and 1860s, and the influx of European immigrants continued in this pattern well into the second decade of the 20th century, until World War I.

The arrival of all of these European immigrants—and the traditions these families instilled in their Texas descendants—coupled with the long, proud heritage left to the inhabitants of Fayette County by the Americans who had came earlier, created a unique environment. La Grange is a prime example of this vibrant, multicultural community that cherishes its historic roots.

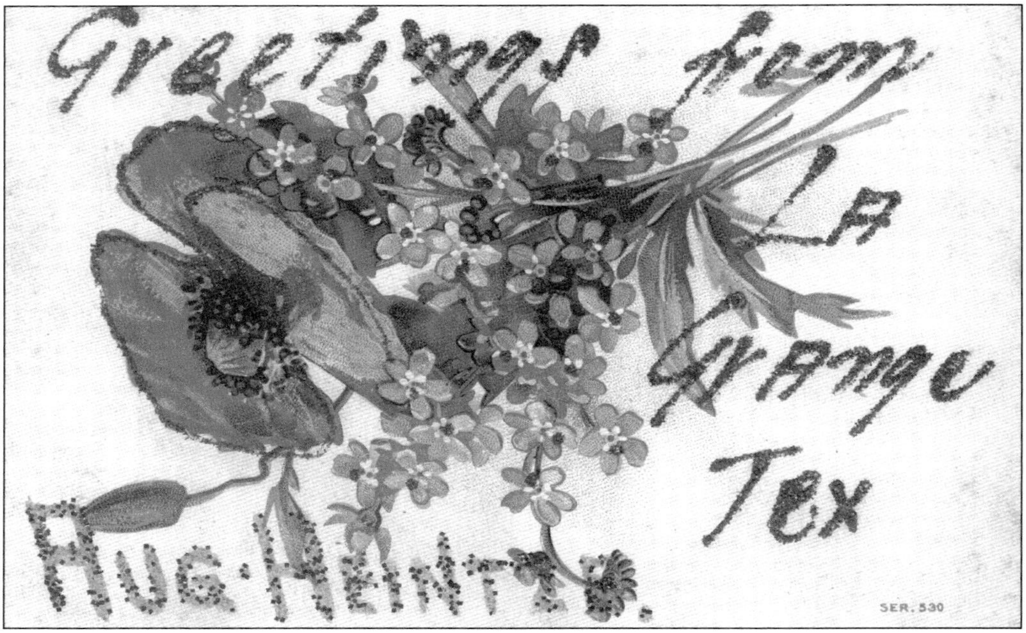

Greetings from La Grange, Tex. Aug Heintze. Shown is a card sold by August Heintze Jr. (1851–1923), a leading retailer in La Grange. Heintze came to Texas from Kappeln, Germany, in 1873, settling first in the Rio Grande valley before moving to Warrenton, in northern Fayette County, where he married Johanna Speckels (1854–1945). In 1888, the couple moved to La Grange, where Heintze ran several businesses, including the Heintze-Speckels Company, located on the east side of the La Grange square. (Gary E. McKee.)

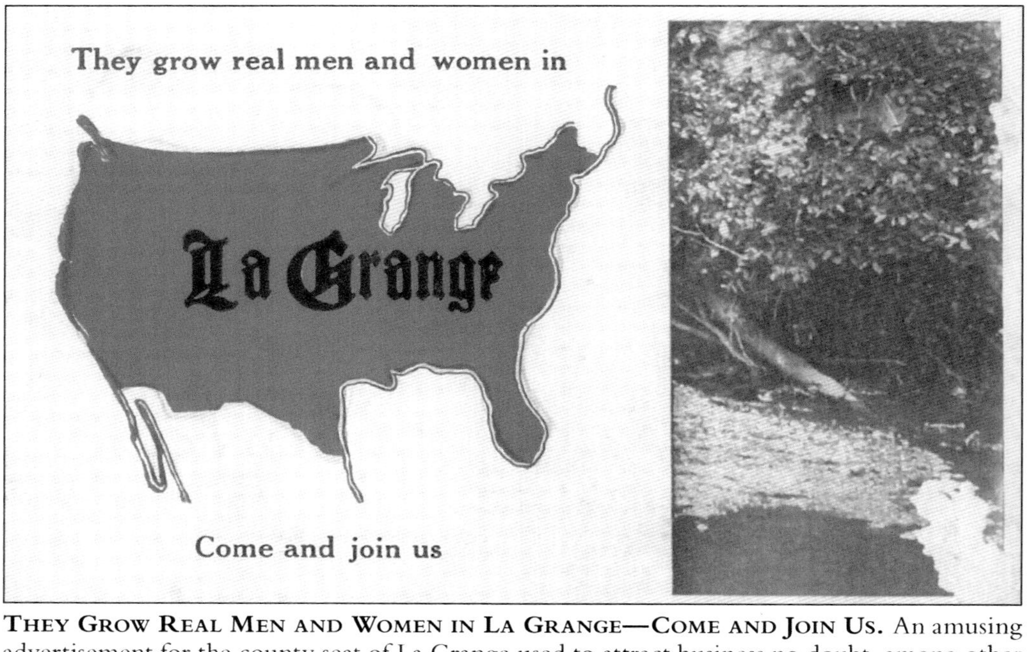

They Grow Real Men and Women in La Grange—Come and Join Us. An amusing advertisement for the county seat of La Grange used to attract business no doubt, among other things. (Author's collection.)

HAVING A LITTLE SPORT IN LA GRANGE, TEXAS. Here is what passes for a racy postcard from the turn of the 20th century. Such postcards were created for numerous localities; however, this one from La Grange is quite rare. Interestingly, it was used not by a La Grange resident, but by someone in Schulenburg, as the card's caption, "Having a Little Sport in La Grange, Texas," has been crossed through and instead states, "Schulenburg." (Gary E. McKee.)

COUNTY COURT HOUSE, LA GRANGE, TEX. The grandest of all of Fayette County's structures is its 1891 Romanesque Revival courthouse, the county's fourth. Designed by James Riely Gordon (1863–1937), it replaced a smaller third courthouse, designed by William von Rosenberg and built by Heinrich Kreische. This current courthouse was built of local blue Muldoon sandstone, red Pecos sandstone, pink Burnet granite, and white Belton limestone at a cost of $99,407.04. Its clock tower rises 100 feet above the square. The courthouse was fully restored in 2006. (Author's collection.)

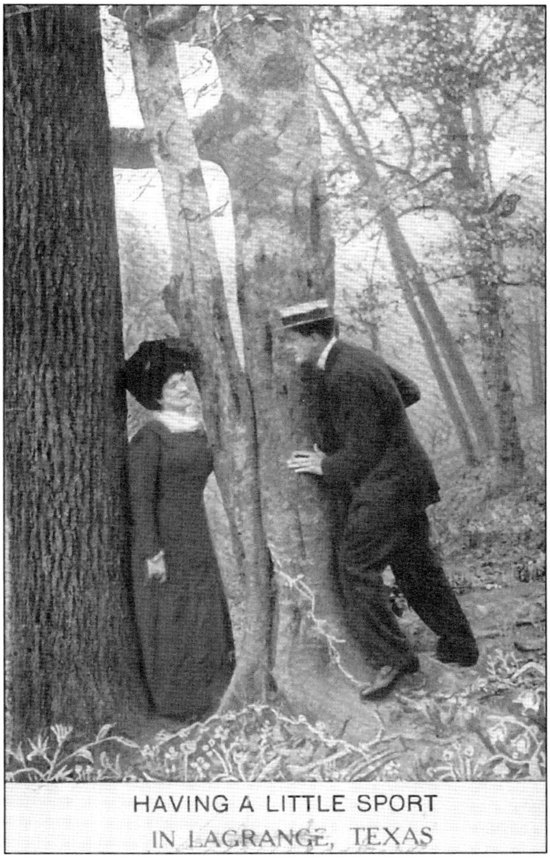

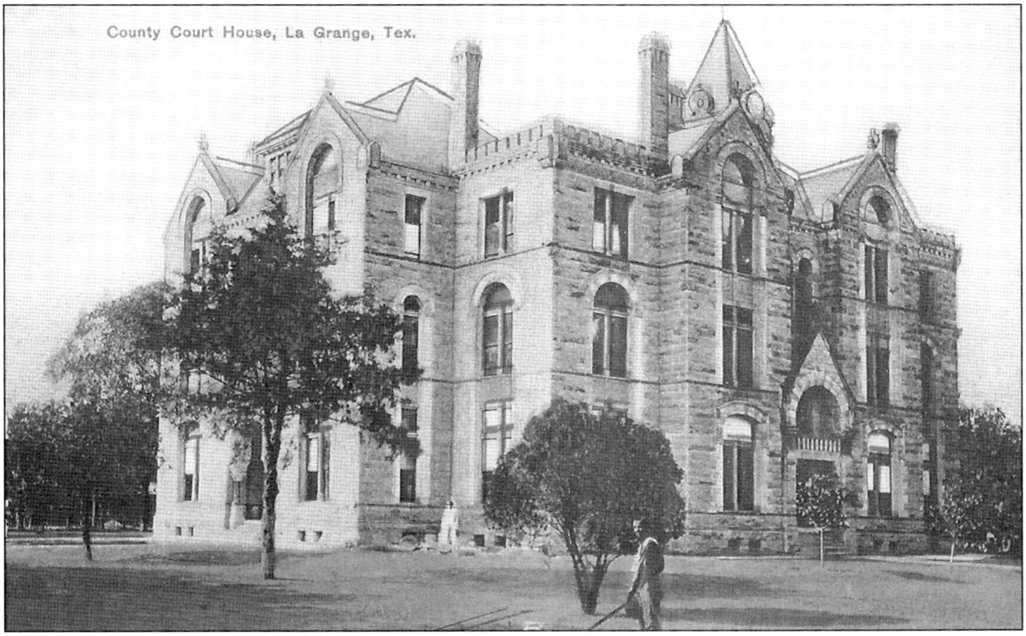

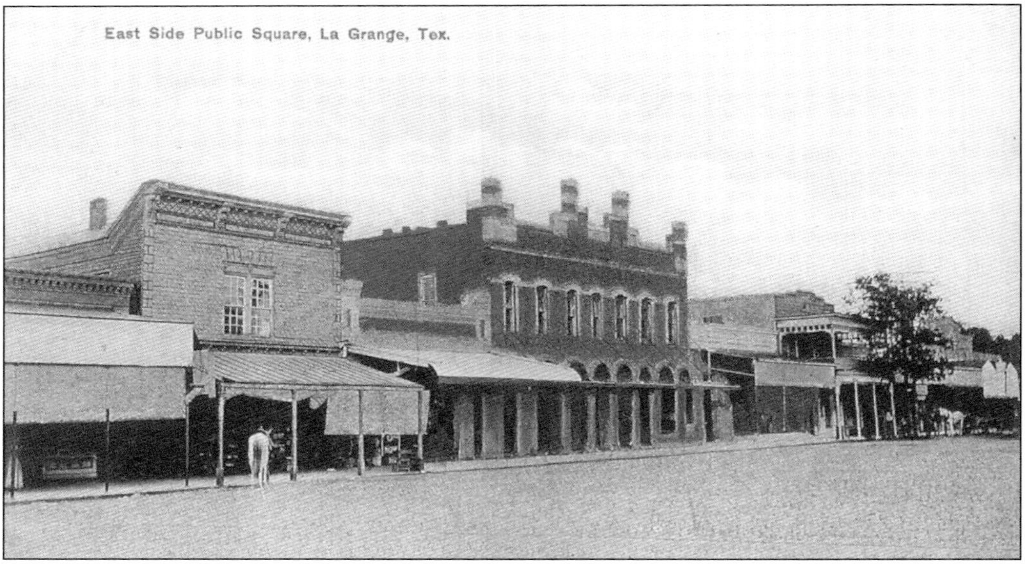

EAST SIDE PUBLIC SQUARE, LA GRANGE, TEX. The eastern side of the La Grange square is visible here. In the center is a large cast stone structure. It was built in 1906–1907 by Dr. William Hermes (1828–1922), who came to Texas from Heidelberg, Germany, in 1846 with his wife, Mary. In 1855, Hermes opened a drugstore with Dr. Albert Hermann Eck (1834–1930) and ran what became the oldest drugstore in continuous operation in Texas. (Fayette Heritage Museum & Archives.)

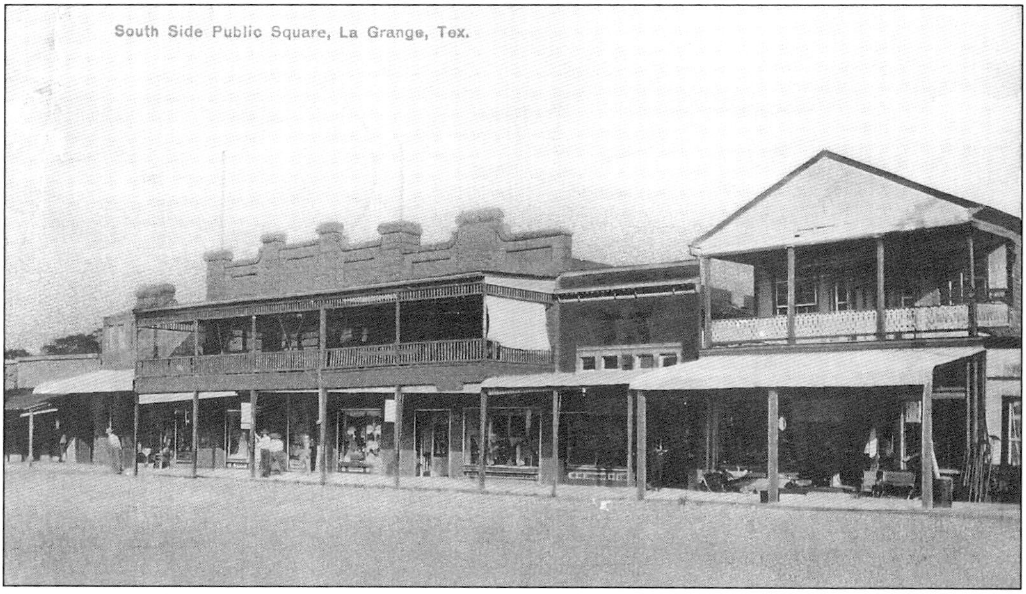

SOUTH SIDE PUBLIC SQUARE, LA GRANGE, TEX. The building pictured in the middle is the Von Rosenberg building, constructed in 1906, in which the Von Rosenberg Company was operated by Carl Johannes "C.J." von Rosenberg (1857–1934) and Alexander Ernst von Rosenberg (1869–1937). Next door is the Farqhuar building. A new Von Rosenberg building replaced these two structures in 1922 and still stands today. The wooden building on the far right housed the La Grange Saddlery and was torn down in the 1940s. (Author's collection.)

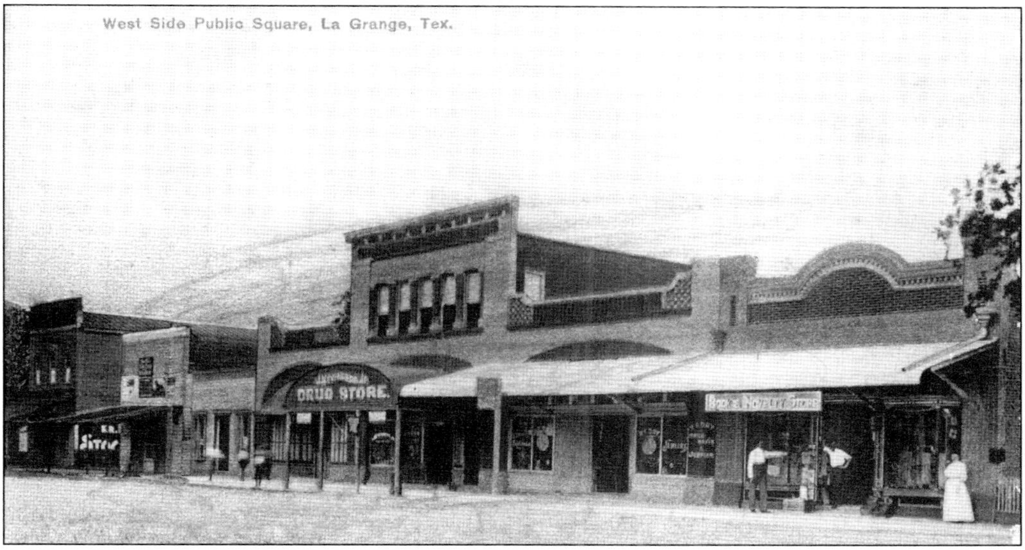

WEST SIDE PUBLIC SQUARE, LA GRANGE, TEX. Pictured is the square's west side. The Meyenberg Drugstore is in the middle, Day's Jewelry and Watch Repair is next door to the right, and closer to the foreground is the Robison Book and Novelty Store. The jeweler was Robert Fulton Day (1836–1919). Day came to Texas from Tennessee before 1860 and married Elizabeth Duncan Chandler (1828–1895), whose first husband was early Fayette pioneer John W. Chandler (1823–1857). Today, the Meyenberg building has been restored and houses Schroeder Drug, and the Lukas Bakery is in the former Robison Book Store. (Fayette Heritage Museum & Archives.)

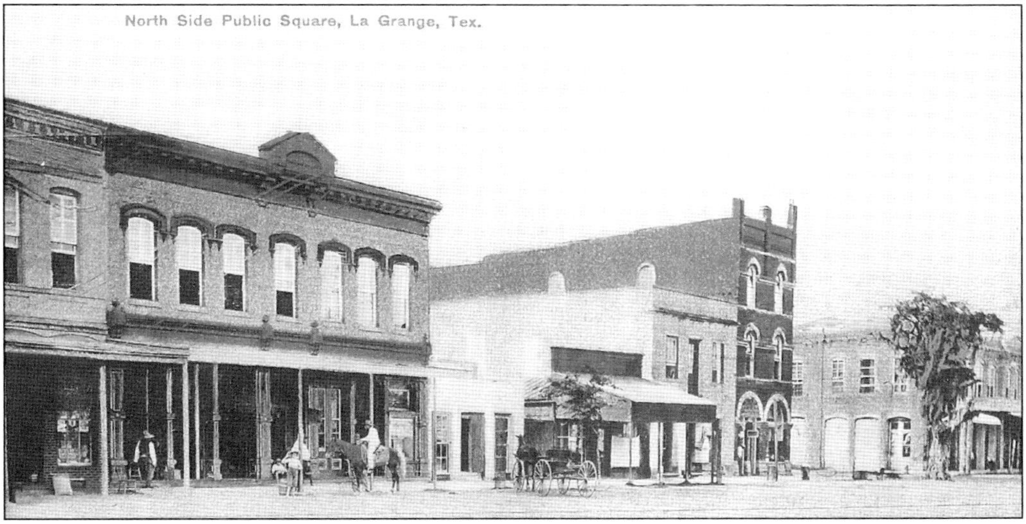

NORTH SIDE PUBLIC SQUARE, LA GRANGE, TEX. The north side of the square is dominated by the Homuth Opera House, Iron Front Saloon, and the John Schumacher Bank building, on the corner of East Colorado and North Washington Streets. Built in 1885 by August Ernst Homuth (1858–1937), the Homuth building had a prefabricated iron edifice, from the Pullis Brothers Company of St. Louis. The Iron Front Saloon was on the first floor and the Homuth Opera House on the second floor. The three-storied Schumacher Bank became the La Grange State Bank, then State Bank, and is today Prosperity Bank. (Author's collection.)

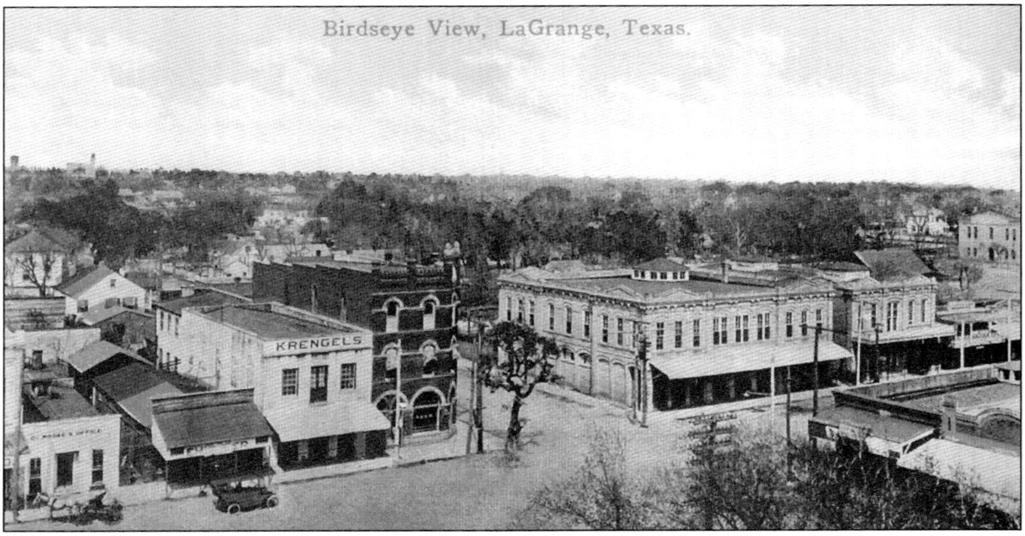

Birdseye View, La Grange, Texas. A bird's-eye view of the northwest corner of the La Grange business district shows the Schumacher Bank and the Lester Hotel in the middle. The Lester Hotel was built in 1885 and was later owned by Gerhard von Minden, who also ran the Cozy Theater, which stood to the right of the hotel on Colorado Street. Both the hotel and theater burned on March 8, 2000. Visible in the background, behind the hotel and bank, are railroad tracks that follow La Fayette Street and the La Grange Casino Building, on the far right of the postcard. (Gary E. McKee.)

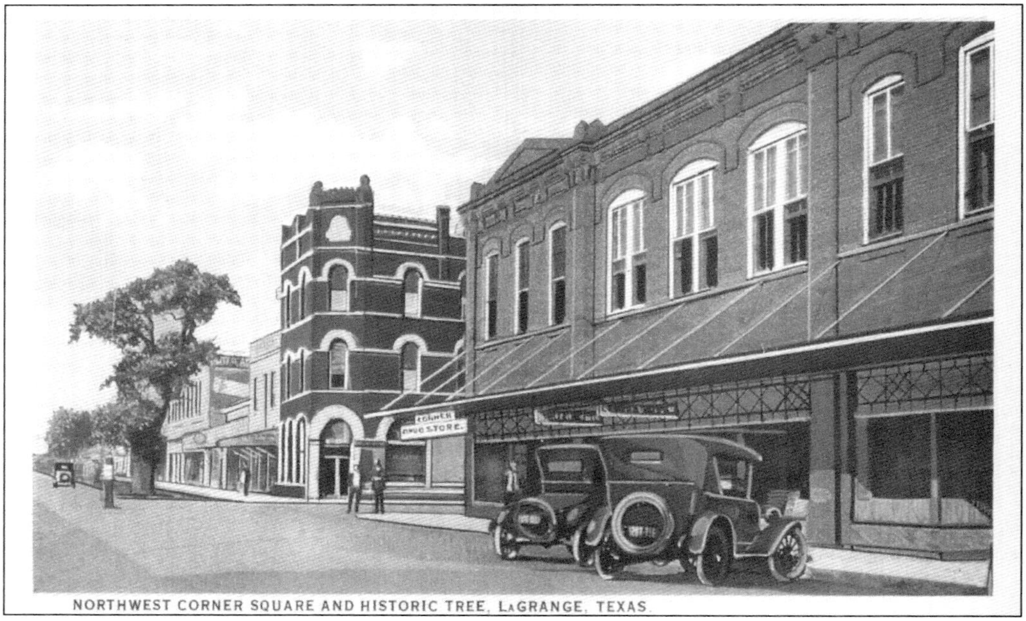

Northwest Corner Square and Historic Tree, La Grange, Texas. The corner pictured is the intersection of North Washington and West Colorado Streets and the location of several noted La Grange landmarks, most notably the Muster Oak. This ancient live oak tree was the place where the 15 men who took part in the ill-fated Dawson Expedition met on Friday, September 16, 1842. (Author's collection.)

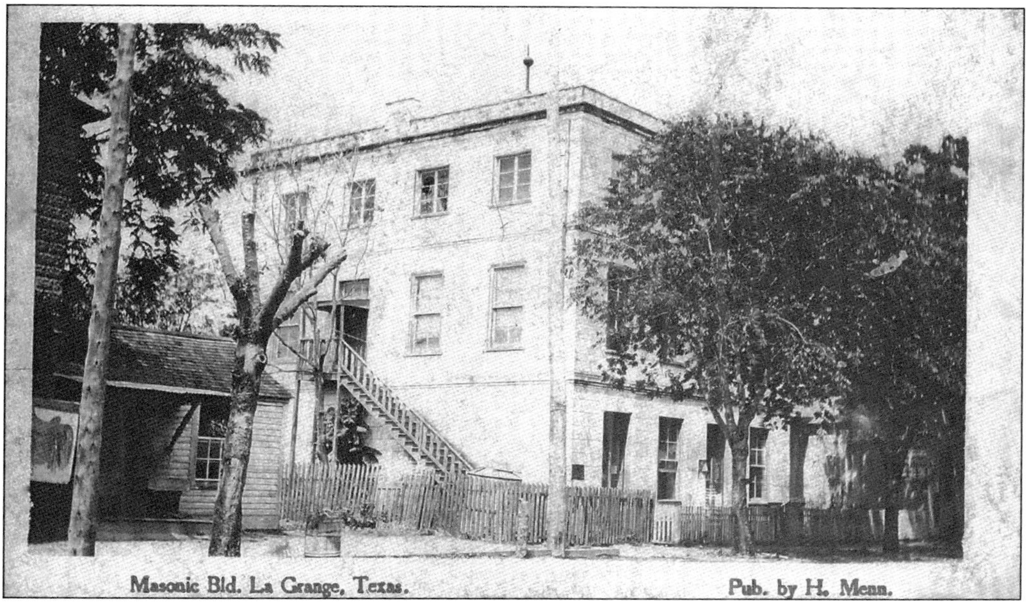

MASONIC BLD. LA GRANGE, TEXAS. Pictured is the old Masonic building, erected in 1860 by Heinrich Rohde (1804–1866), and one of the oldest buildings still standing in La Grange. Rohde came to Texas from Lauenberg, Germany, with his wife, Henrietta. After Rohde died, Henrietta married Rohde's business partner, August Kleinert. The Rohdes' daughter Louise Henrietta Rohde (1863–1932) married William von Rosenberg (1859–1919), who became Travis County judge in Austin. Rohde's will gifted the building to La Grange's Masonic Lodge, which occupied it until 1939. (Fayette Heritage Museum & Archives.)

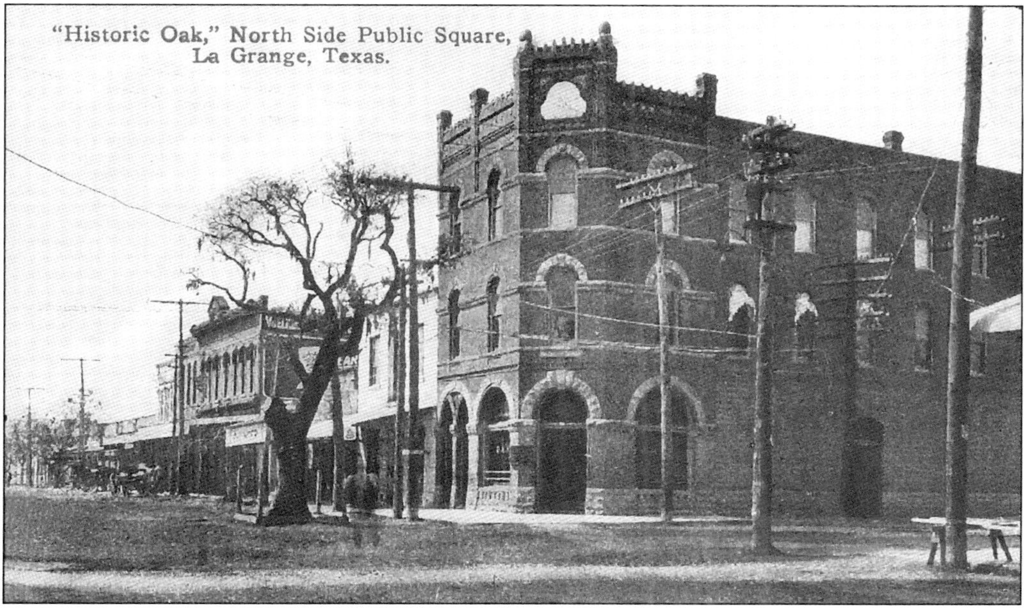

"HISTORIC OAK," NORTH SIDE PUBLIC SQUARE, LA GRANGE, TEXAS. Shown is the John Schumacher Bank building, located at the corner of West Colorado and North Washington Streets, with the historic Muster Oak standing outside its entrance. (Carolyn Heinsohn.)

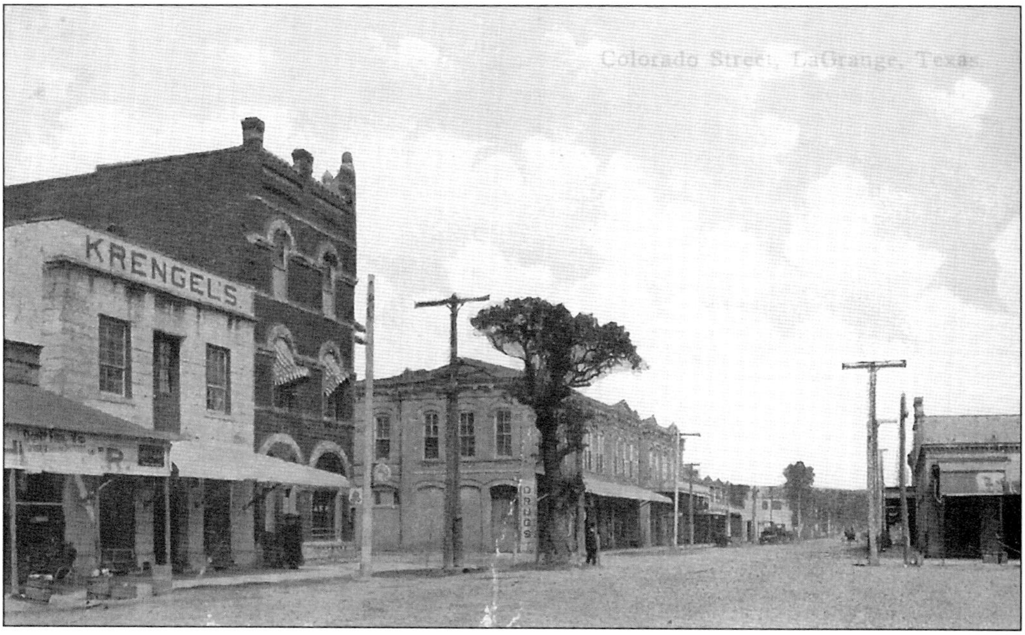

COLORADO STREET, LA GRANGE, TEXAS. Shown is another view of the John Schumacher Bank building, next door to Krengel's Store, with the historic Muster Oak in the middle. The Lester Hotel, also known as the Lester House, can be seen across North Washington Street from the bank. (Author's collection.)

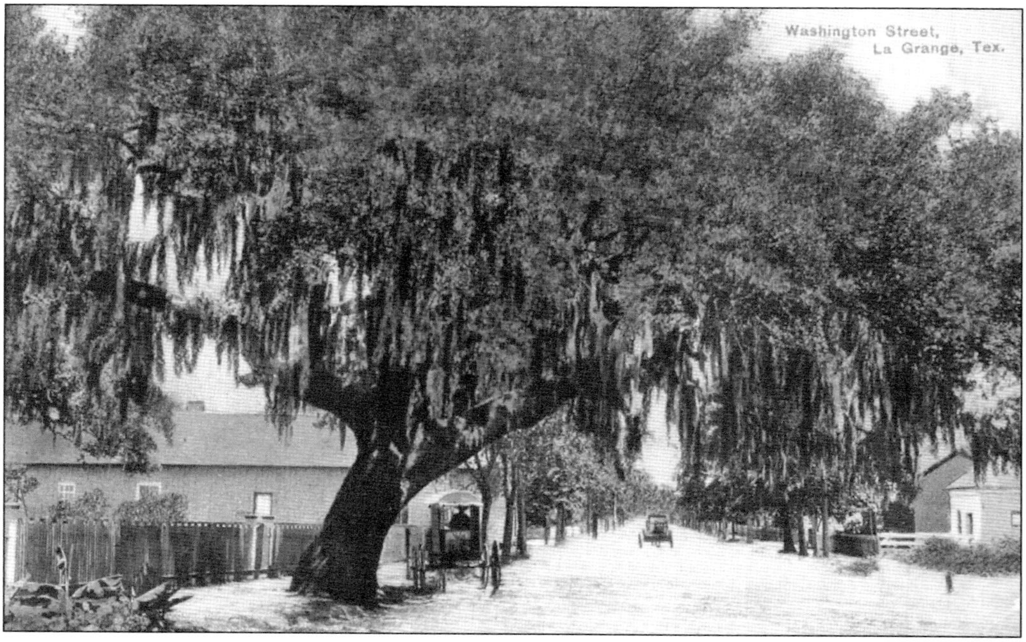

WASHINGTON STREET, LA GRANGE, TEX. This majestic live oak was located on South Washington Street between West Travis and West Crockett Streets, just outside the fenced yard of the home of Abram Alexander (1823–1898). (Fayette Heritage Museum & Archives.)

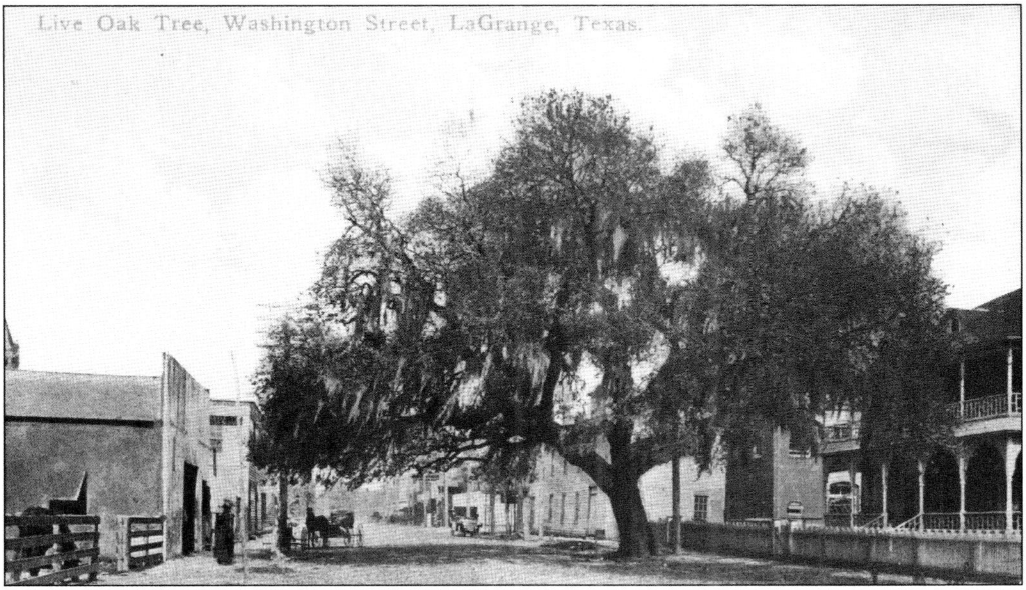

LIVE OAK TREE, WASHINGTON STREET, LA GRANGE, TEXAS. This is the same live oak in front of the Alexander residence, which is now the location of the Fayette County Record. The two-story wooden structure behind the tree was Fayette County's second courthouse. Purchased by Judge Augustin Haidusek (1845–1929), this building housed his Czech language newspaper, the *Svoboda*. Haidusek came to Texas in 1856 and became La Grange's mayor in 1875 (the first such honor for a man of Czech descent in the United States) and county judge in 1884. (Fayette Heritage Museum & Archives.)

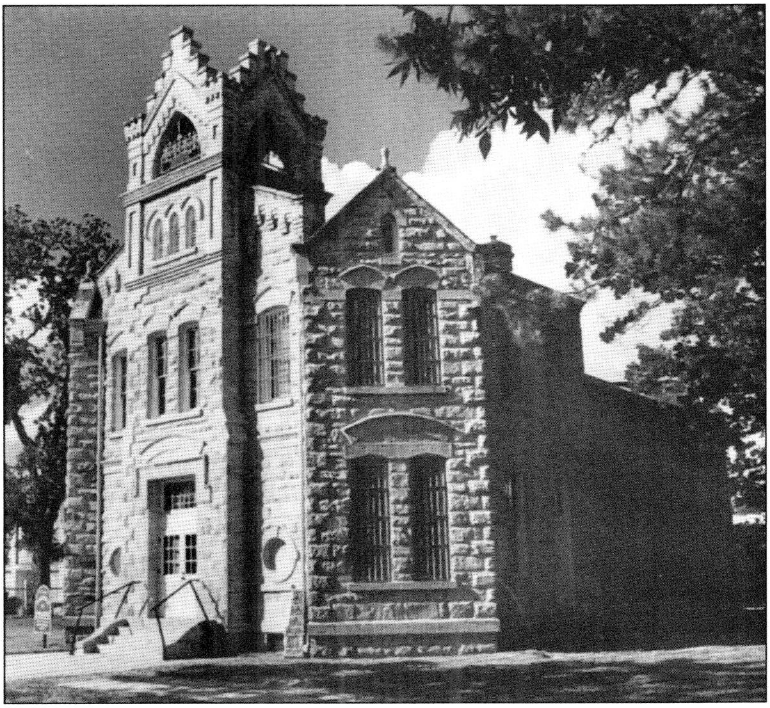

FAYETTE COUNTY JAIL IN LA GRANGE, TEXAS. Built in 1883, this was the third official Fayette County Jail. The first was built in 1838 and the second in 1853. John Andrewartha and James Wahrenberger of Austin designed the 1883 Victorian Gothic edifice. Built of blue Muldoon sandstone by Fritz Schulte, with the aid of Tillman Eaves, the new jail cost approximately $30,000 and served the county until 1985. (Gary E. McKee.)

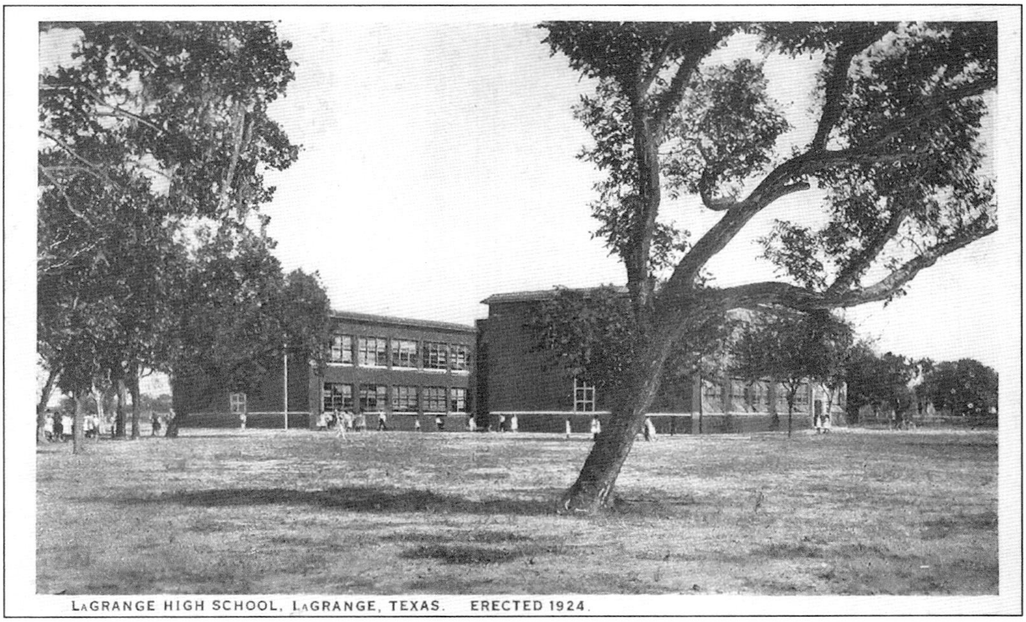

La Grange High School, La Grange, Texas, Erected 1924. Pictured is the then new La Grange High School, which opened in 1924. Today, this structure, located on East Travis Street between South Vail and South Jackson Streets, serves as the La Grange Middle School. (Author's collection.)

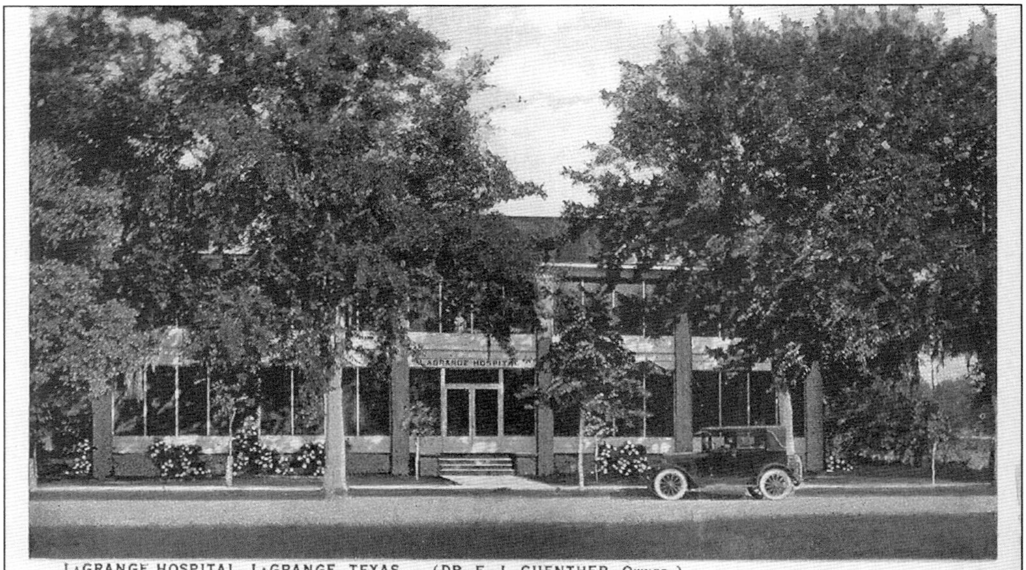

La Grange Hospital, La Grange, Texas, Dr. F.J. Guenther, Owner. The La Grange Hospital was established by Dr. Frank Joseph Guenther (1885–1949) when he purchased the home of Delphine Estell Byrnes (1851–1924), located at the intersection of North Jackson and East Guadalupe Streets in 1920. In 1951, the hospital became a nonprofit and changed its name to the Fayette Memorial Hospital. In 1967, a new hospital was built, and in 2005, St. Mark's Medical Center replaced that. (Author's collection.)

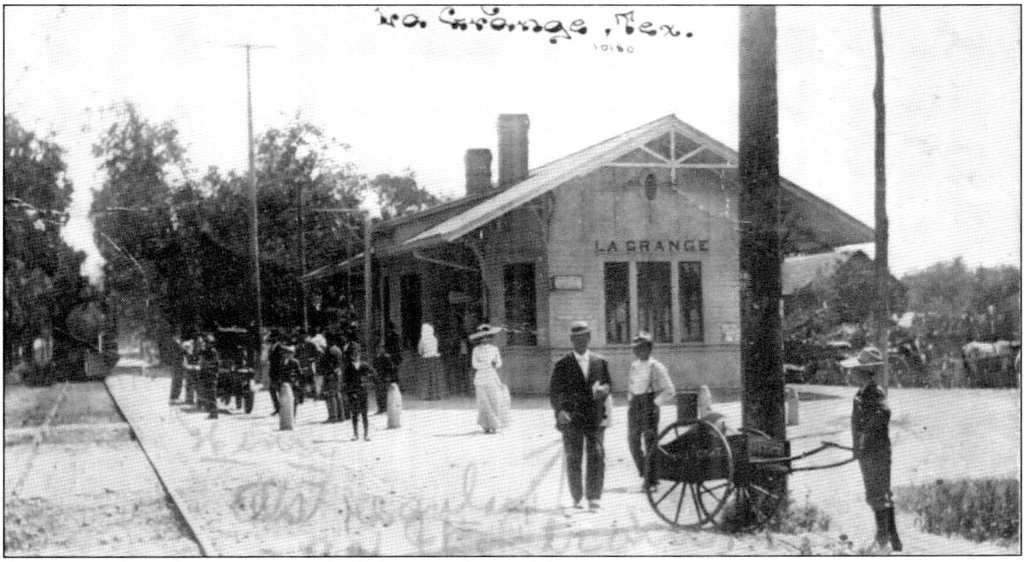

MKT DEPOT, LA GRANGE, TEX. La Grange's first passenger depot opened in 1887, when the Taylor, Bastrop & Houston Railway came through the city. This depot was located at the intersection of West La Fayette and North Washington Streets and was the second train depot in La Grange. Pictured is the 1897 Missouri, Kansas & Texas (MKT) depot, which replaced the first structure that burned earlier that same year. Today, this depot is a museum. (Fayette Heritage Museum & Archives.)

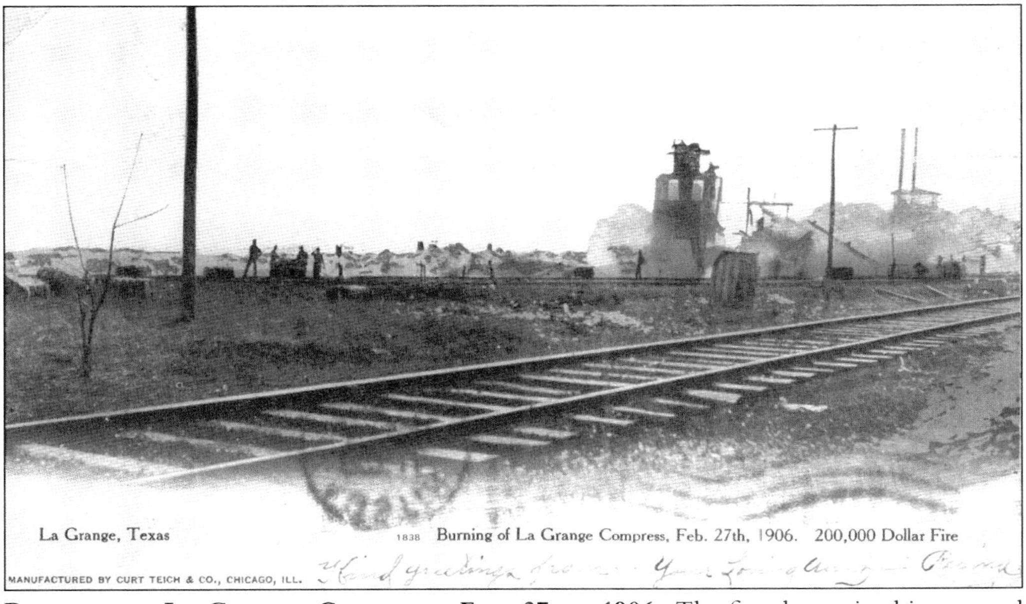

BURNING OF LA GRANGE COMPRESS, FEB. 27TH, 1906. The fire shown in this postcard occurred February 26–27, 1906, at the La Grange & Lockhart Compress Company, located on East La Fayette Street and operated by John Schumacher and C. J. von Rosenberg. The fire was caused by sparks from a locomotive, which ignited the compress building and 2,400 cotton bales next to the rails. The neighboring Alamo Lumber Company building and all of its lumber also burned. The fire caused $200,000 in damages—in 1906 currency. (Author's collection.)

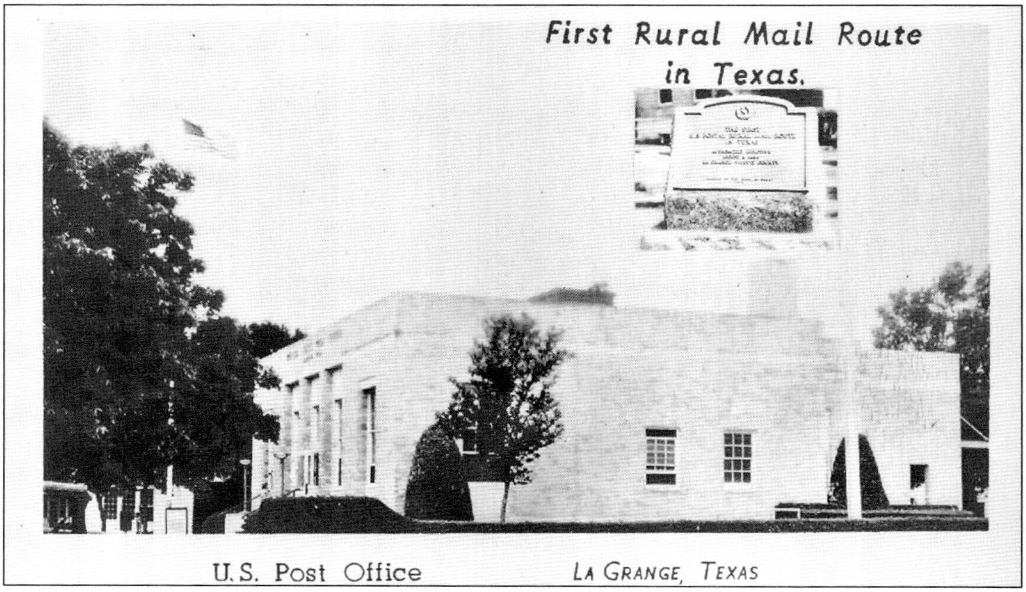

US POST OFFICE LA GRANGE, TEXAS. La Grange's first post office was established in 1838 and was located in the postmaster's place of business, wherever that may be. The first US Post Office in town was established in 1846, and in 1899, the first US rural postal route in Texas was implemented in the La Grange area. The Art Moderne post office shown here was erected in 1937, at the corner of West Colorado and North Jefferson Streets, and still serves La Grange today. (Author's collection.)

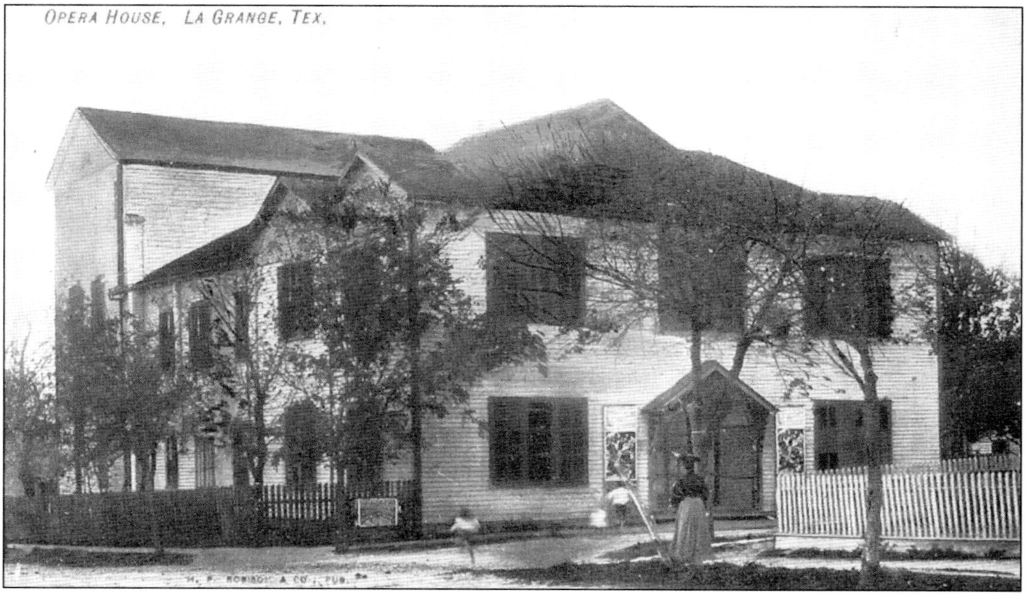

OPERA HOUSE, LA GRANGE, TEX. Built in 1894, the La Grange Opera House was at the intersection of North Franklin and East Colorado Streets, the present site of La Grange's city hall. It was used for civic functions as well as for-profit theatrical presentations. The theater on the first floor was managed by Frederick William Flato (1820–1899) and later by Victor Dunn Alexander (1877–1932). (Author's collection.)

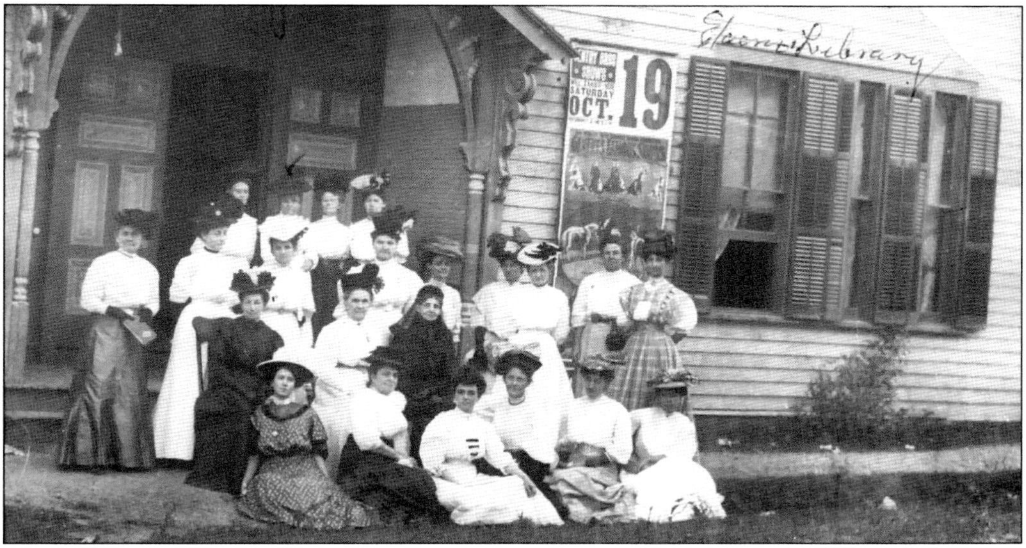

Liane Tuttle's Birthday at Old Opera House, 1907. Pictured are members of the Etaerio Club, created in 1902, celebrating the birthday of Liane de Lassaulx Tuttle (1832–1922). She was born in Koblenz, Germany, and came to Texas in 1849 with parents Otto and Margarethe de Lassaulx. She married Georg Willrich, of Bluff, and then George Tuttle, of Pin Oak. Her grandfather was J.C. von Lassaulx (1781–1848), architect to the Prussian Court in Koblenz. Her son George Willrich Jr. was county judge from 1903 to 1918. Her sister Clementine de Lassaulx Struve is the author's great-great-grandmother. (Fayette Heritage Museum & Archives.)

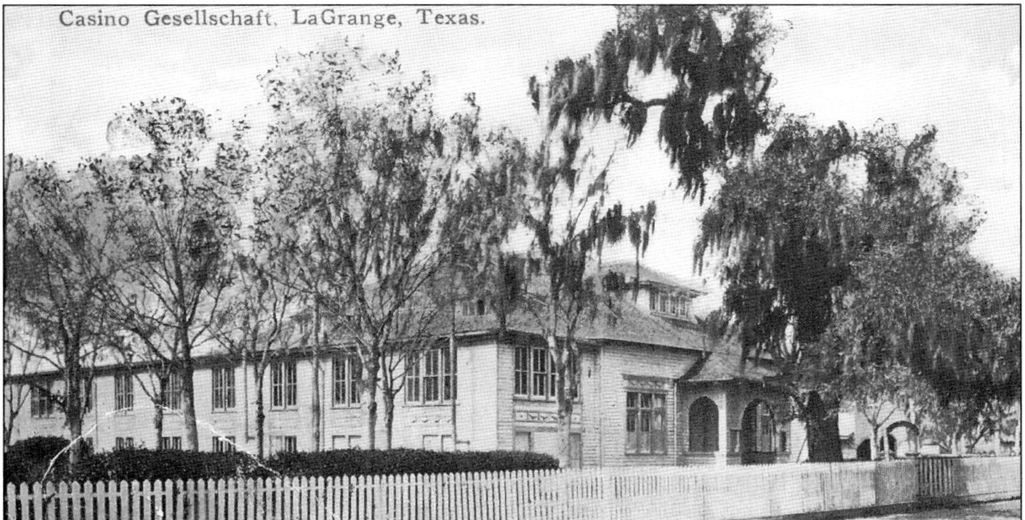

Casino Gesellschaft La Grange, Texas. Pictured is the Casino Gesellschaft, which was located on North Main Street. It was a social hall and meeting place that hosted the Flower and Industrial Fair, forerunner of the Fayette County Fair, which began in 1902. It also housed the American Legion Post 102, organized in 1919, which was initially named for Hugo Ehlers (1893–1918), who died in the Battle of the Argonne. The building burned in 1977. (Fayette Heritage Museum & Archives.)

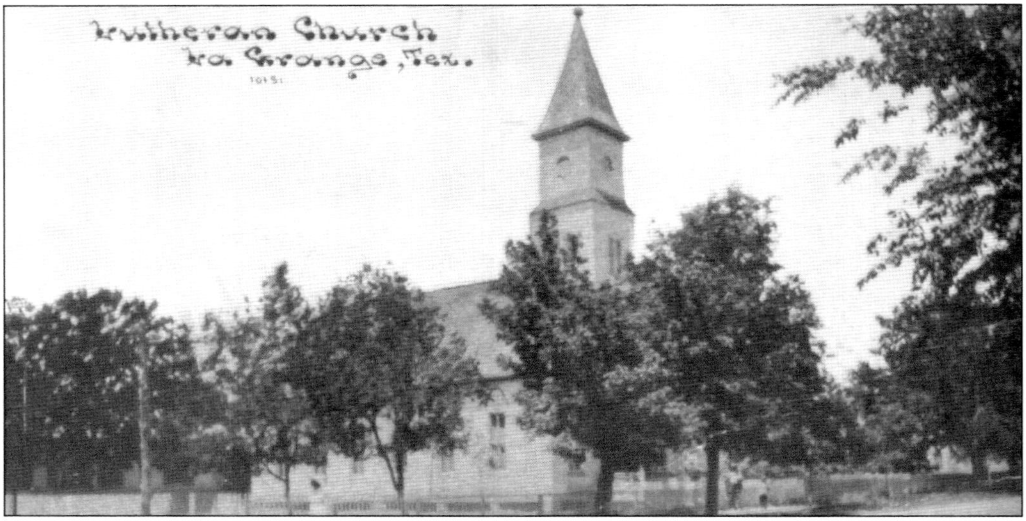

Lutheran Church, La Grange, Texas. What is known today as the St. Paul Evangelical Lutheran Church began in 1903 as the German Evangelical Lutheran Church. This chapel was constructed at the corner of South Jefferson and West Crockett Streets and dedicated on November 23, 1907. In 1950, the church moved to its present location at South Jefferson and West Walnut Streets, where a new brick church was dedicated on November 25, 1952. (Fayette Heritage Museum & Archives.)

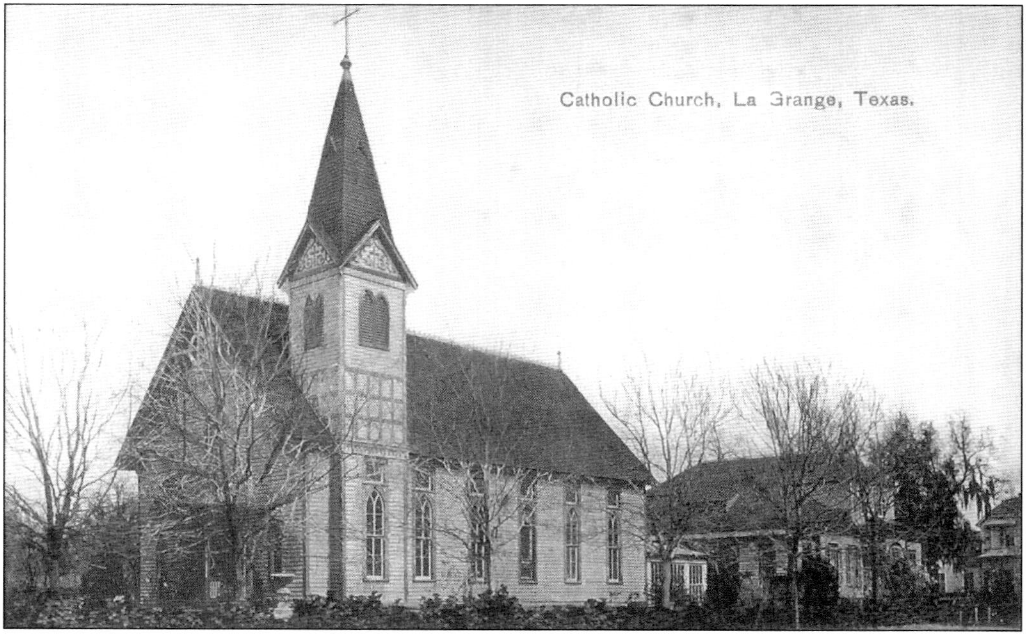

Catholic Church, La Grange, Texas. The first Catholic Mass in La Grange was held by visiting priests from Fayetteville and Hostyn Hill in the home of Dennis and Cibela Hans, on North Franklin Street. A permanent church was needed, and local Catholics had Carl Michaelis build this church in 1887. The chapel was expanded several times before being replaced in 1973 by the nearby Sacred Heart Catholic Church. The pictured chapel was demolished in 1982 to make room for a new Parish Center. (Gary E. McKee.)

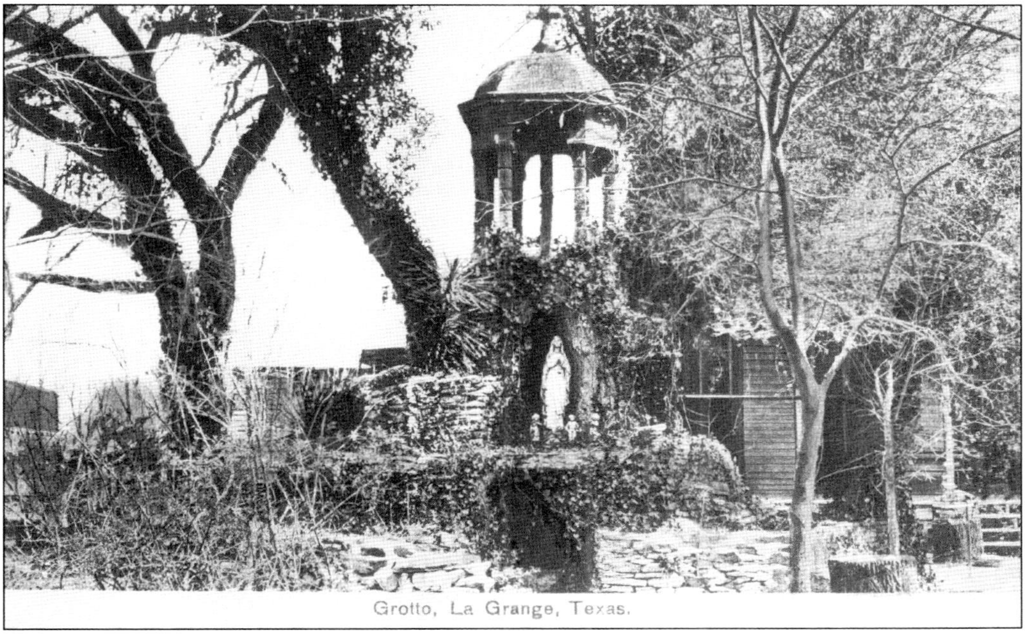

GROTTO, LA GRANGE, TEXAS. Pictured is the Sacred Heart Grotto, which was located at the first site of the Sacred Heart Catholic Church of La Grange in the northern section of the city. In the 1930s, the church was moved roughly three blocks to the northeast, where it was later expanded, and then replaced by a newer building in 1973. (Fayette Heritage Museum & Archives.)

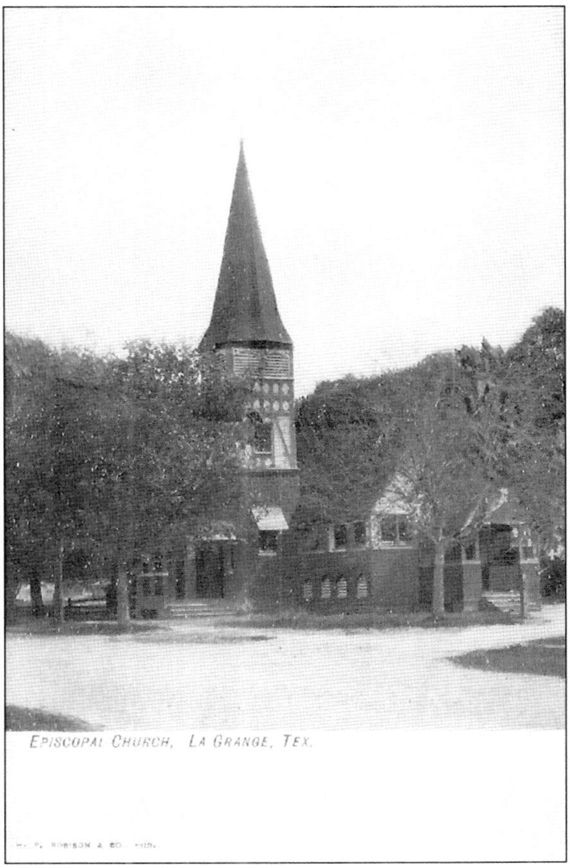

EPISCOPAL CHURCH, LA GRANGE, TEX. The St. James Episcopal Diocese was formally organized in 1856; however, the Saint James Episcopal Church shown here was built by Carl Michaelis in 1885, in the Queen Anne style, on the southeast corner of East Colorado and North Monroe Streets. This beautiful structure was designed by Richard M. Upjohn, of New York, and survives to this day. (Author's collection.)

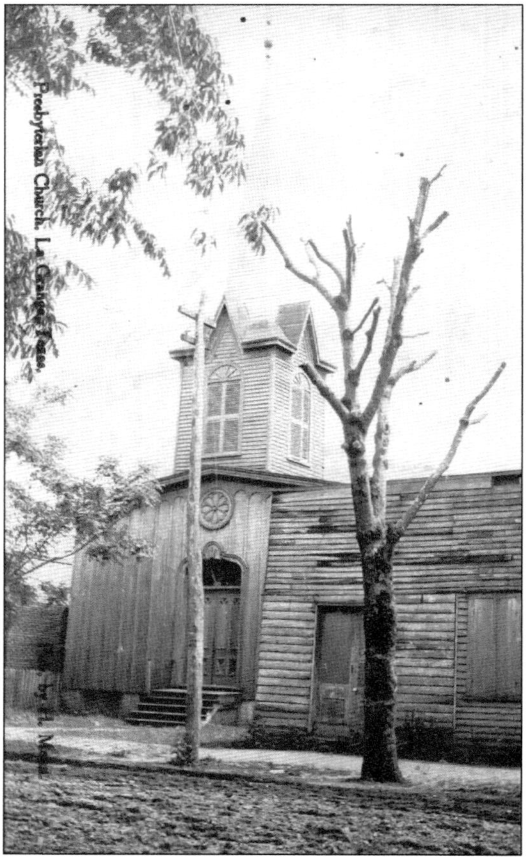

PRESBYTERIAN CHURCH, LA GRANGE, TEXAS. Built in 1852–1853 and perhaps the oldest in Fayette County, this chapel was once known as the Union Church and is today St. Paul's African Methodist Episcopal Church. Used by Episcopal, Lutheran, Baptist, and Presbyterian congregations, the Presbyterians gained title when the La Grange Baptist Church of Christ allowed the Presbyterians to gain full title in 1884. The Presbyterians used the chapel until 1954, when it was moved from Travis Street to East Guadalupe Street. (Fayette Heritage Museum & Archives.)

FIRST PRESBYTERIAN CHURCH, LA GRANGE, TEXAS. Organized in 1848, La Grange's Presbyterian congregation first met in what was known as the Union Church, located on Travis Street. That chapel was likely the oldest Presbyterian church in Texas. Under the guidance of Rev. Calvin Owen, the Gothic-style sanctuary shown here was designed and built in 1953 by Arthur H. Pohl (1899–1964) on the southeast corner of East Crockett and South Franklin Streets. (Author's collection.)

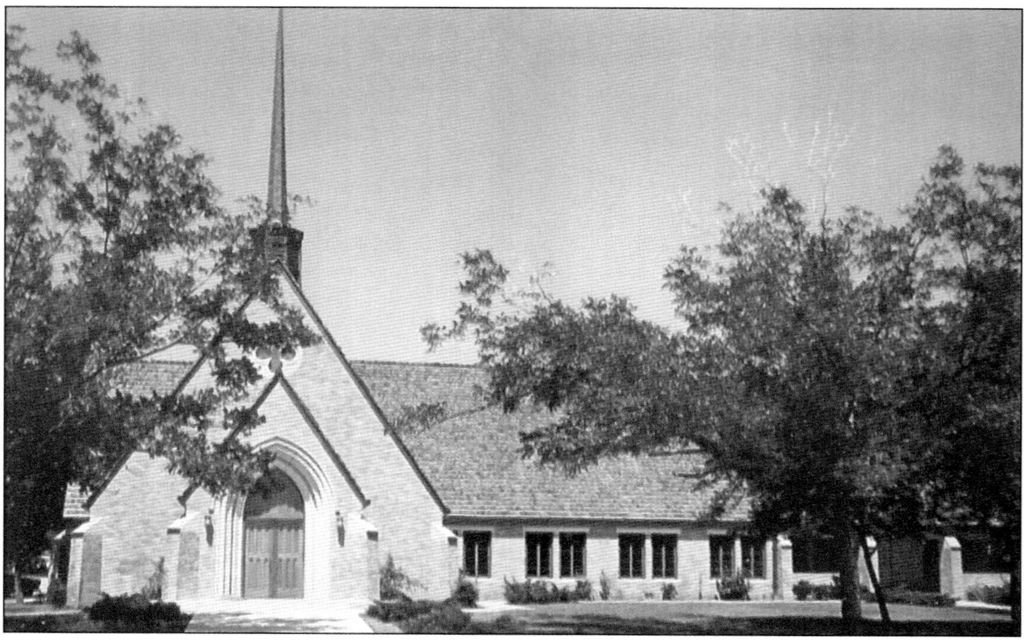

METHODIST CHURCH LA GRANGE, TEXAS. Begun in 1839 as the Methodist Episcopal Mission Church of La Grange, the city's first Methodists were a satellite to the larger Methodist community in Rutersville, and services were held in a dilapidated structure on South Washington Street. In 1883, a new church was built and called Travis Street United Methodist Church. It was sold in 1994 and moved to the Festival Hill complex in Round Top. A new First United Methodist Church now exists on North Von Minden Street. (Author's collection.)

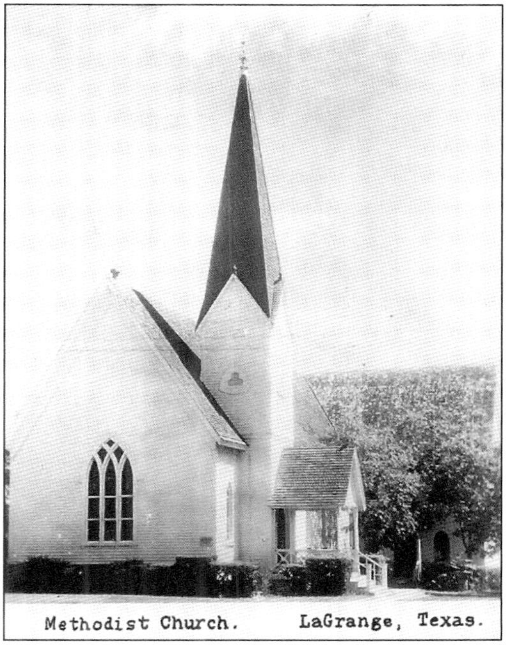

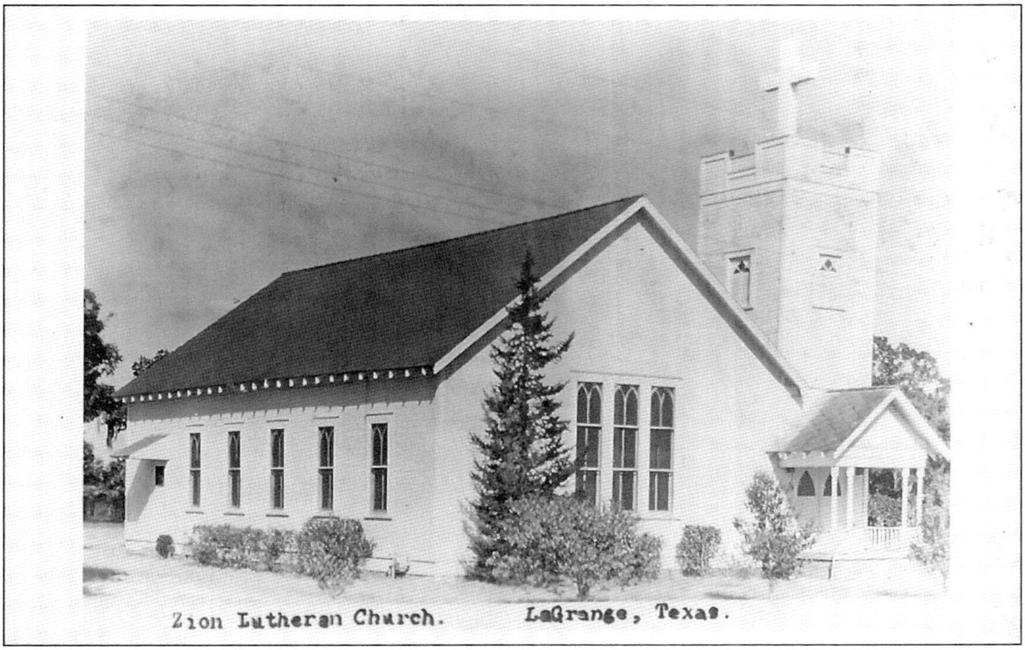

ZION LUTHERAN CHURCH, LA GRANGE, TEXAS. Shown here is the former Zion Lutheran Church, which was located at North Franklin and East Vine Streets. This church was dedicated on June 28, 1928, as a member church of the Missouri Synod. In 1962, Trinity Hill Lutheran, in the rural Plum area, and Zion Lutheran Church, in La Grange, merged into Mount Calvary Lutheran Church. The old Zion Lutheran Church building was torn down and replaced with a newer sanctuary designed by Travis Broesche, of Houston, which was dedicated on May 2, 1965. (Author's collection.)

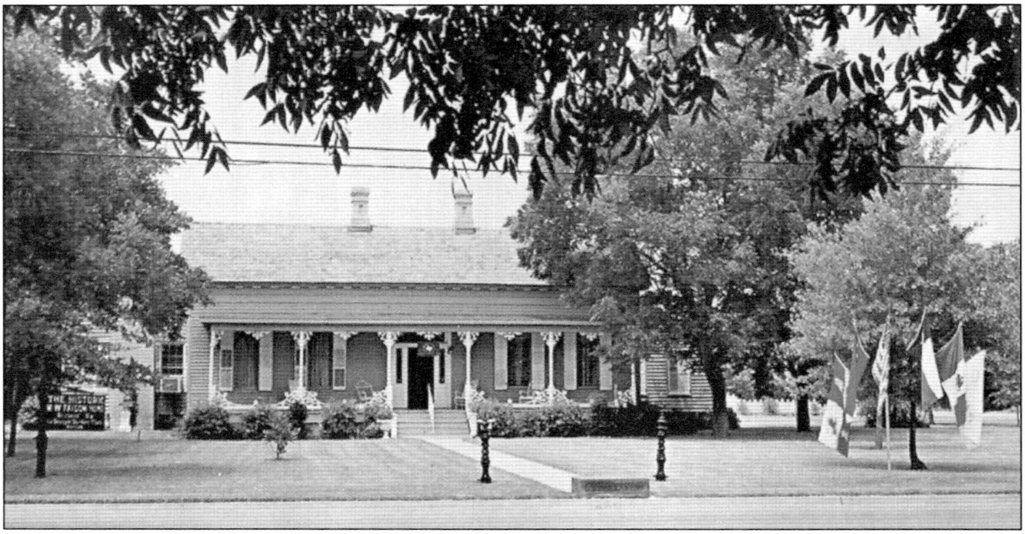

FAISON HOME, LA GRANGE. Located on South Jefferson Street is the Faison home, pictured here. It was built in 1841 as a two-room structure and then enlarged by Sylvester Stansbury Munger (1820–1901). Nathaniel W. Faison (1817–1870) purchased the home in 1866. On his death, Faison deeded the home to his African American housekeeper, Louisiana "Lou" Brown, who sold it to Peter Faison. Julia Ogden Faison lived there until her death in 1961, when the property was sold to the La Grange Garden Club, which opened it up to the public. (Rox Ann Johnson.)

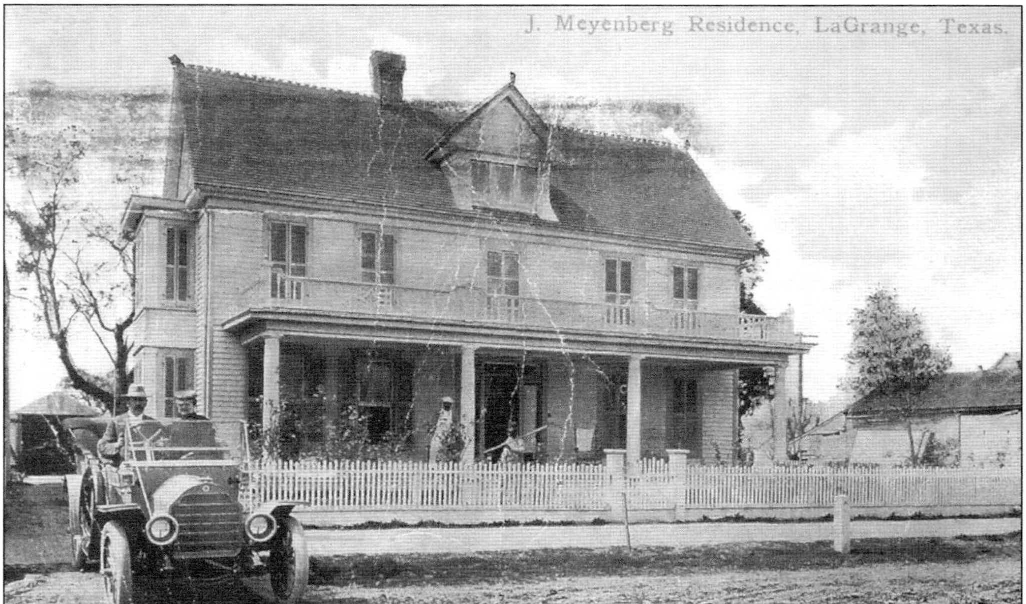

J. MEYENBERG RESIDENCE, LA GRANGE, TEXAS. Julius S. Meyenberg (1819–1908) came to Texas from Celle, Germany, in 1844 and married Kunigunde Oske (1828–1867) in 1850. Meyenberg settled in La Grange in 1865, built a home on the west side of the square, and worked as a druggist. The Meyenberg home was purchased by Austin Savings and Loan and moved to the corner of West Travis and North River Streets, where today it is a restaurant. A replica of the Meyenberg home was rebuilt on the old square lot. (Carolyn Heinsohn.)

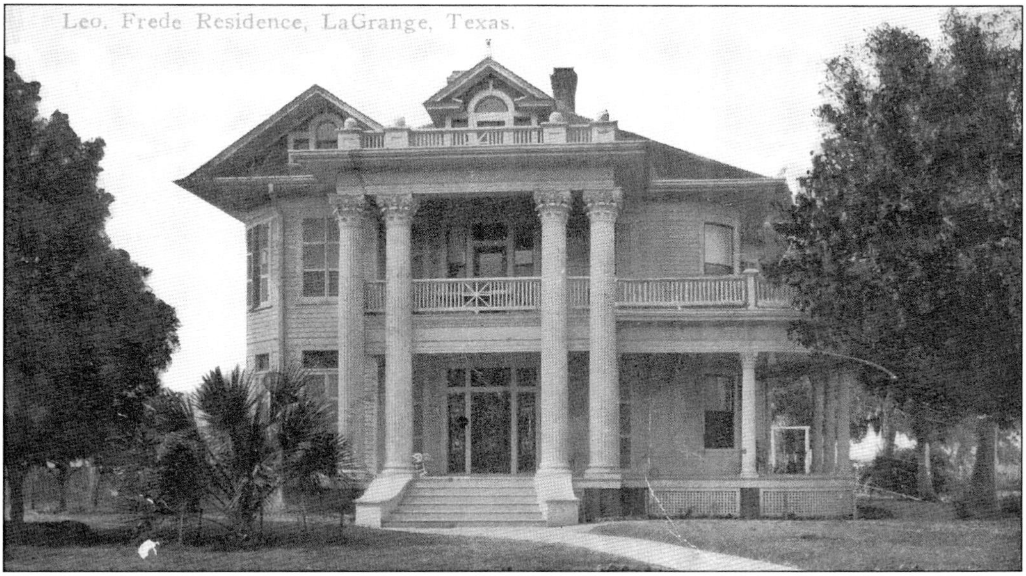

LEO. FREDE RESIDENCE, LA GRANGE, TEXAS. Leopold H. Frede (1866–1946) was born in La Grange to August and Barbara Fink Frede, who both died in the 1867 yellow fever epidemic. Frede was raised by his aunt and uncle John and Louise Schumacher. Schumacher operated the Schumacher Bank, where Frede was first cashier and later president until his death. Frede built the home pictured here in 1906 at the corner of South Washington and West Pecan Streets. (Carolyn Heinsohn.)

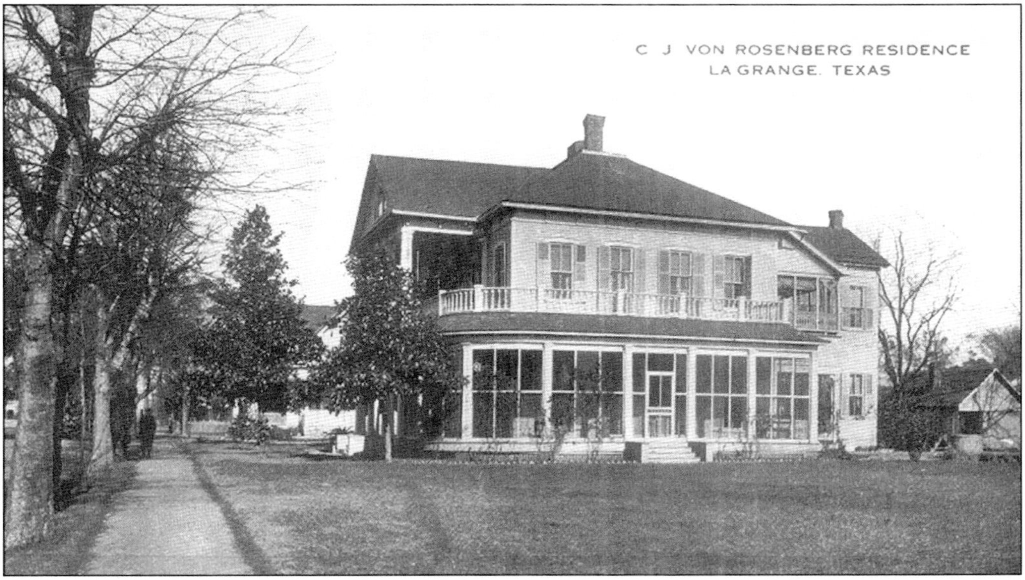

C.J. VON ROSENBERG RESIDENCE, LA GRANGE, TEXAS. Carl Johannes "C.J." von Rosenberg (1857–1934), son of Johannes and Julie Groos von Rosenberg, was a member of the influential German family that immigrated to Texas from East Prussia in 1849. C.J.'s grandfather Peter Carl von Rosenberg was a veteran of the Battle of Waterloo and owned a large portion of the Nassau Plantation in northern Fayette County. C.J. founded the Von Rosenberg Company in La Grange and lived in the home pictured here. (Author's collection.)

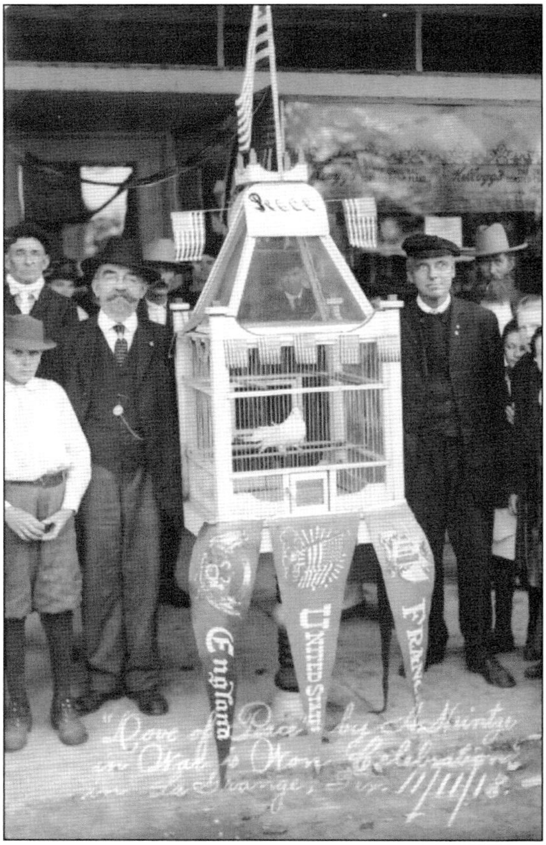

DOVE OF PEACE BY A. HEINTZE. Shown is the dove of peace, a symbol of the Armistice reached at the end of the World War I, as exhibited by August Heintze on November 11, 1918, during the city's War is Won Celebration. Below the dove's cage fly the banners of the Allied powers: England, the United States, and France. Interestingly, the banner of Russia is missing, probably because of the Russian Revolution of 1917. (Fayette Heritage Museum & Archives.)

LA GRANGE CITIZEN'S BAND. Members of the La Grange Citizen's Band are pictured. The third boy from the left in front is John Blackburn Alcorn (1892–1964), who was raised by his grandfather Louis Joseph Struve (1839–1921) after he was orphaned by the deaths of his parents, John Rugby Alcorn (1868–1908) and Elise Struve Alcorn (1869–1905). Louis Struve immigrated to Texas with his father, Heinrich Ludwig von Struve (1812–1898), in 1848, along with his stepmother and siblings. (Fayette Heritage Museum & Archives.)

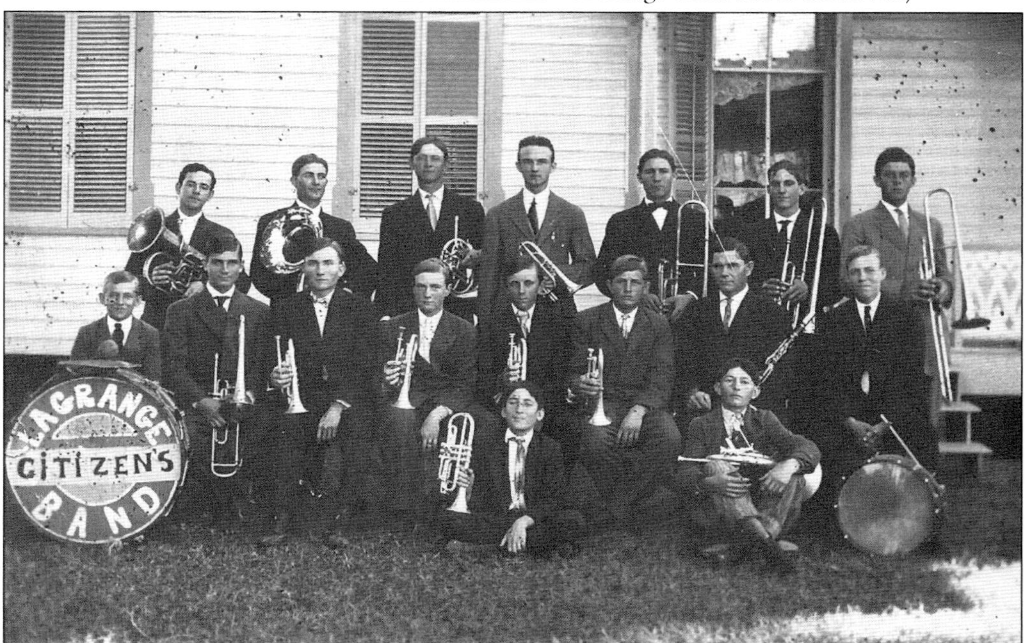

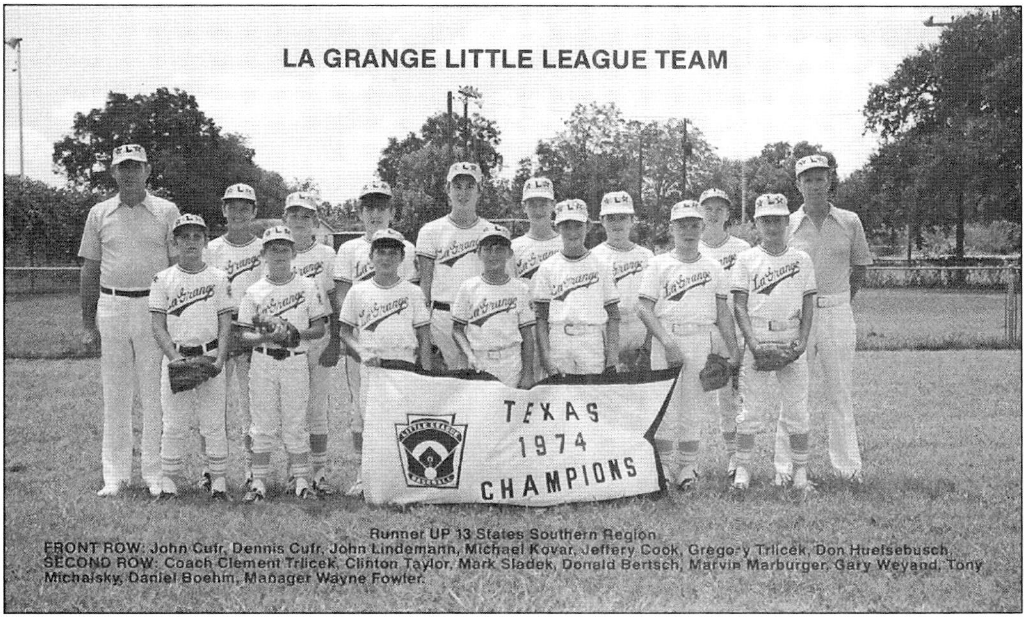

La Grange Little League Team. Here is the 1974 State Champion La Grange Little League team. The caption states: "Runner Up 13 States Southern Region." La Grange made it to the championship game but lost to the Jackson, Tennessee, American Little League team, 0-1. (Rox Ann Johnson.)

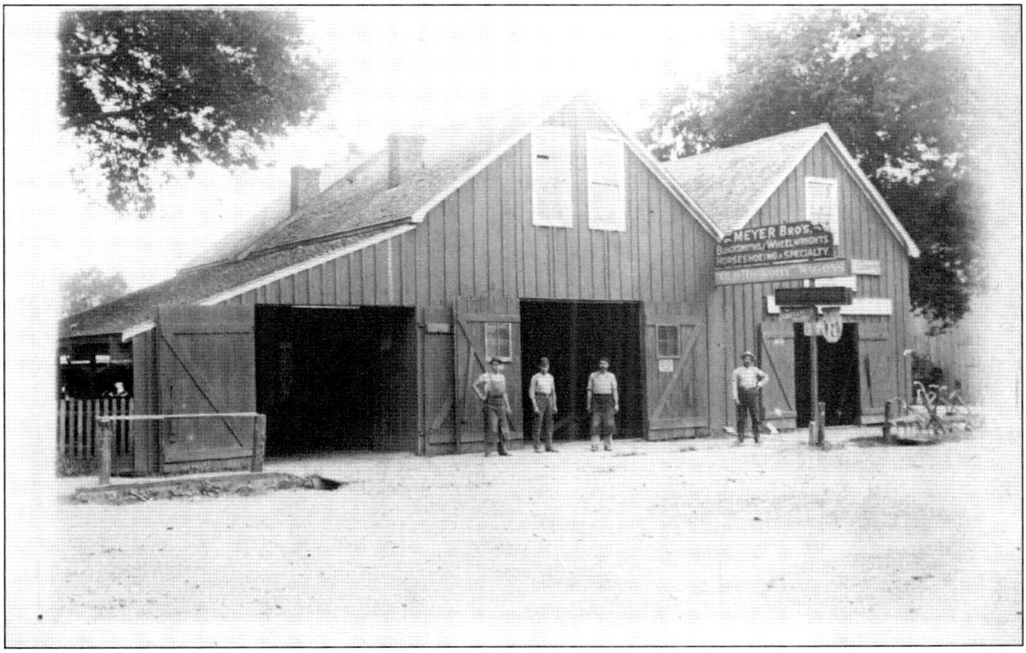

Meyer Bro's. Blacksmiths/Wheelwrights. Located at the corner of North Jefferson and West Colorado Streets, near the present US Post Office, Meyer Bro's. Blacksmiths was owned and operated by Henry and Alfred Meyer. (Fayette Heritage Museum & Archives.)

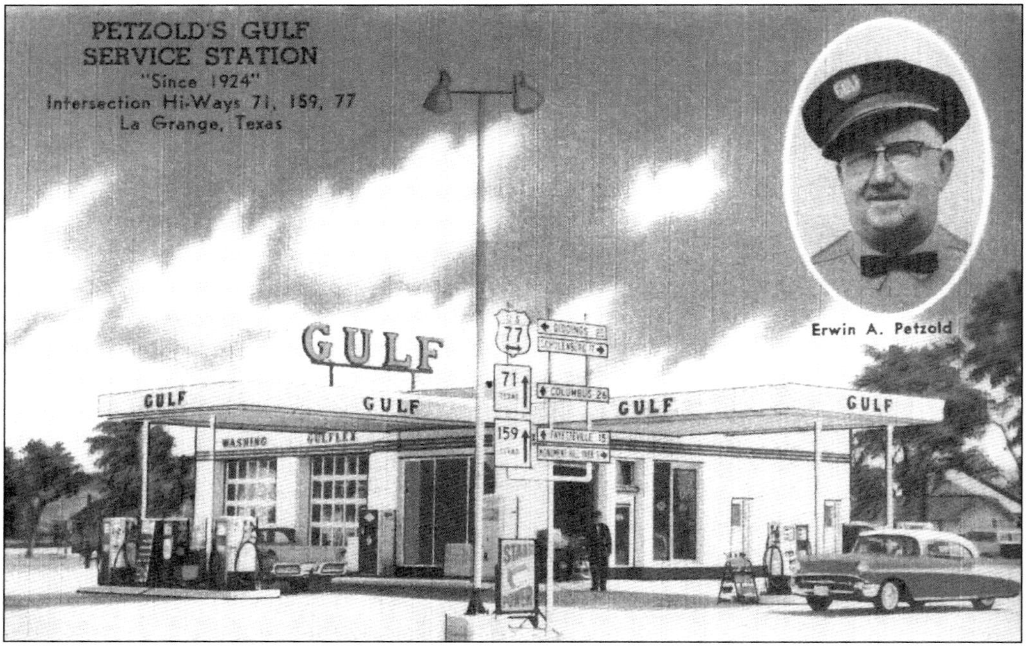

Petzold's Gulf Service Station. Located at the southeast corner of the intersection of Jefferson and Travis Streets, Irwin A. Petzold's Gulf Service Station was the prototype filling station, serving up gas with a smile. In operation since 1924, the station today is gone, replaced by a parking lot for Auto Zone. (Gary E. McKee.)

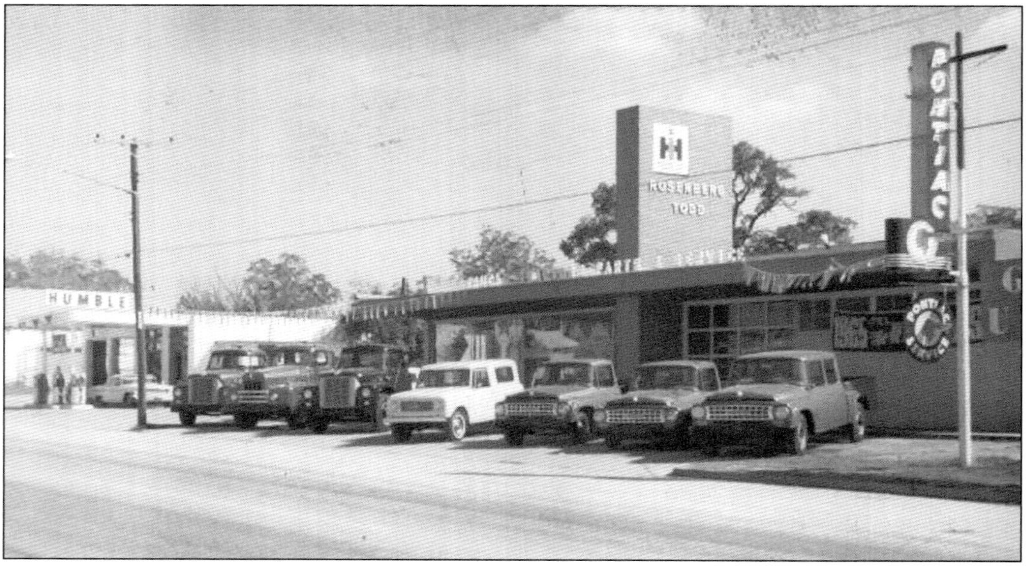

Rosenberg-Todd Dealership. Located on West Travis Street, the Rosenberg-Todd Dealership sold International Harvester trucks and farm equipment, plus Pontiacs and Oldsmobiles. Begun in 1952 by Berger and Lois von Rosenberg Todd, the author's grandparents, and Lois's brothers Sam and Lester von Rosenberg, it became Bohot-Todd after Todd bought out his brothers-in-law in 1966 and brought in his son-in-law Harvey Roland Bohot. The car franchise was sold to Brasher Motors in 1989. (Author's collection.)

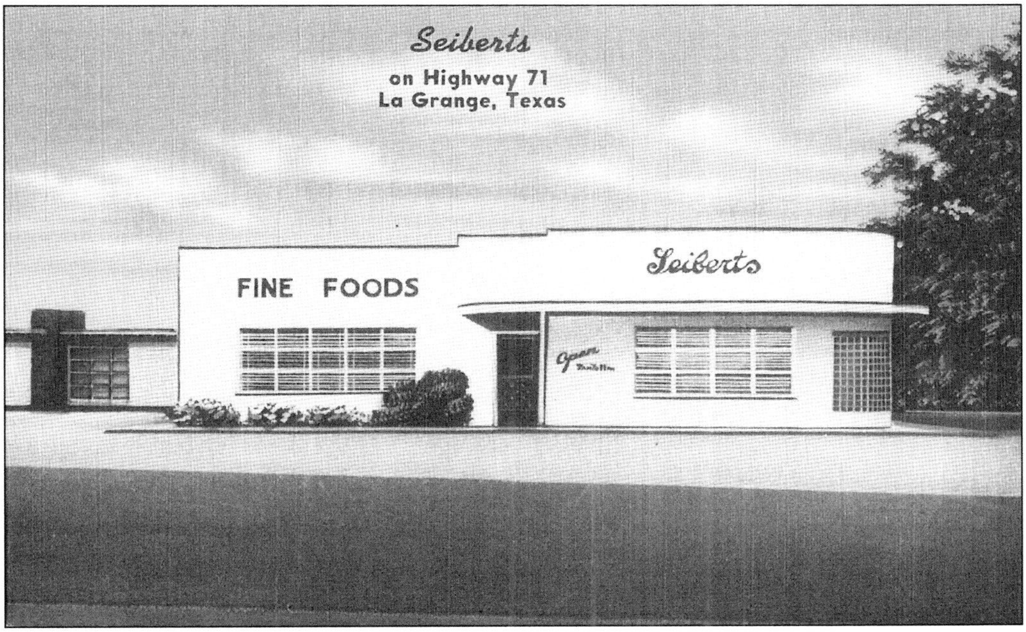

SEIBERT'S ON HIGHWAY 71, LA GRANGE, TEXAS. Shown is Seibert's Fine Foods, which was a popular La Grange eatery on Travis Street in the 1930s and 1940s. The café was owned by Arthur Henry Seibert (1903–1958) and his wife, Deloise Briggs Seibert. (Author's collection.)

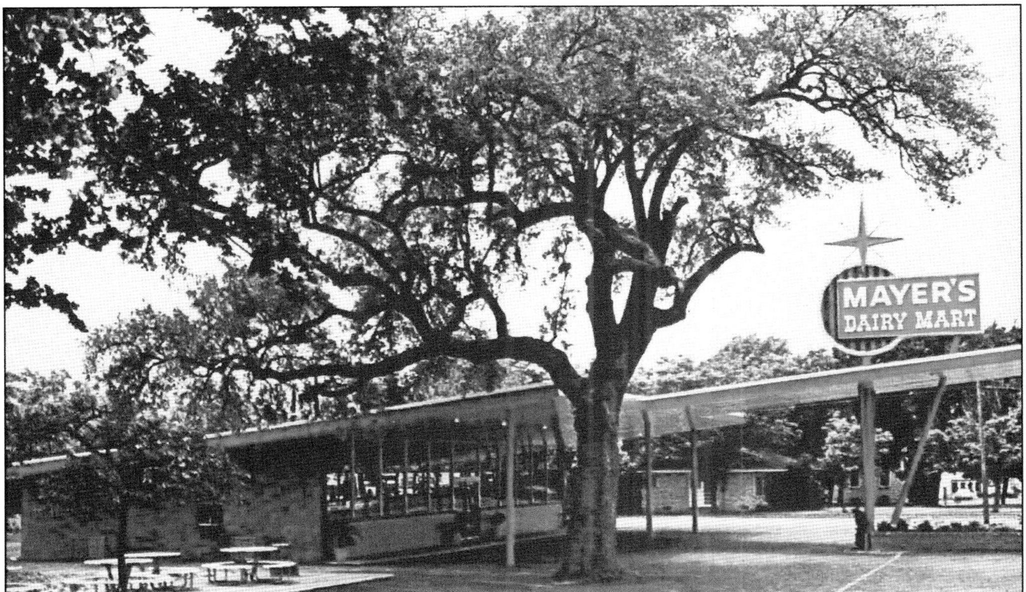

MAYER'S DAIRY MART. Here is Mayer's Dairy Mart, which was located on Travis Street, where the H-E-B supermarket parking lot exists today. (Rox Ann Johnson.)

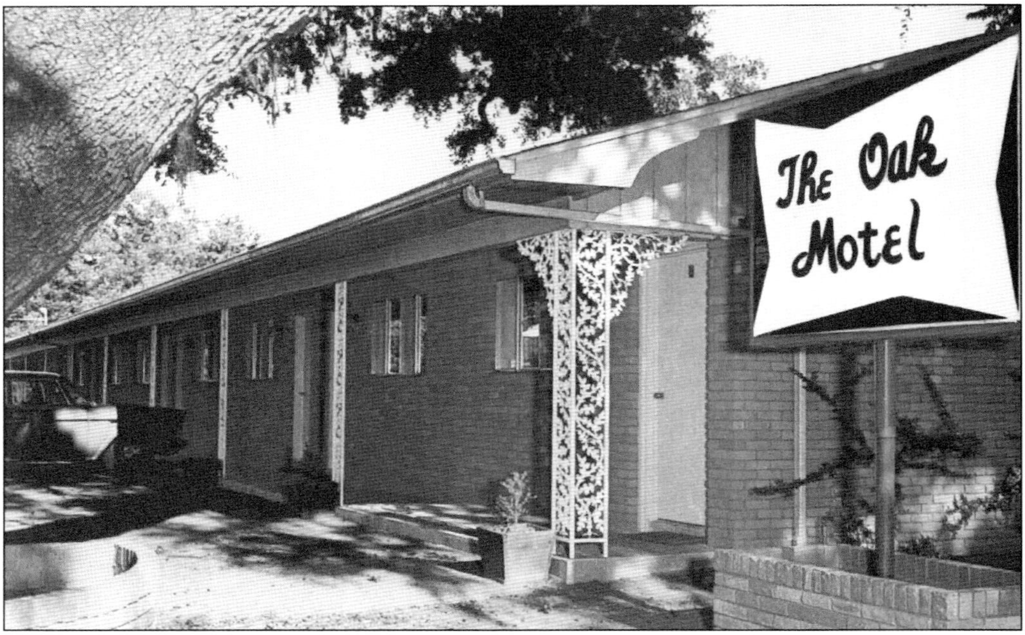

The Oak Motel. The Oak Motel is located in La Grange, at the intersection of Jefferson and Crockett Streets. The main part of the motel lobby is in an older home; however, the rooms themselves are in a 1960s-era, drive-up motel with 18 rooms. The motel is still in operation and open for business. (Fayette Heritage Museum & Archives.)

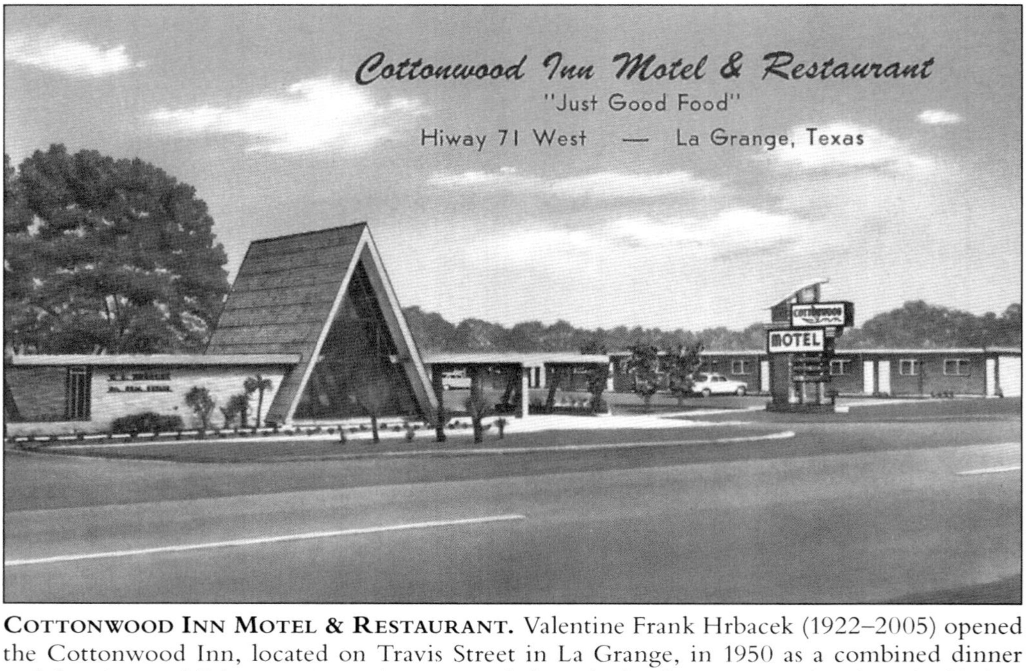

Cottonwood Inn Motel & Restaurant. Valentine Frank Hrbacek (1922–2005) opened the Cottonwood Inn, located on Travis Street in La Grange, in 1950 as a combined dinner and dancing establishment. It was later expanded, with the drive-in motel and pool added in 1962–1964 and a cocktail bar, the El Patron Club, completing the Cottonwood Inn complex in 1974. (Author's collection.)

Three

SCHULENBURG
THE TOWN THE RAILROAD BUILT

Unlike La Grange, Schulenburg did not organically grow into the city it currently is. Like so many Texas communities, the Galveston, Harrisburg & San Antonio Railroad virtually created Schulenburg overnight out of whole cloth.

In the early 1870s, the railroads were intent on expanding across Texas. The Galveston, Harrisburg & San Antonio Railroad needed a line connecting its namesake commercial centers. By 1870, it had laid track as far west as Alleyton/Columbus, in Colorado County, and was looking for its next stop when its agent Maj. James Converse traveled to High Hill to determine if the then burgeoning community should be the next stop.

After the German revolutions of 1848, a great number of German immigrants who came to Texas made their home in and around what become known as High Hill. Following the Germans closely in the 1850s and 1860s were Moravian and Austrian immigrants. By the time Major Converse visited High Hill in 1870, it seemed the logical choice for the next stop after Columbus. However, the railroad chose to situate the new station four miles to the southeast. Not a great distance today, but in 1870, it was High Hill's death knell.

There are several theories as to why High Hill was passed by in favor of a nonexistent locale. One strain of thought suggests that the residents of High Hill were not unified in their desire to have the new rail line come thundering through their town. Another is the railroad's surveyors determination that it would be too costly to run track through the elevated terrain of High Hill and opted to run the line where the prairie leveled out.

Whatever the actual reason, the decision was made and on March 1, 1873, Converse purchased 450 acres of land and a house from Louis Schulenburg, adding adjacent land donated by Christian Baumgarten, Franz Stanzel, F.A. Stanzel, and John Wittbecker. A new depot was built and called Schulenburg's Station, in honor of the man who had previously owned the depot's locale, but the work on laying the track from Columbus to the new station was slow.

The railroad finally arrived in Schulenburg on December 8, 1873, when the depot opened for business. Many of the residents of Schulenburg's early competitor moved from High Hill to the new community, literally, by having their physical homes lifted and transported to lots alongside the tracks. By 1874, Schulenburg claimed over 700 residents, and the town was officially incorporated on May 24, 1875.

Since that time, the town has never looked back and continued to grow and thrive as a commercial center well into the 20th century. While the railroad ceased passenger operations in the 1940s, the city still boasts a multicultural citizenry, like its sibling city to the north, welcoming large Anglo, German, and Czech communities.

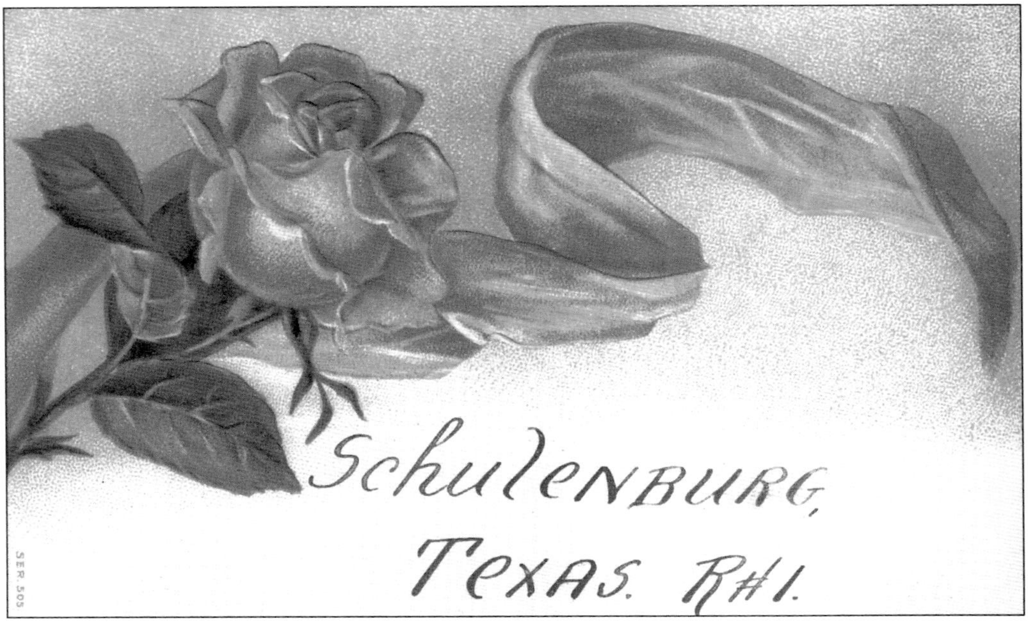

Schulenburg, Texas R#1. Here is a charming hand-labeled postcard, from about 1910, depicting a beautiful yellow rose of Texas over a blue ribbon. The equally charming town of Schulenburg is in the southern part of Fayette County. (Gary E. McKee.)

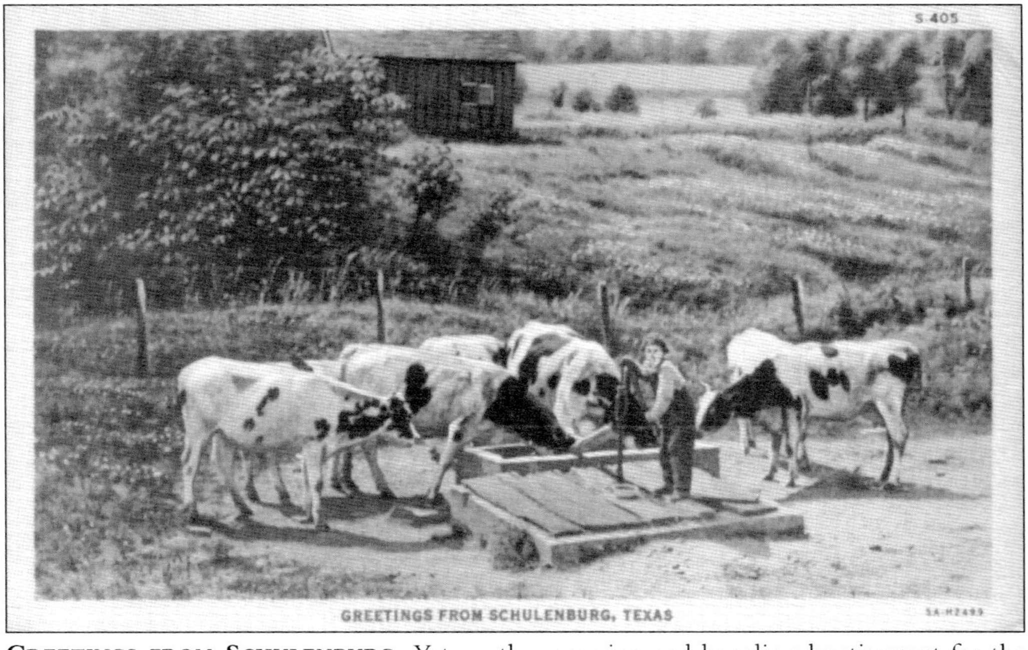

Greetings from Schulenburg. Yet another amusing and bucolic advertisement for the town of Schulenburg showing off their dairy business. (Gary E. McKee.)

SEE WHAT I CAUGHT IN SCHULENBURG, TEX. This whimsical postcard was sent by an admirer in La Grange to Mary Janacek (1896–1993), the daughter of Peter Janacek (1861–1926) and Mary Pratka Janacek (1871–1915). (Gary E. McKee.)

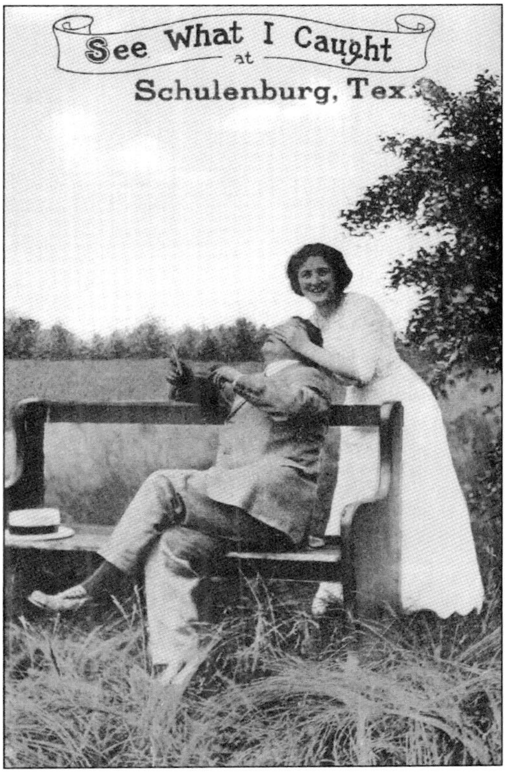

SCHULENBURG, TEXAS. Shown here is a bird's-eye view of Schulenburg, from the south. In the upper left can be seen the passenger depot of the Galveston, Harrisburg & San Antonio Railroad, and to its immediate right across the street is the railroad's freight depot. In the foreground inset is the original St. Rose of Lima Catholic Church. (Gary E. McKee.)

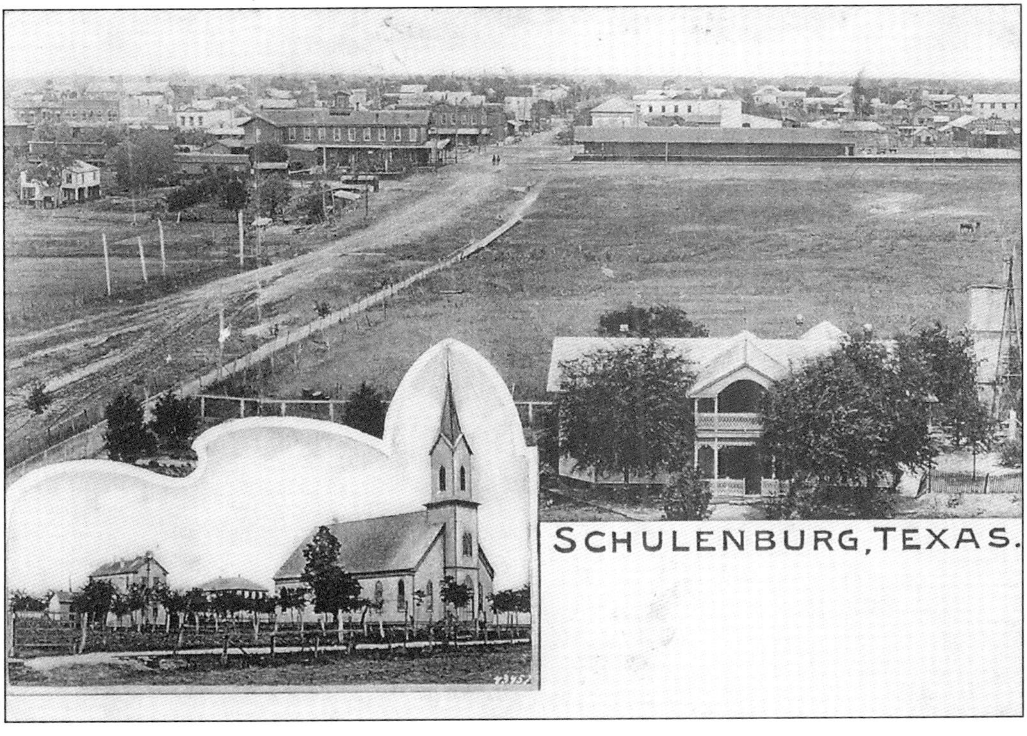

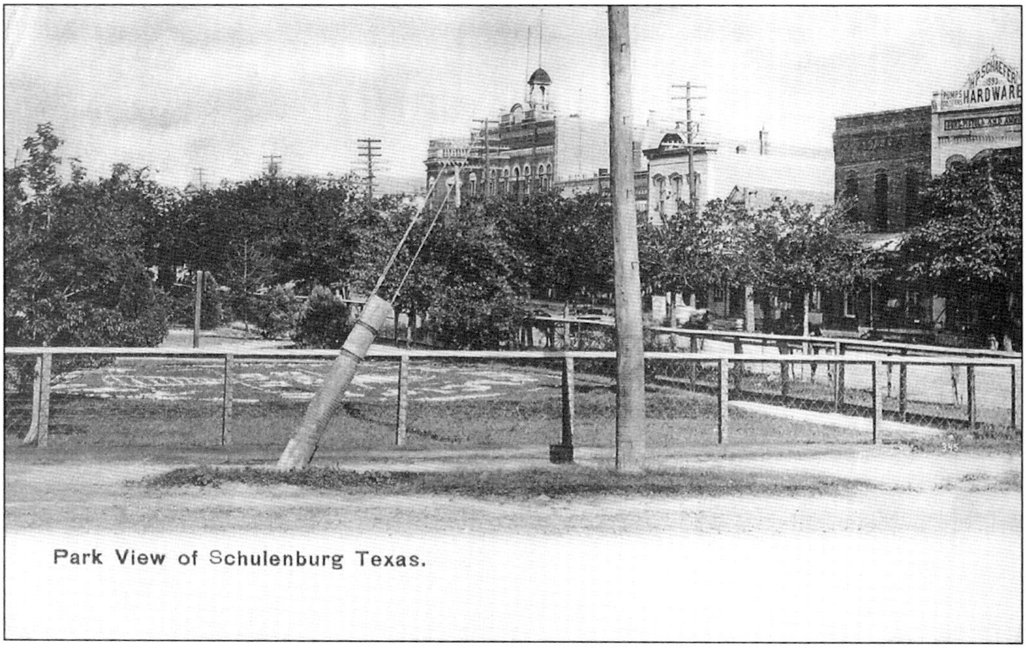

PARK VIEW OF SCHULENBURG, TEXAS. The park shown was located between the main passenger depot and the businesses along North Main Street at Lyons Avenue. The park had flowers, sycamore trees, palms, and cedars, as well as hitching posts for horses and wagons. In the center of the park, planted by Harry Adams, was the emblem of the Southern Pacific Railroad, which later acquired the railroad and depot. (Author's collection.)

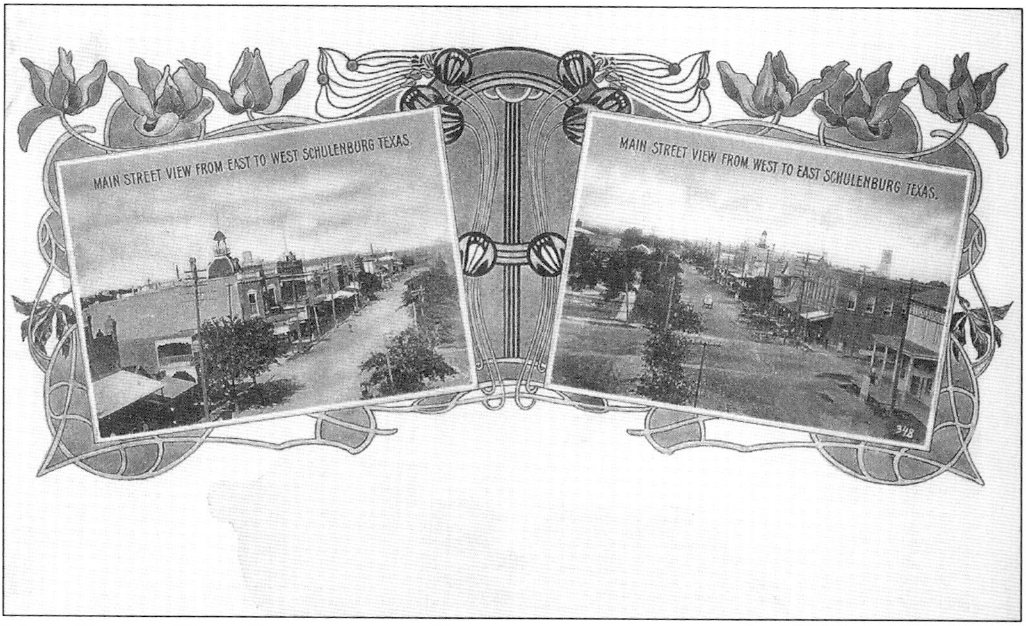

MAIN STREET VIEW, SCHULENBURG, TEXAS. Here are two Main Street views of downtown Schulenburg, looking from opposite directions, from about 1910. (Carolyn Heinsohn.)

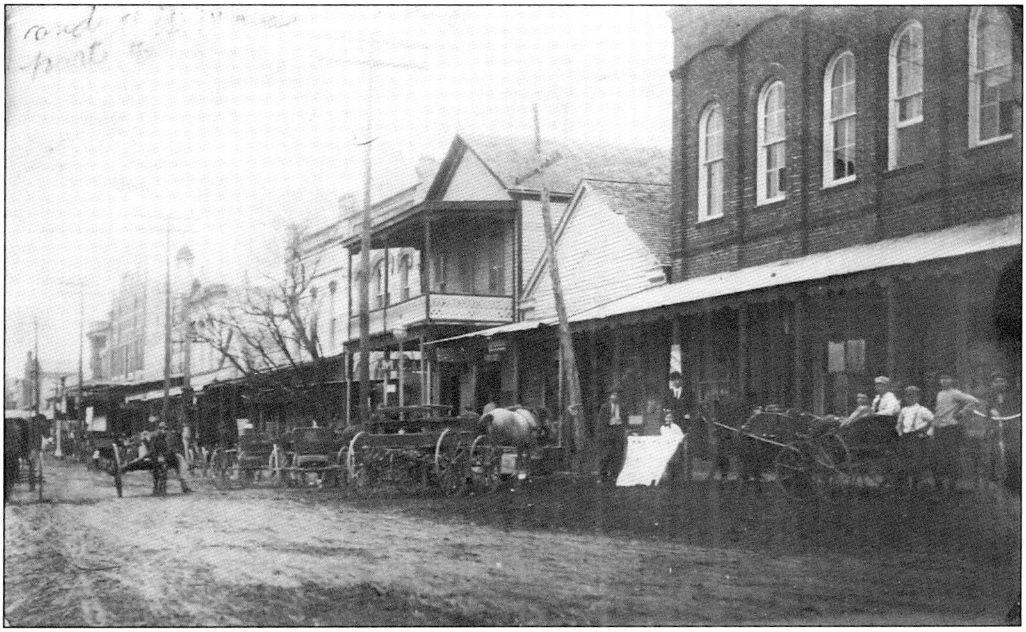

SCHULENBURG, TEXAS, BEFORE 1910. Again, the bustling activity once common to downtown Schulenburg's North Main Street is shown, this time looking west from the intersection of North Main Street and Lyons Avenue. (Carolyn Heinsohn.)

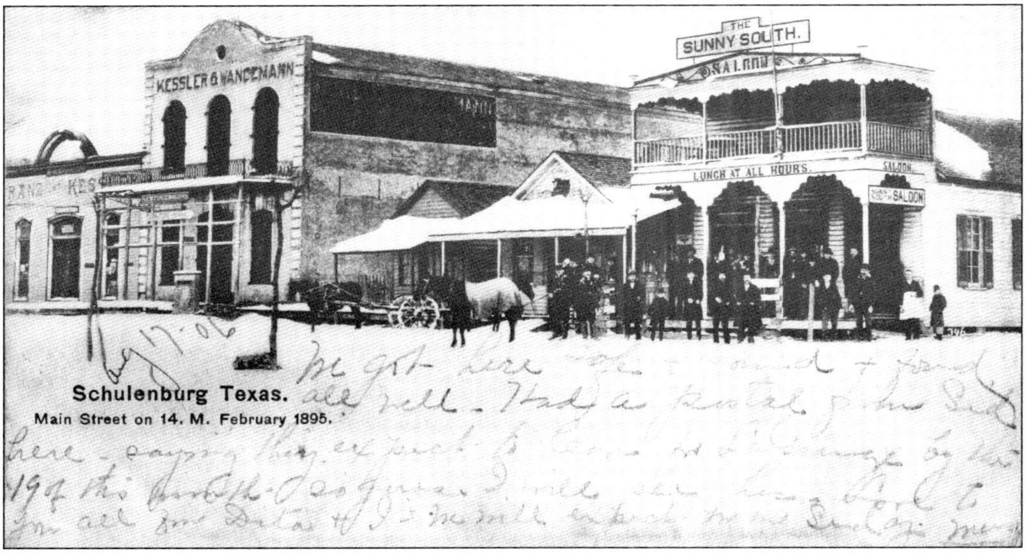

SCHULENBURG, TEXAS, MAIN STREET ON 14. M. FEBRUARY 1895. Interestingly, the scene depicted in this photo postcard is a snowfall in Schulenburg on Valentine's Day in 1895. The businesses shown are Cranz and Kessler, Kessler & Wangemann, and the Sunny South Saloon, run by H.F. Starke. The Cranz, Kessler, and Wangemann families were related by marriage. Cranz and Kessler was run by Gustav "Gus" Cranz (1848–1943) and his brother-in-law Edmund B. Kessler (1858–1922). Cranz's daughter Lillie married oil tycoon Hugh Roy Cullen (1881–1957) after he came to Schulenburg in 1897 to go into the cotton brokering business. (Fayette Heritage Museum & Archives.)

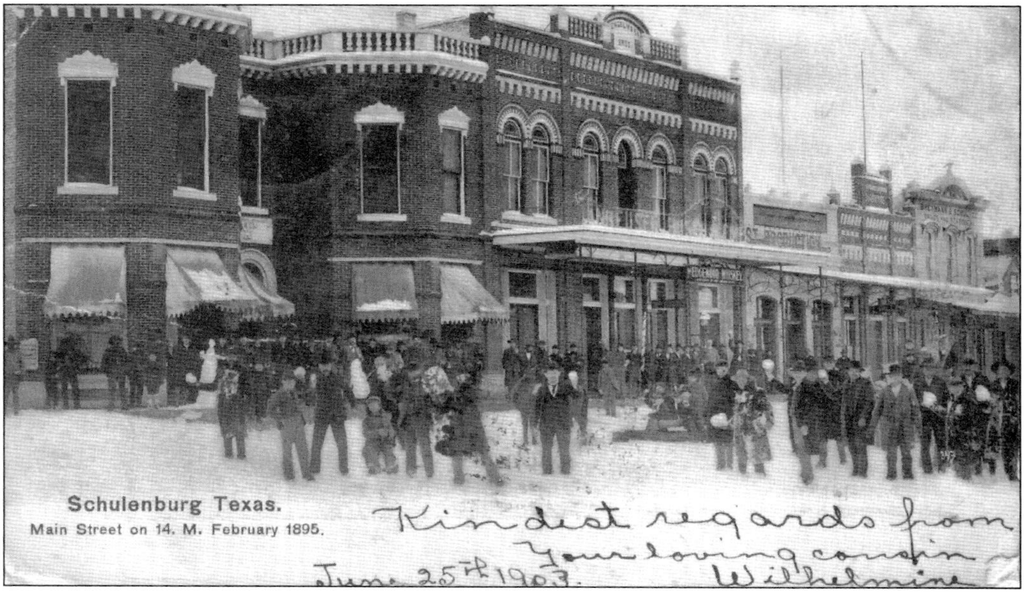

SCHULENBURG, TEXAS, MAIN STREET ON 14. M. FEBRUARY 1895. Here is another scene from Valentine's Day in 1895, showing the Russek family's building at the corner of North Main and Upton Streets. In 1869, Franz Russek (1816–1895) immigrated to Texas from the Czech Republic. He worked with the Galveston, Harrisburg & San Antonio Railroad as an agent assisting Czech and German immigrants. Russek met immigrants in Galveston, assisted them through customs, and accompanied them to Schulenburg, often lending them money. His son Ignaz Russek (1856–1908) founded the First National Bank of Schulenburg. (Gary E. McKee.)

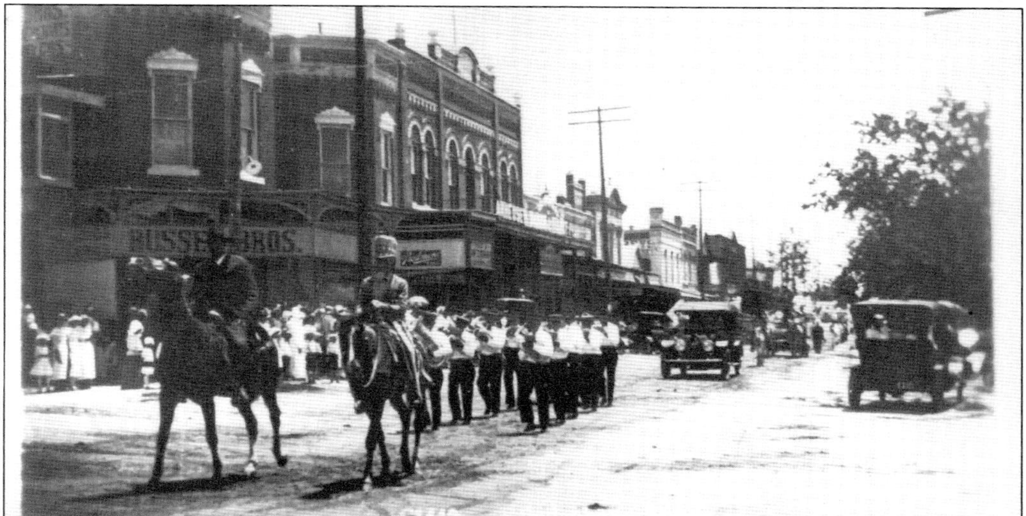

FOURTH OF JULY PARADE. Depicted in this scene is a Fourth of July parade, from about 1925, with Frederich Bruns, as Uncle Sam, leading the festivities. The Russek Brothers building and the Two Brothers Saloon, owned by Charles and Gustav Sengelmann, are visible in the background. These two buildings were constructed in 1894, after a fire on October 10, 1893, devastated much of the western downtown district along Upton Avenue, between North Main and Anderson Streets. (Gary E. McKee.)

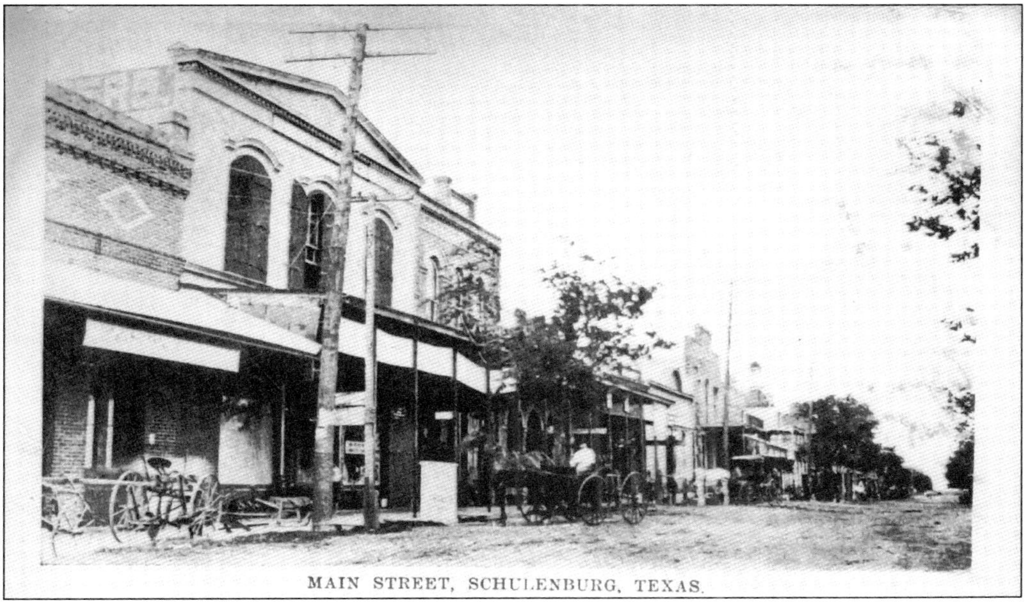

MAIN STREET, SCHULENBURG, TEXAS. Here again is Schulenburg's downtown. The structure with the peaked capital and shuttered windows was the Bohms building, where Gerhard Bohms (1834–1896) ran a store. The Bohms building later changed hands in the family and displayed the Wolters name. Bohms came to Texas from Jaderberg, Germany. His daughter Anna married Robert Anton Wolters (1858–1940), whose brothers Ferdinand Carl Wolters (1862–1910) and Ernest Jacob Wolters (1856–1910) ran a saloon and saddlery one door and two doors down from Bohms, respectively. (Gary E. McKee.)

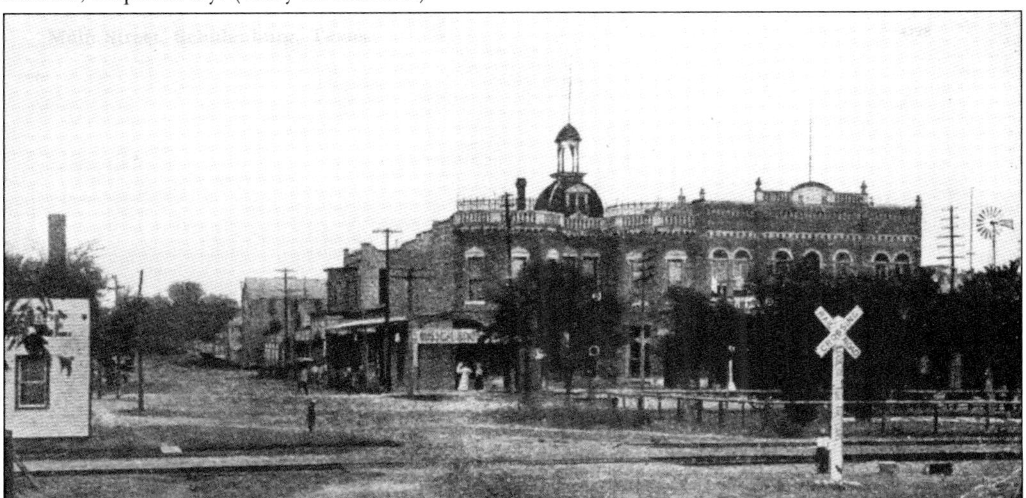

MAIN STREET, SCHULENBURG, TEXAS. Schulenburg started as a railroad depot in 1873, when the Galveton, Harriburg & San Antonio Railroad extended its line from its western terminus at Alleyton/Columbus in Colorado County on to San Antonio. In choosing to locate its depot at Schulenburg, the railroad extinguished the growth of the High Hill community. Located four miles to the northwest, High Hill is from where many of Schulenburg's earliest residents came and is often referred to as the "Mother of Schulenburg." (Author's collection.)

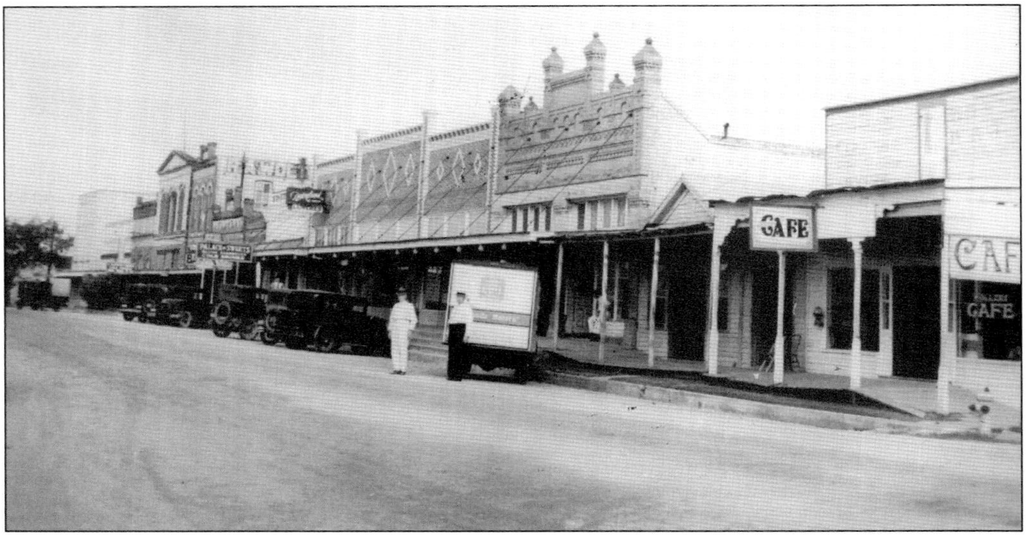

DOWNTOWN SCHULENBURG. The gentleman in dark trousers by the delivery truck is Otto Bruno Schwenke (1877–1940), who came to Texas in 1882 from Germany with his parents, Ernst and Theresa Kobert Schwenke. Schwenke initially farmed in the Freyburg vicinity, but he later moved to Schulenburg to work as an embalmer with the Baumgarten Company, which was a lumber, hardware, and furniture business, but which also constructed coffins, thus the need for an embalmer. Schwenke later began the Schwenke-Baumgarten Funeral Home in Schulenburg, which is still in existence today. (Gary E. McKee.)

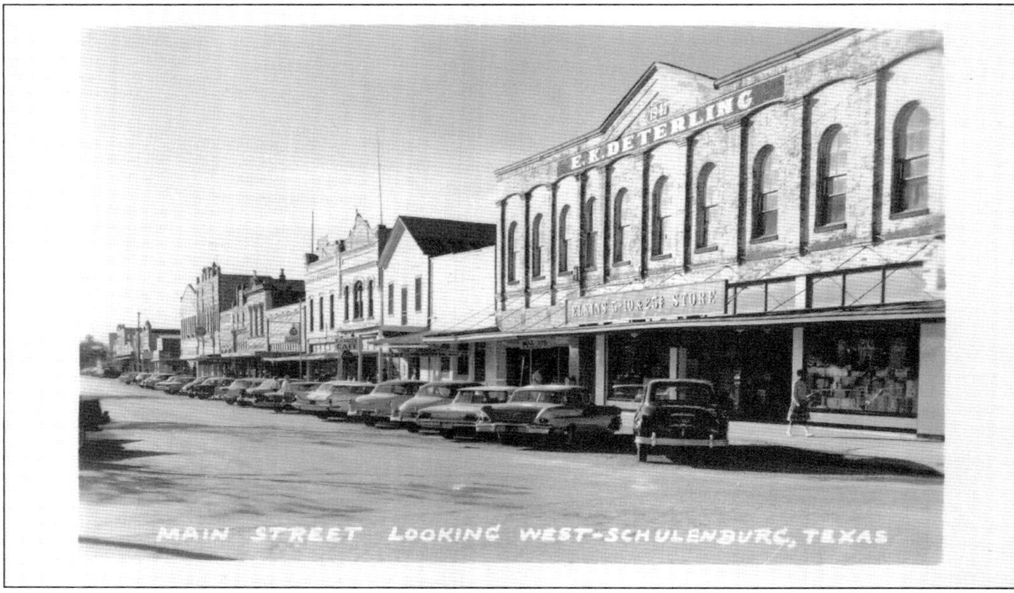

MAIN STREET LOOKING WEST, SCHULENBURG, TEXAS. Prominent in this postcard is what is labeled the E.K. Deterling Building in which the Elkins five-and-dime store is located. Atop the peaked molding is the painted date of 1947, however, the building dates to much earlier than that, as it appears distinctly in a hand-drawn, bird's-eye-view map by Augustus Koch from 1881. The structure was built by Johann Carl Proetzel (1825–1887), who ran a business there. The Family Dollar store is located there today. (Gary E. McKee.)

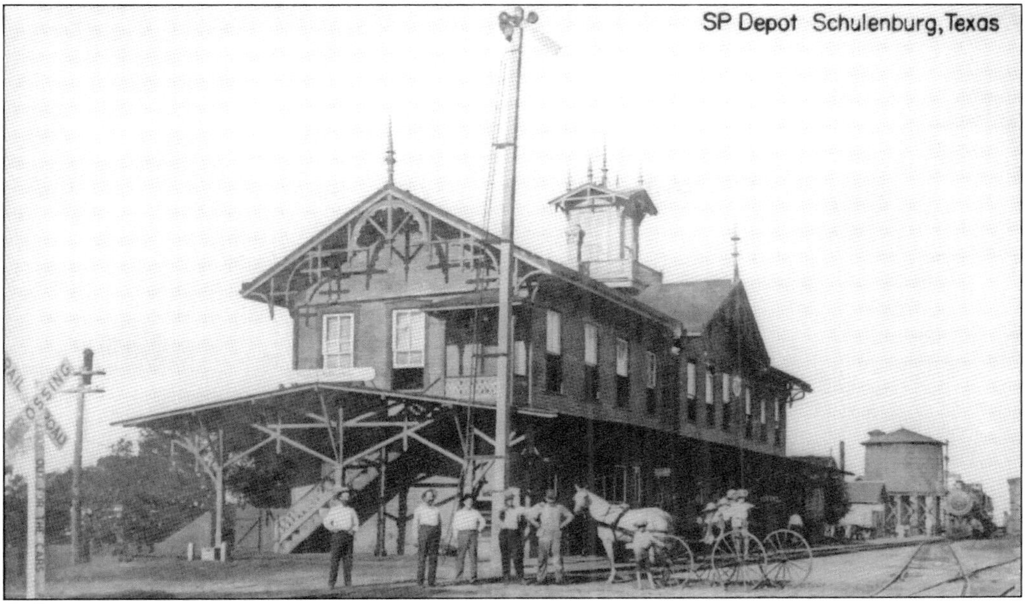

SP Depot, Schulenburg, Texas. When Maj. James Converse came to High Hill in 1873, the residents of High Hill did not want what he offered, a train from Galveston through Harrisburg (Houston) to San Antonio. What High Hill passed up, the residents of Lyons jumped at. Thus it was that Louis Schulenburg, Johann Christian Baumgarten, the Stanzel brothers, and Johann Heinrich Wittbecker aided in the founding of Schulenburg. Baumgarten was especially enthusiastic and allowed many of the Irish laborers building the railroad to stay in his log home, and for this he is known as the "Father of Schulenburg." (Gary E. McKee.)

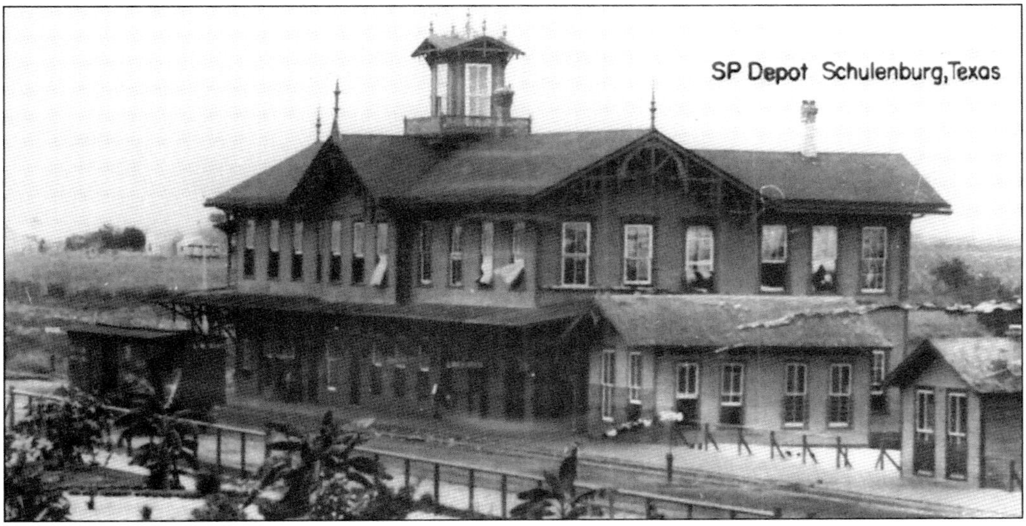

SP Depot Schulenburg, Texas. Built in 1881 alongside the tracks, the beautiful High Victorian–style passenger depot was a sight to behold. It housed a hotel as well as a dining room, and Schulenburg residents were often seen awaiting the trains from Galveston and Houston in their finest attire. The depot was demolished in 1940 and replaced with a smaller passenger depot, which itself was demolished when passenger service ceased altogether in the 1970s. (Carolyn Heinsohn.)

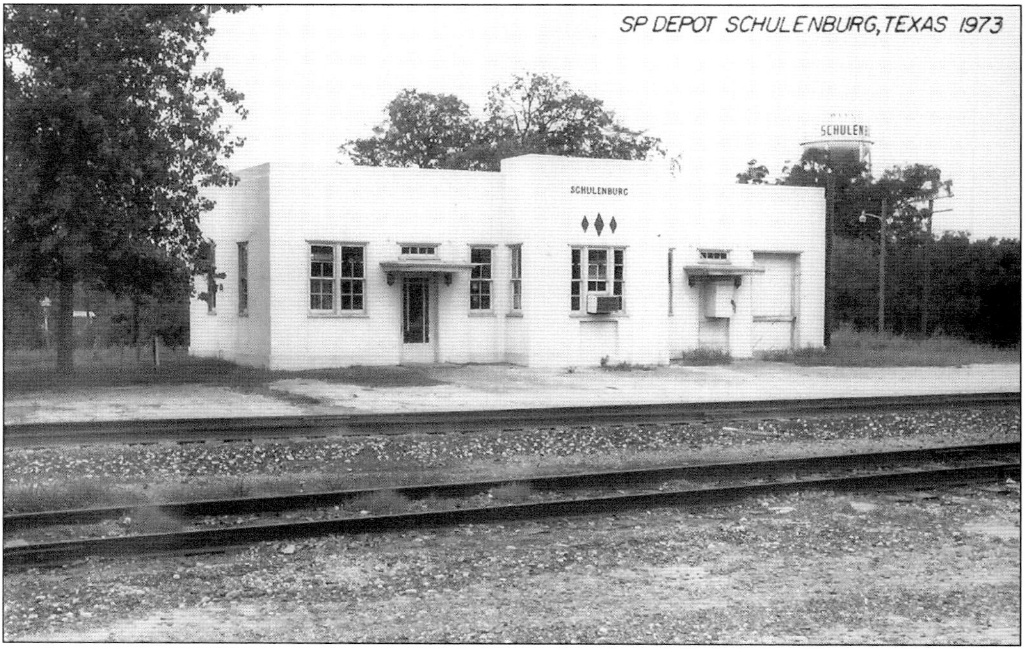

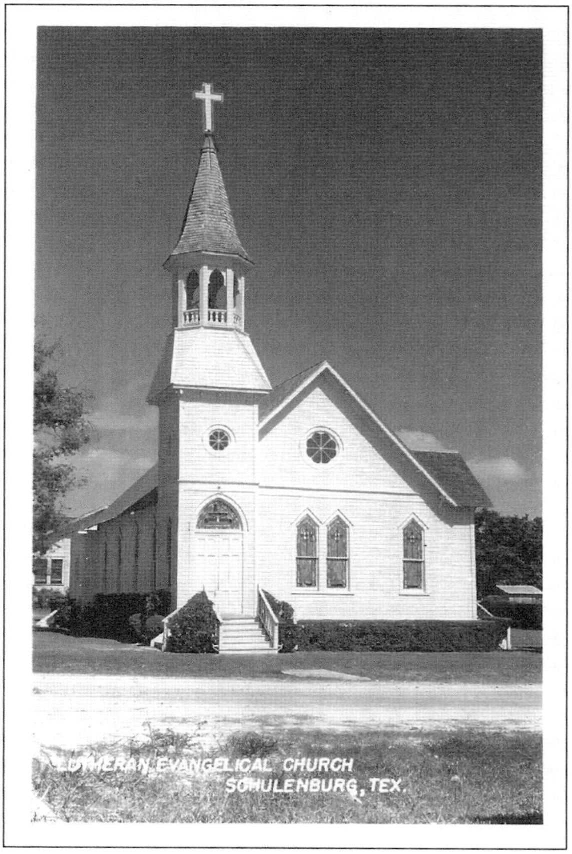

SP DEPOT, SCHULENBURG, TEXAS, 1973. Erected on the site of the former ornate Victorian passenger depot when it was demolished in 1940, this Southern Pacific Depot also was torn down eventually, when passenger traffic ceased in Schulenburg. (Author's collection.)

LUTHERAN EVANGELICAL CHURCH, SCHULENBURG, TEX. Pictured is the Lutheran Evangelical Church in Schulenburg, located at the intersection of West Summit Street and Hillje Avenue. Today, this is in fact the St. Paul Presbyterian Church. (Author's collection.)

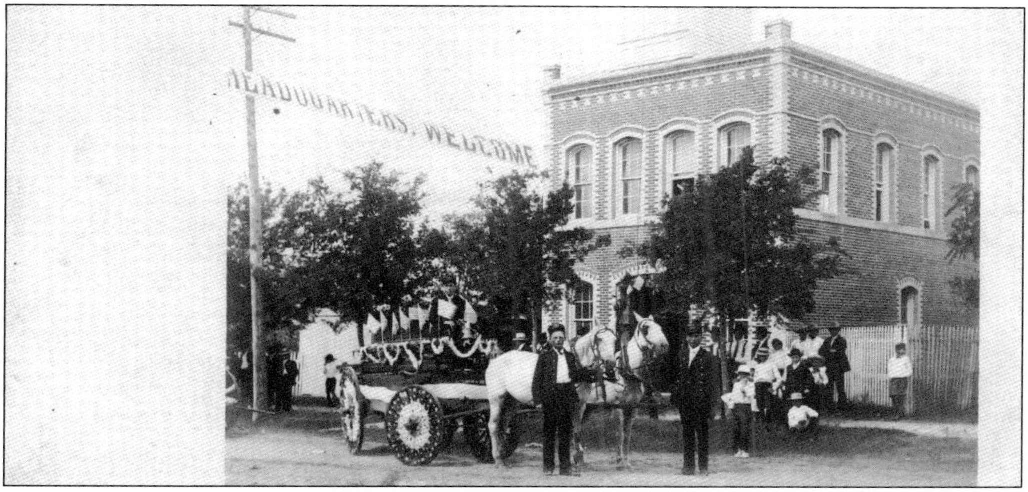

FIRE STATION AND JAIL, SCHULENBURG, TEXAS. Here is Schulenburg City Hall and Fire Station, built about 1905. It was believed that the steeple atop the structure (barely visible in this image) was from an area church that had been wrecked in a hurricane on July 21, 1909. A bell tower later was blown off the building in a storm, and the firehouse, which also housed the city jail, was demolished in the early 1960s. Following the fire of 1893, Schulenburg took fire safety very seriously, and in 1903, with the aid of Gus Depmore, it inaugurated a volunteer fire department, members of which are shown here. (Gary E. McKee.)

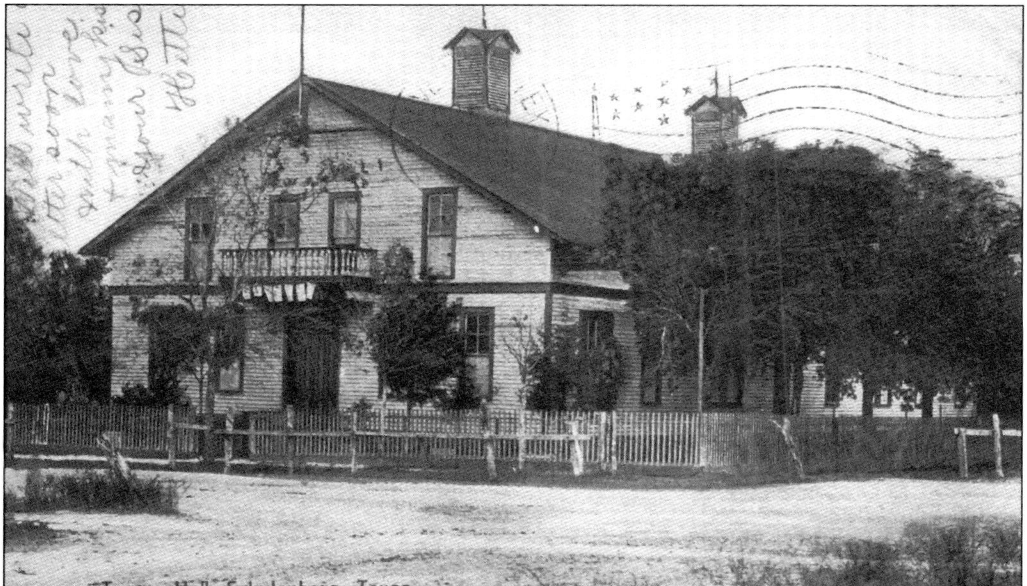

TURNER HALL, SCHULENBURG, TEXAS. Built in 1886 by Heinrich W. Bohlmann (1845–1926) and at the direction of the Schulenburg Turnverein, a German athletics and social club, Turner Hall hosted numerous activities, including theatrical performances, musical concerts, and social events. The building was alternately called the Opera House, the City Auditorium, the Turnverein, the Tri-Association Hall, and ultimately the American Legion Hall, after that organization acquired the structure in 1936. It was originally located at the corner of Summit and Upton Streets but has been situated in Wolters Park since 1937. (Gary E. McKee.)

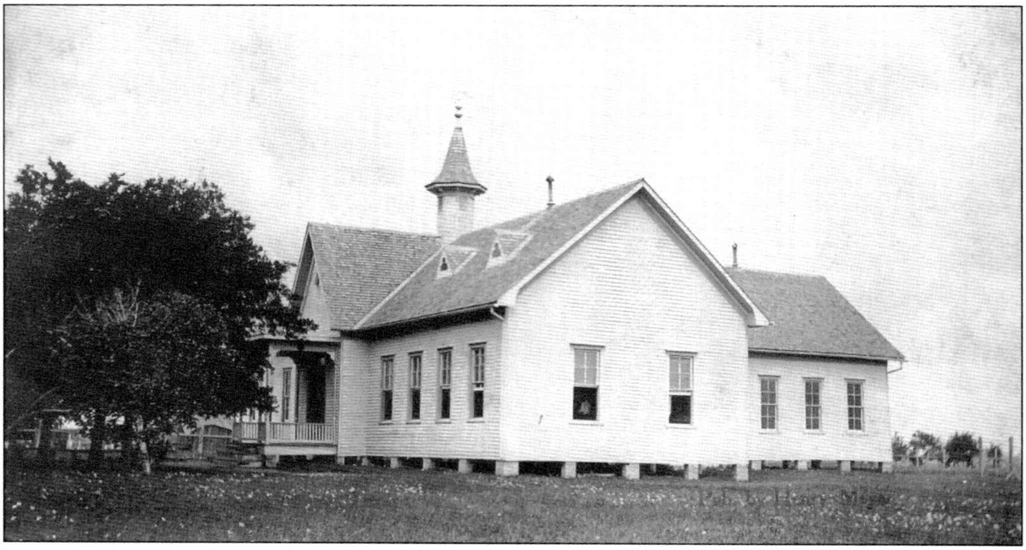

PUBLIC SCHOOL. Pictured is the Schulenburg Public School house, built in 1900. Before then, school was taught in the old Lyons Lodge building, which had been moved to Schulenburg from High Hill. In front of the school was a water well, which was covered by a latticed gazebo called a summerhouse. The school had four rooms with desks for both the students and the teachers. By 1915, the school had 268 students studying up through the 10th grade—its highest level. (Gary E. McKee.)

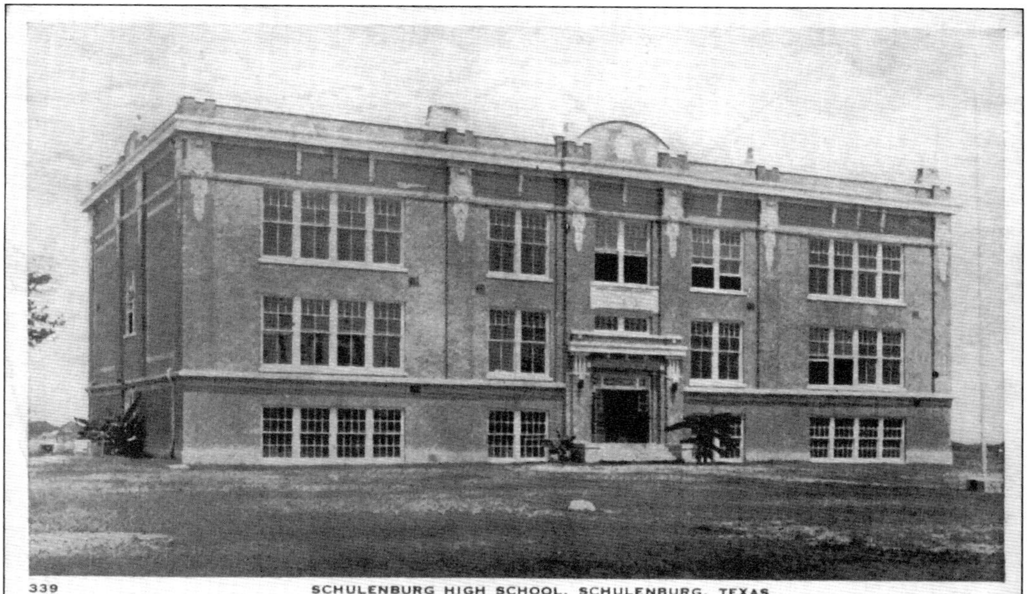

SCHULENBURG HIGH SCHOOL, SCHULENBURG, TEXAS. By the early 1920s, Schulenburg had outgrown its four-room school, and on February 26, 1921, the Schulenburg School District was formed. In 1923, the school shown here was dedicated. Now known as the Old Main, the new school had 12 classrooms and an auditorium. The old schoolhouse was divided in two. Half was transferred to the Julia Anne Green School, which was Schulenburg's African American school, and the other half was used as an external classroom. (Gary E. McKee.)

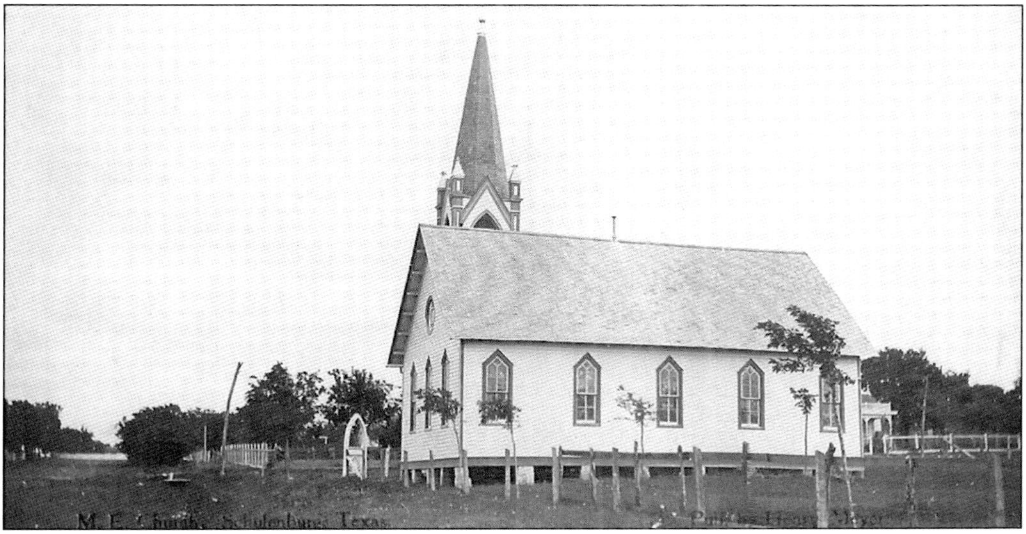

M.E. CHURCH, SCHULENBURG, TEXAS. This is a photo postcard of Schulenburg's Methodist church, built in 1905. The church was aligned with the older Freyburg Methodist Church, which had existed in the nearby Freyburg community since 1879. At that time, the Methodist church performed missionary work in their surrounding vicinity, and the Freyburg pastor would come to Schulenburg on a bimonthly basis to preach and raise converts. This outreach resulted in a large-enough congregation in Schulenburg that the newly constructed church shown was dedicated on October 29, 1905. (Author's collection.)

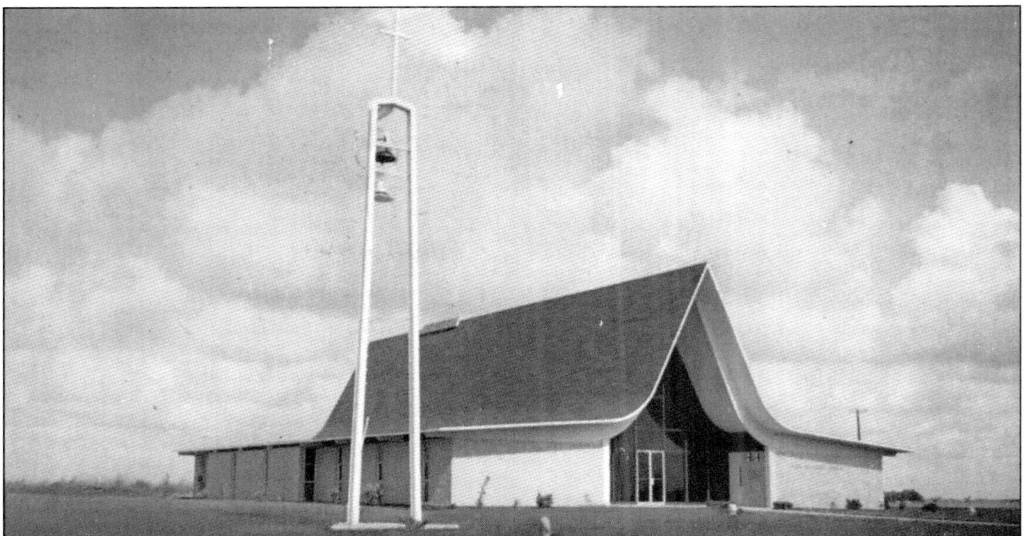

FIRST METHODIST CHURCH. Wilhelm Thurmann, of the Freyburg Methodist community, donated funds to have a bell commissioned for the new Schulenburg Methodist church. The bell was cast in Ohio and inscribed with the text, "This bell is a gift for the German Methodist Church from Wilhelm Thurmann, born September 22, 1833, in Klein Brese, Brandenburg, Germany, died June 8, 1906, Schulenburg, Texas. F. Bohmfalk, Pastor." The bell still rings today in the steel tower shown in front of the current First United Methodist Church of Schulenburg. (Gary E. McKee.)

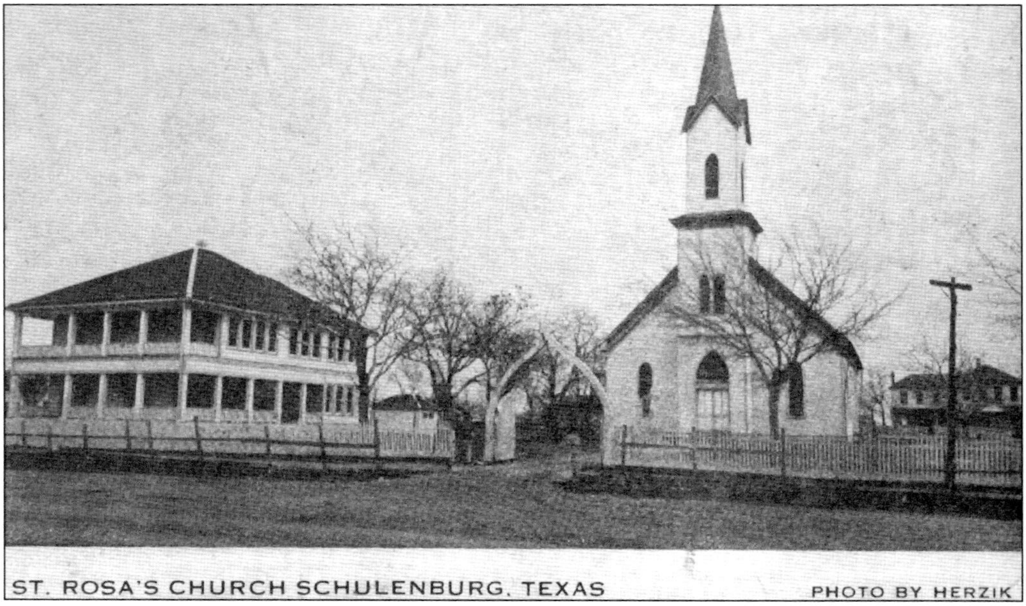

St. Rosa's Church, Schulenburg, Texas. St. Rose of Lima Church was the first Catholic Church in Schulenburg and was dedicated on October 23, 1889, in honor of the first American saint. The first chapel was built by Heinrich Bohlmann. The land for the church was donated by Franz (1839–1928) and Rosina Guenther Stanzel (1830–1912), who, along with Franz Andreas Stanzel (1834–1889), donated land to the railroad to jump-start the founding of Schulenburg. The Stanzel brothers came to Texas from Pohl, Czech Republic, in 1867. (Gary E. McKee.)

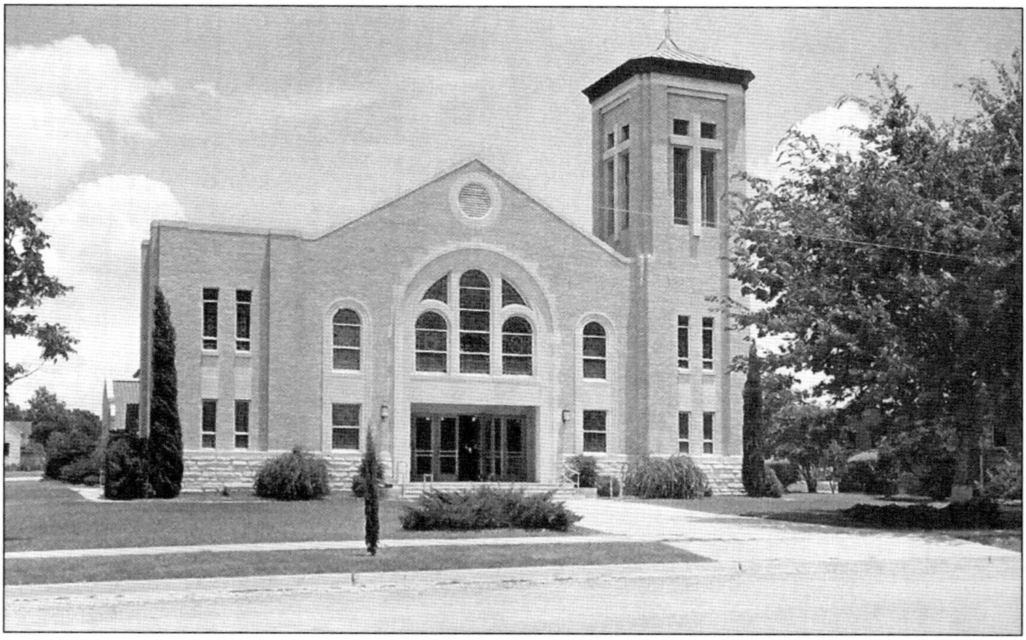

St. Rose of Lima Catholic Church. On June 15, 1952, the present Spanish-style yellow brick and limestone edifice shown here was dedicated as the replacement for the former St. Rose of Lima chapel. (Author's collection.)

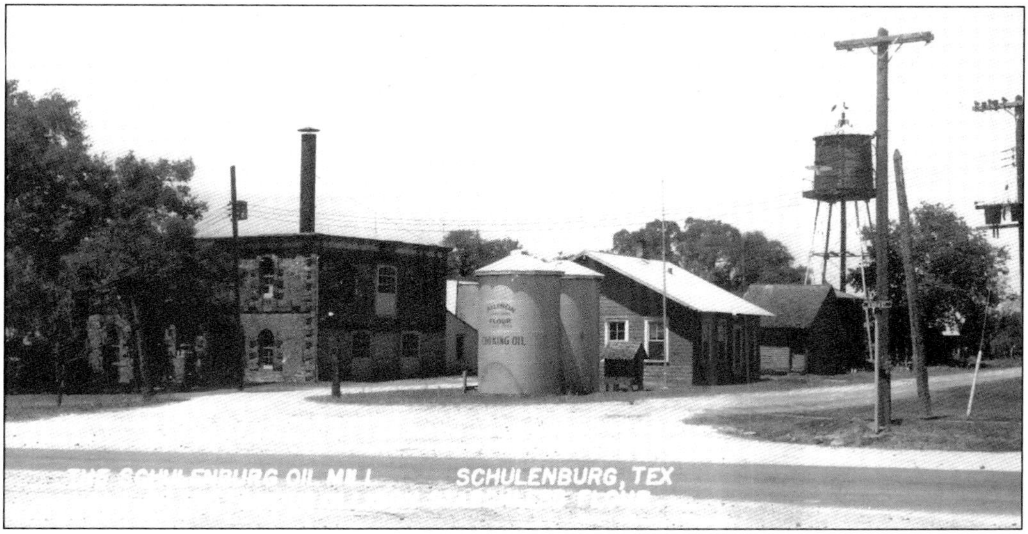

THE SCHULENBURG OIL MILL, SCHULENBURG, TEX. Built in 1883 as a replacement for an earlier mill in High Hill, which had begun in 1866, the Schulenburg Oil Mill was operated by Johann Christian Baumgarten and his son Gus. Known as the "Home of the Famous Allison Starchless Flour," through Gus's management, the mill was instrumental in the creation of Allison Flour, made from cottonseed as a substitute for wheat flour. During World War I, Baumgarten shipped more than 60,000 pounds of Allison Flour to the Peerless Biscuit Company in Pittsburg. (Gary E. McKee.)

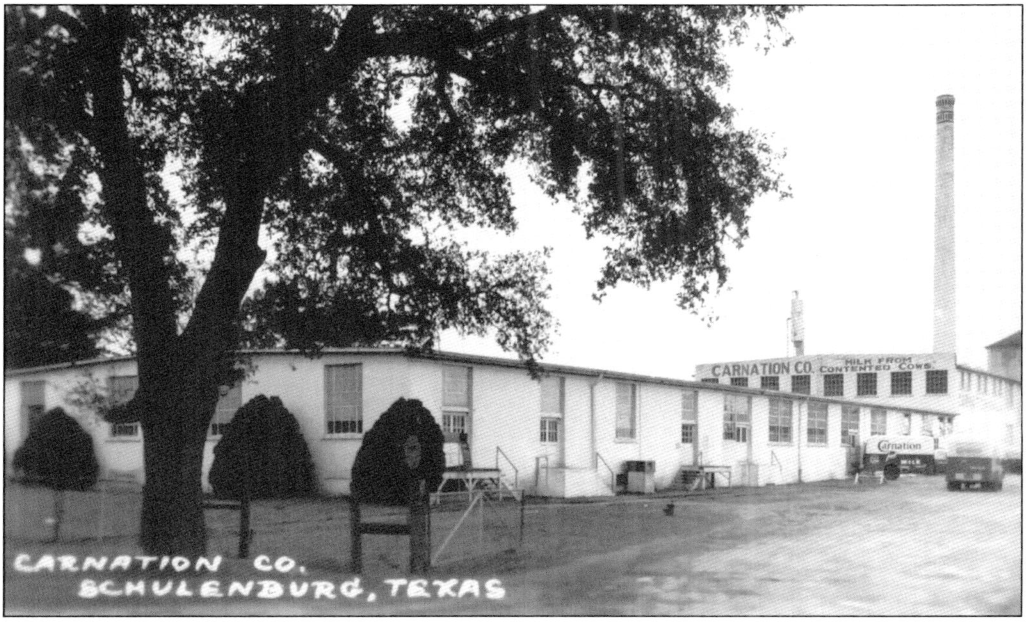

CARNATION CO., SCHULENBURG, TEXAS. In 1929, the Carnation Company located its first Texas milk-processing plant in Schulenburg. At its ground-breaking ceremony on April 3, 1929, the company flew in the then famous "Flying Bull" from Wisconsin for a crowd of 30,000 people who had come to celebrate the event. The Carnation plant brought jobs and prosperity on the eve of what would, later that year, become the Great Depression. (Gary E. McKee.)

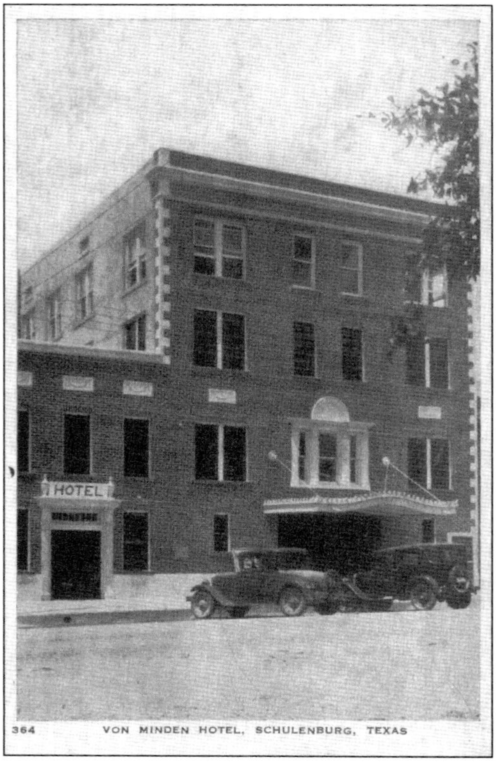

Von Minden Hotel, Schulenburg, Texas. Opened on May 22, 1928, the Von Minden Hotel was built by Gerhard von Minden (1875–1948) for his daughter Leonida Katrina Speckels and her husband, Irwin J. Speckels. The hotel and adjoining Cozy Theater, which opened in November 1927, were welcome attractions. They were companions to von Minden's Lester Hotel and Cozy Theater in La Grange. The Von Minden Hotel is the last of the hotel/theater combinations in Texas. The Speckels resided in a three-bedroom apartment in the hotel from 1928 until 1979. The hotel and theater are still in operation today. (Author's collection.)

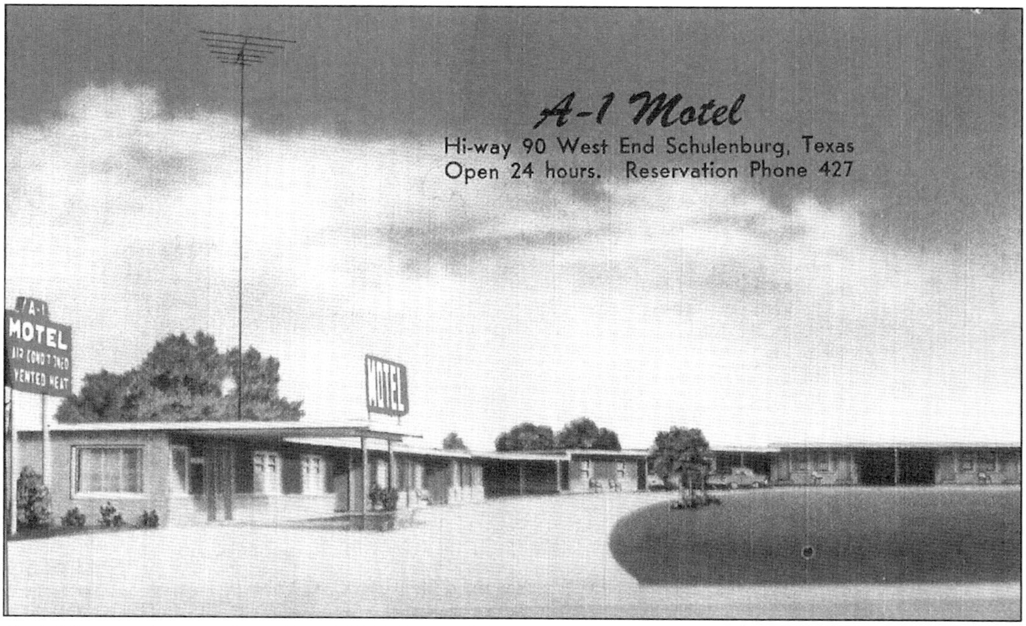

A-1 Motel. Located on the old Highway 90 connecting Weimar to Schulenburg and Flatonia is the A-1 Motel, which existed at 1321 West Summit Street in Schulenburg. Advertising rooms with air-conditioning and vented heat, it was owned by Frank and Mary Kurtin. The building was demolished in 2008. (Author's collection.)

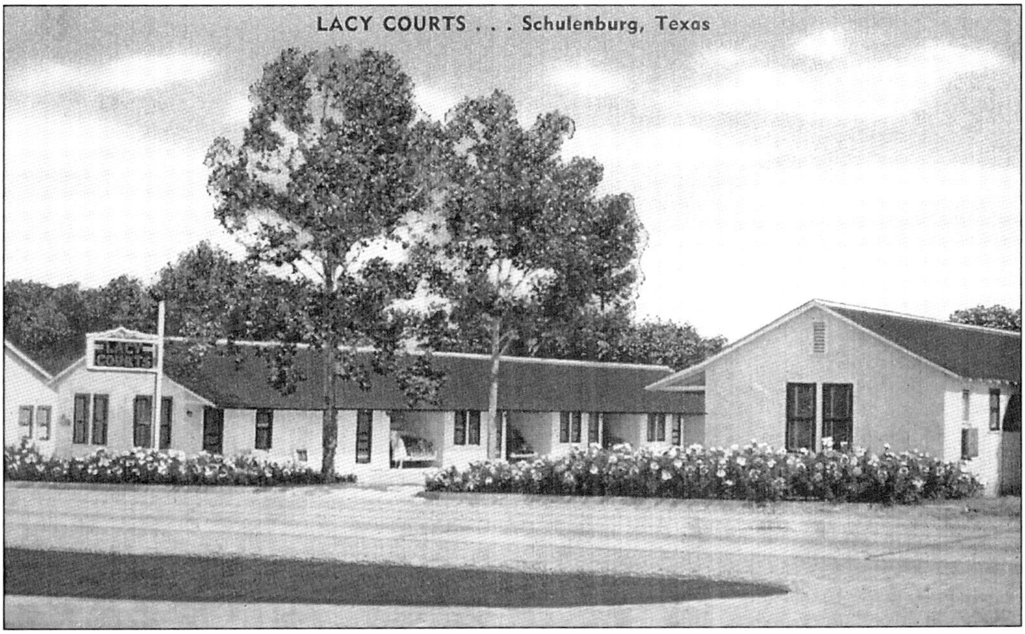

Lacy Courts . . . Schulenburg, Texas. The Lacy Courts property was located at the northeast corner of West Summit Street and James Avenue. Today, it is an apartment complex. (Author's collection.)

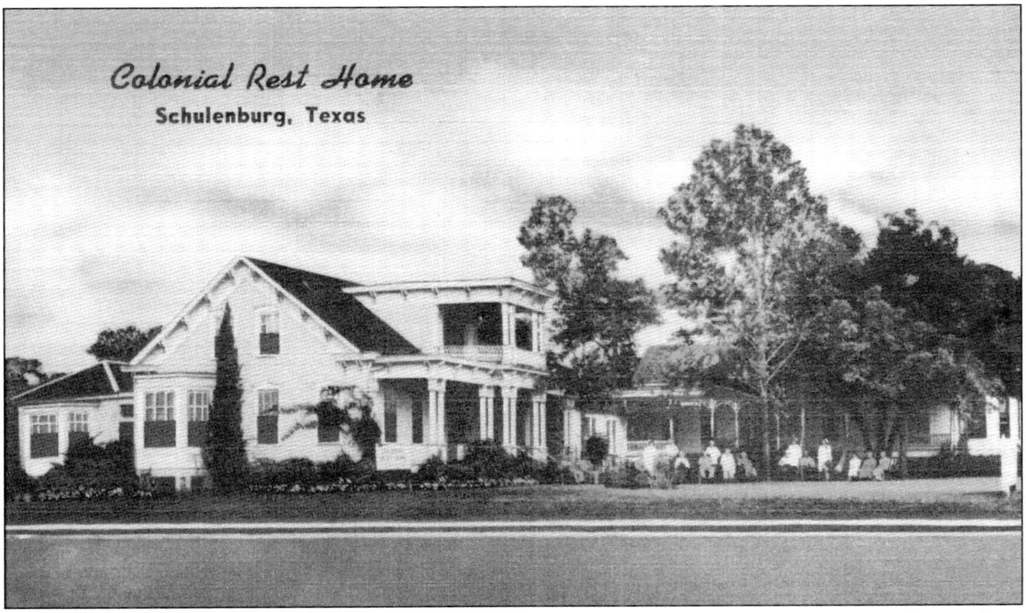

Colonial Rest Home, Schulenburg, Texas. The Colonial Rest Home was located on West Avenue in Schulenburg. Originally, this building was the home of Fayette County pioneer Charles A. Kessler (1834–1910), who came to Texas in 1845 from Nassau, Germany. The adjoining building was the home of Lillie and Robert Boettcher, Kessler's daughter and son-in-law. In 1944, the homes were purchased by Dr. Gene Schulze and used as the Schulze Hospital. The hospital closed in 1956, when it became the Colonial Rest Home. (Gary E. McKee.)

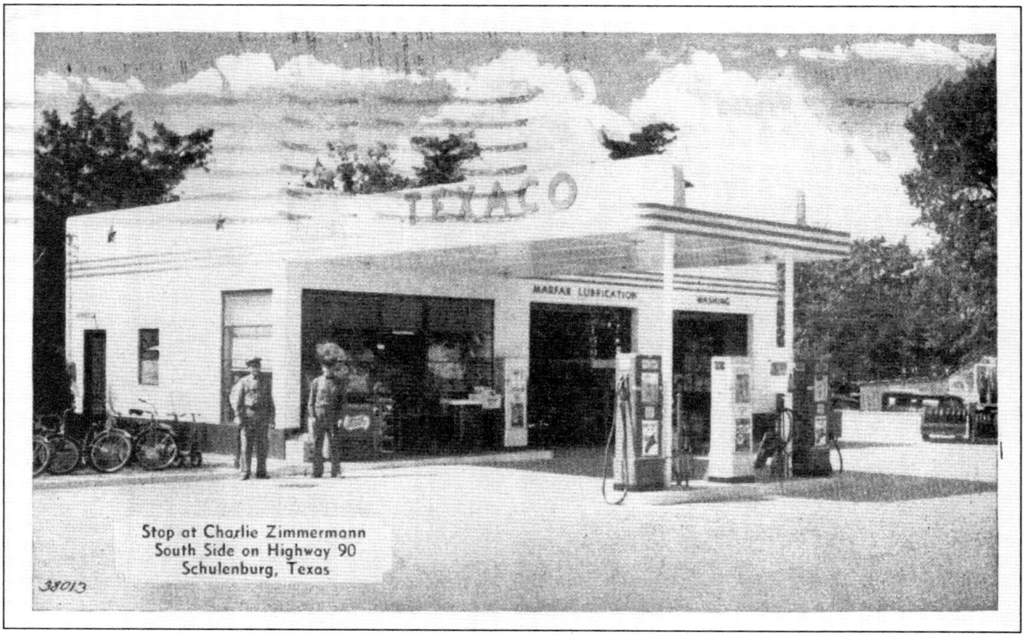

STOP AT CHARLIE ZIMMERMANN. Charlie Zimmermann's Texaco service station is pictured here in the 1940s. The station was located on the southwest corner of the intersection of West Summit Street and Upton Avenue. Today, the carport and gas pumps have been removed, but the building still exists. (Gary E. McKee.)

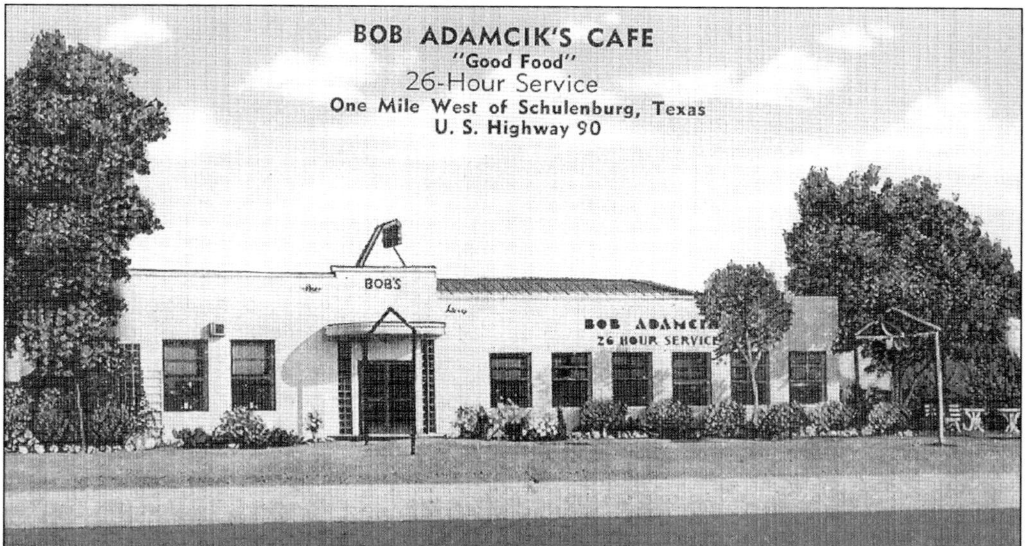

BOB ADAMCIK'S CAFE. Located one mile west of Schulenburg on Highway 90, Bob Adamcik's Café gave the other eateries in town a run for their money. Beginning in the early 1930s with a filling station, Robert Joseph Adamcik (1903–1967) was a consummate salesman who used witty pitches and humorous tactics to lure customers. Some of his marketing strategies included the phrase, "26 hour service;" a blue parrot outside his restaurant; and a monkey named Bob Jr. The Adamciks came to Texas from Frenstat, Czech Republic. (Author's collection.)

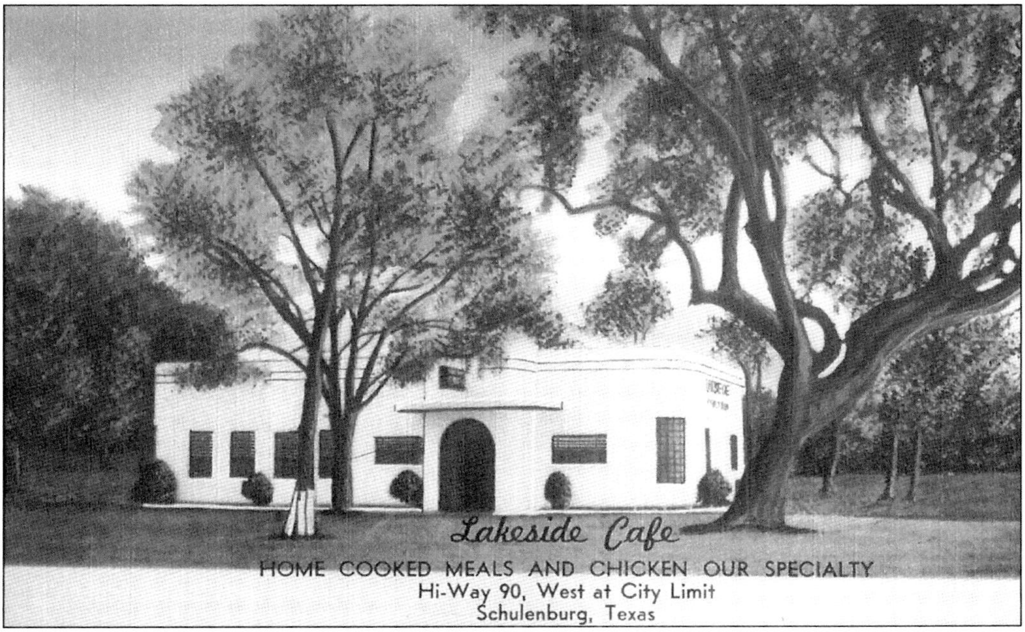

LAKESIDE CAFÉ . Joining the other hamburger joints in Schulenburg was the Lakeside Café, which was located next to a small tank on the south side of West Summit Street, east of Shultz Avenue. The tank had fish that patrons could catch—if they had time to kill. (Author's collection.)

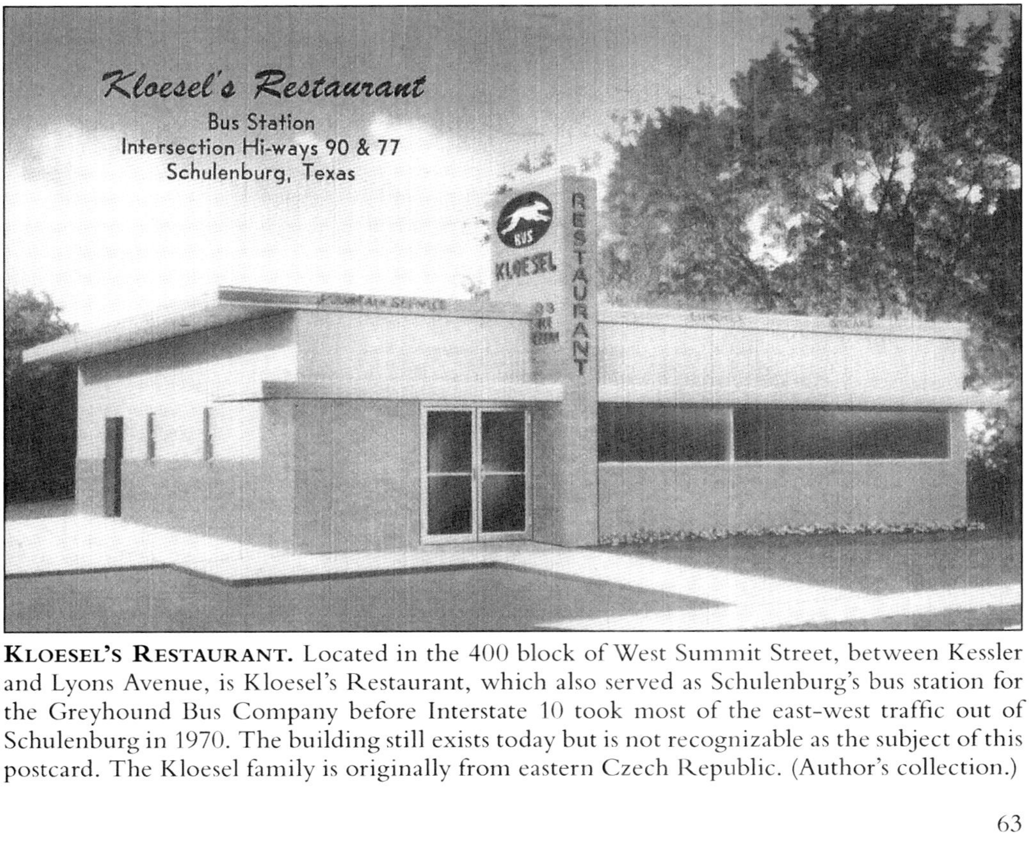

KLOESEL'S RESTAURANT. Located in the 400 block of West Summit Street, between Kessler and Lyons Avenue, is Kloesel's Restaurant, which also served as Schulenburg's bus station for the Greyhound Bus Company before Interstate 10 took most of the east-west traffic out of Schulenburg in 1970. The building still exists today but is not recognizable as the subject of this postcard. The Kloesel family is originally from eastern Czech Republic. (Author's collection.)

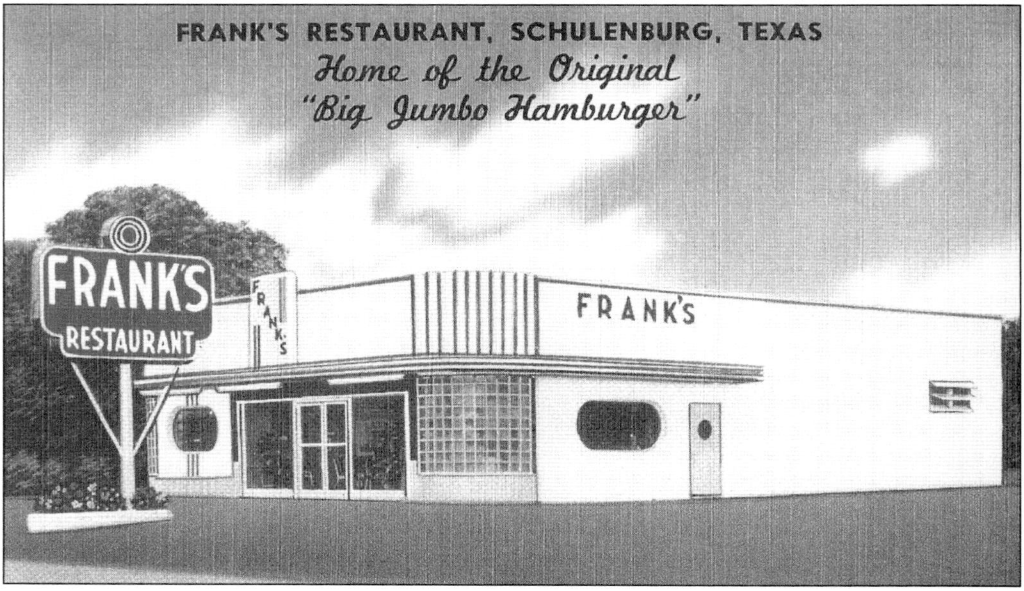

Frank's Restaurant, Schulenburg, Texas. Located, at the time of this postcard, in the 400 block of West Summit Street, Frank's Restaurant has become a staple for interstate travelers. Begun in 1929 by Frank John Tilicek (1905–1941), the café shown here was the second incarnation of Tilicek's business, which began on North Main Street in Schulenburg's downtown. The business moved to West Summit Street in 1934 and then to Interstate 10 in the 1970s, where it still hosts hundreds of patrons daily. (Author's collection.)

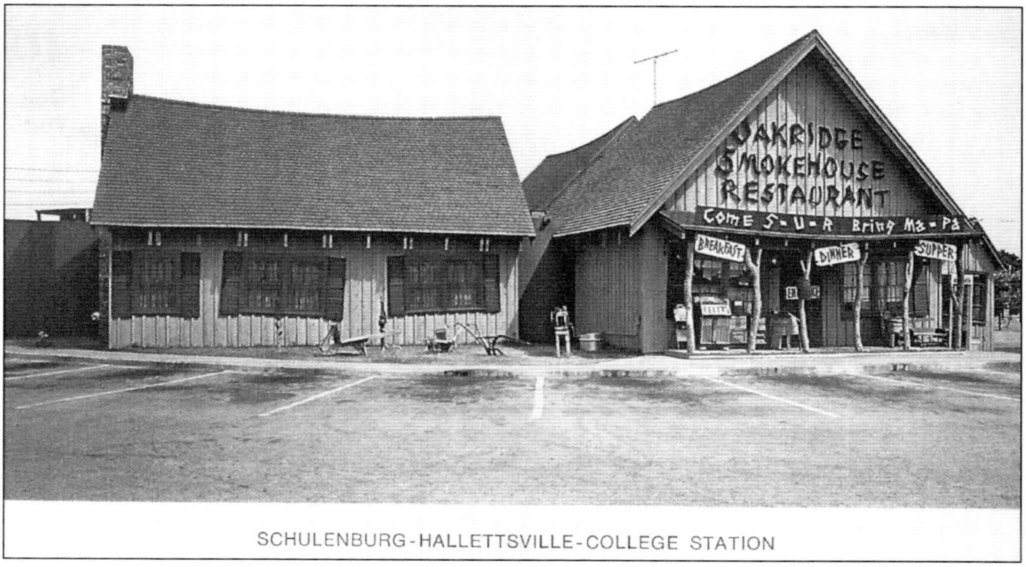

Schulenburg-Hallettsville-College Station. The Oakridge Smokehouse Restaurant, located at the intersection of Interstate 10 and Highway 77, opened for business in 1969. The business, which includes a motel and gas station, was started by Roy Bucek as an offshoot of Bucek's meat locker business, which he entered into in 1950. Bucek and his wife, Vera Veenstra Bucek, ran the business until 1994, when the business was sold to Robert Besetzny, who still runs it today. (Author's collection.)

Four

Flatonia
The Railroad's Other Progeny

The largest population center in the southern part of Fayette County is Flatonia, so named for one of its founders, Frederick William Flato, who, along with his syndicate partners John Kline and John Lattimore, purchased the land upon which the current town is located from the Faires family.

William Alexander "Alex" Faires (1806–1885), originally from South Carolina, came to Texas from Tennessee in 1834 as part of Stephen F. Austin's "Old Three Hundred." Faires and his wife, Ada McClure Faires (1810–1874), settled in southern Fayette County near West Point and raised eight children. The Faires family participated in the Runaway Scrape, and Alex wrote a firsthand account of this violent episode in Texas and Fayette County's early history. The land that Alex Faires patented upon his arrival to Texas was the object of the Flato, Kline, and Lattimore Syndicate's plans for southern Fayette County.

In 1873, at the same time that Schulenburg was being formed by its railroad sponsor, Flatonia was being created by the Southern Pacific Railroad, which entered into the Flato, Kline, and Lattimore Flatonia partnership. Before that time, a small settlement called Old Flatonia was located a mile to the southeast, and an even smaller hamlet called Oso was three miles to the northwest. Both communities disappeared when they transferred their populations and many of their buildings to the new, larger rail station. Thus New Flatonia, as it was once known, grew swiftly as the railroad brought prosperity to southern Fayette County.

The initial settlers in New Flatonia were Anglo Americans, drawn to the venture by the opportunities the railroad brought, along with the inexpensive property that could be had in the newly platted town site. Shortly thereafter, however, waves of German and Czech immigrants, as well as a few Greek and Italian residents, made Flatonia home.

Strangely, the 1887 arrival of the San Antonio & Aransas Pass Railway (SAP), the second rail line enticed to come through Flatonia, caused growth to slow. Other stops along the SAP drew business away from Flatonia and into the new settlements along that line (Muldoon to the north and Moulton in Lavaca County to the south), but not to such an extent as to completely dampen Flatonia's success and well-being. Flatonia continues to thrive as a commercial center, located at the exact halfway point between San Antonio and Houston on Interstate 10.

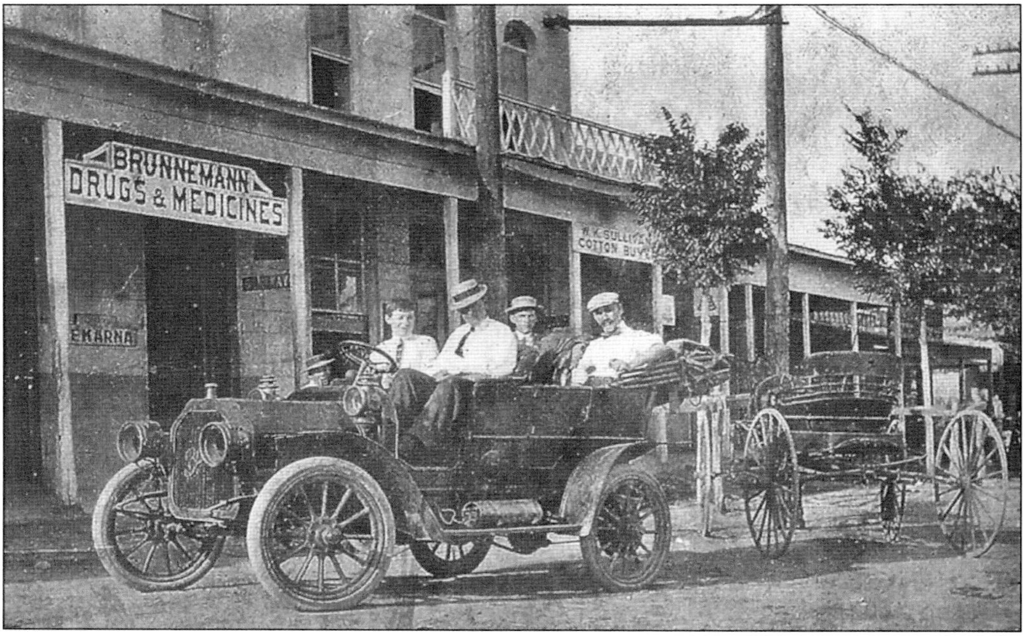

BRUNNEMANN DRUGS & MEDICINES. Shown is one of the first automobiles to grace Flatonia, a 1909 Buick Model F touring edition. The drugstore behind it is the Brunnemann Drugs & Medicine shop, run by August Julius Eduard Brunnemann (1855–1938) and his father-in-law Dr. Hugh McNary Cadwell (1832–1900). Brunnemann came from the Rhineland region of Germany. Next door can be seen the office of Wesley Kinston Sullivan (1862–1938), who was a cotton buyer and originally from Mississippi. (Author's collection.)

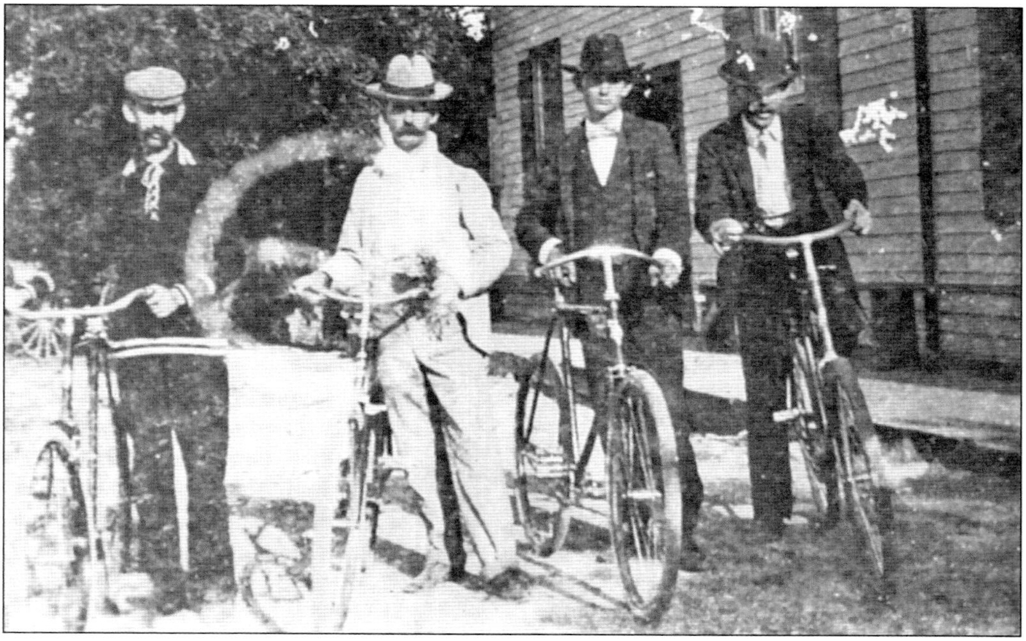

FLATONIA BICYCLISTS. While they do not have a fancy automobile, these four gentlemen certainly make a striking pose with their bicycles. (E.A. Arnim Archives & Museum.)

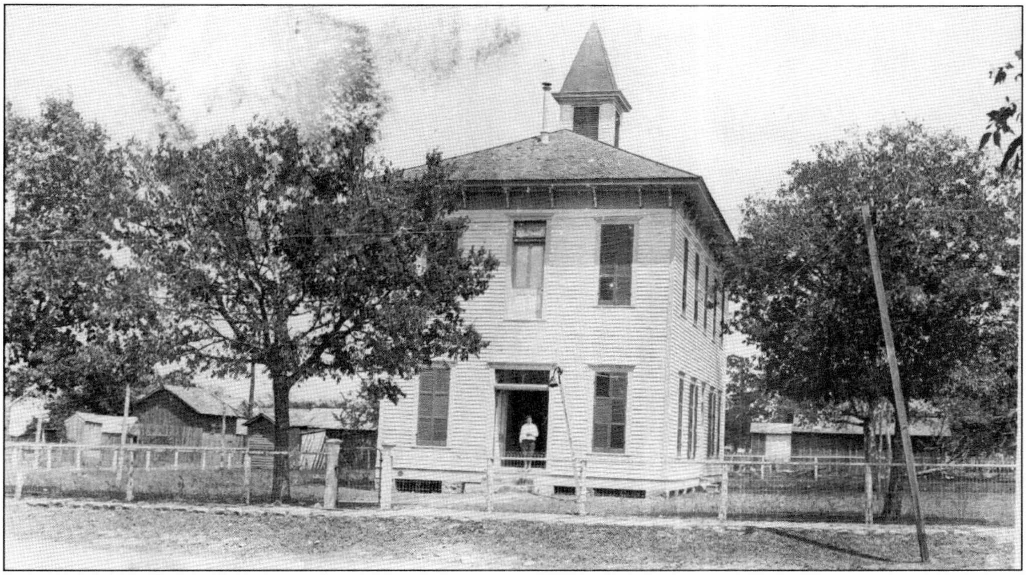

COURT HOUSE, FLATONIA, TEXAS. Along with Round Top, Fayetteville, Winchester, and Schulenburg, Flatonia was unique in Texas in that it had a precinct courthouse, as few counties built such structures. This courthouse was built in 1888 as a dual-purpose facility, serving both as precinct courthouse and Masonic Lodge. The building is located on South Market Street, across from the Olle Hotel. It is still utilized by Flatonia's Masonic Lodge No. 426 today. (E.A. Arnim Archives & Museum/Greive family.)

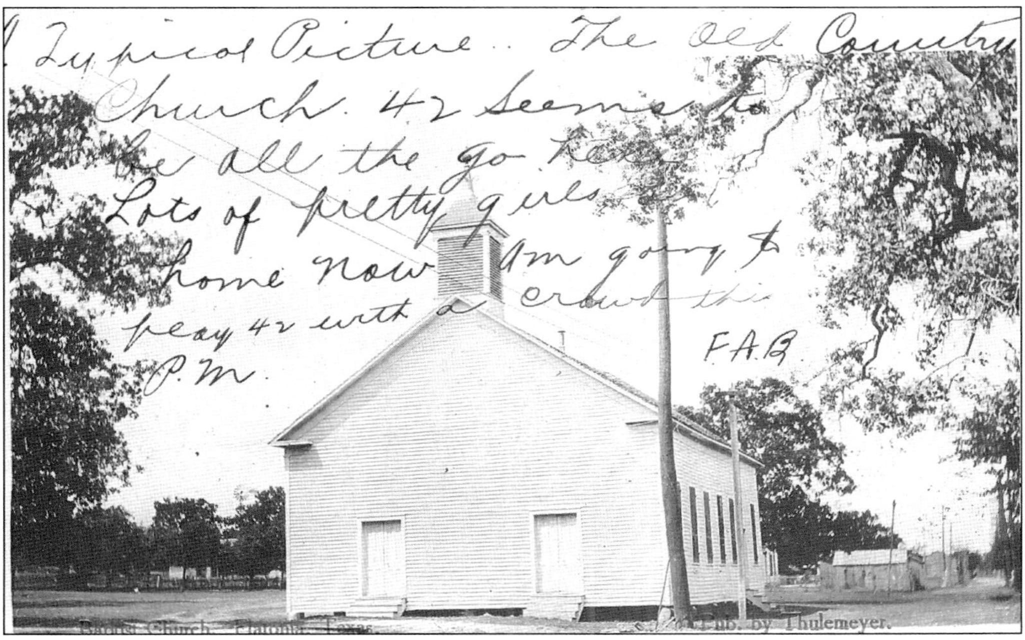

BAPTIST CHURCH, FLATONIA, TEXAS. Built in 1878 by Flatonia's Baptists, the structure pictured was the first church in town. It was located on Converse Street, between South Main and Sixth Streets, and was shared with other faiths. The structure was razed to make way for the current sanctuary, which was dedicated in 1965. (Robby and Kelly Wehmeyer.)

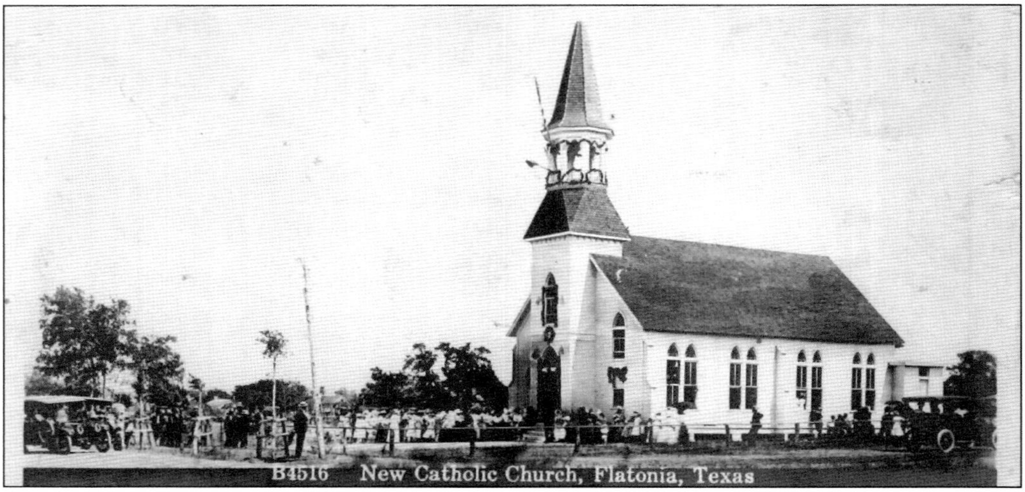

NEW CATHOLIC CHURCH, FLATONIA, TEXAS. At first, Flatonia only had a Baptist church and a Methodist church. In 1912, a Catholic church was added. Sacred Heart Catholic Church was dedicated on September 17, 1912. Sermons were held in English, Czech, and German. In 1933, the church was moved across the street from its original location to South Faires Street. This church building no longer exists, as it was razed to make room for a new sanctuary, which was dedicated in 1978. (E.A. Arnim Archives & Museum/Louis and Edna Brunner collection.)

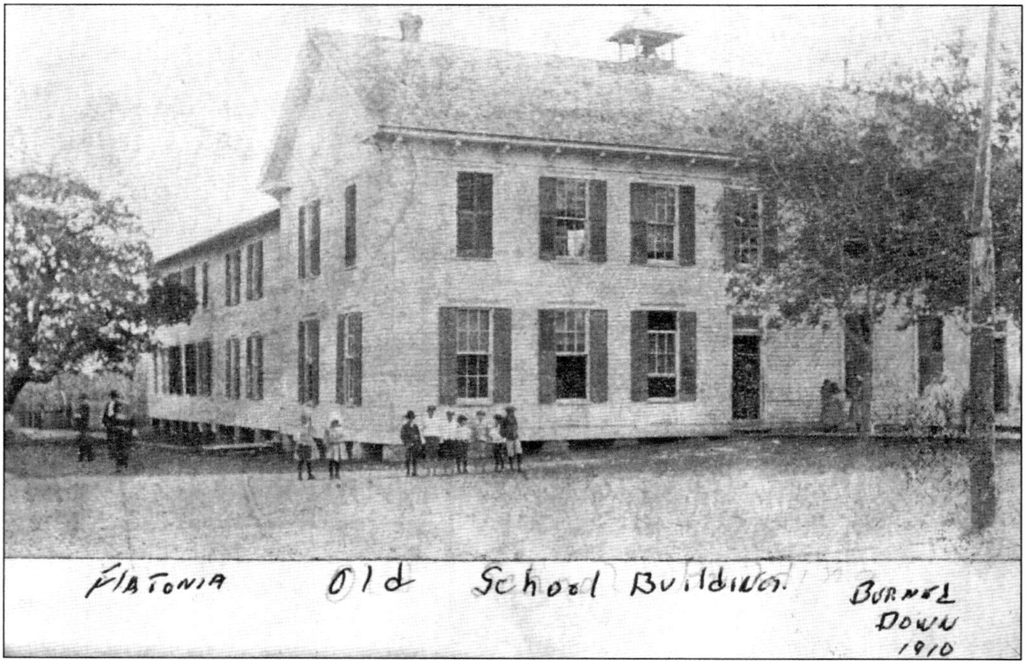

FLATONIA OLD SCHOOL BUILDING. The original Flatonia school building was constructed in 1884. This old Flatonia schoolhouse burned in 1910, and a new public school was opened on September 2, 1912, near the site of the former school. The elementary school was on the first floor, and the high school was on the second floor. The 1912 school building has since disappeared. The site of the original 1884 school is now the location of the Flatonia School District tennis courts. (E.A. Arnim Archives & Museum/Sweet and Betty Mueller collection.)

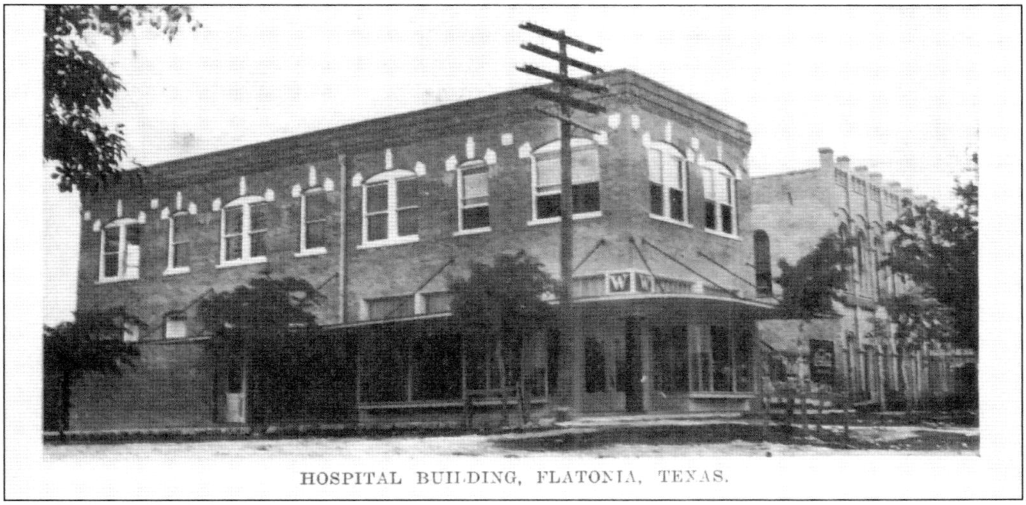

HOSPITAL BUILDING, FLATONIA, TEXAS. The building shown in the foreground is the Wheeler Building, located on West South Main Street. It was built in 1907 for William Harrison Wheeler (1840–1926) and his wife, Emma Arnim Wheeler (1854–1930), sister to Flatonia notable Edward Alexander "E.A." Arnim. To the right is Flatonia's Romanesque Revival hospital, built in 1897 by Dr. George Washington Allen (1849–1903). The hospital's second floor became Flatonia's Opera House in 1910. In 1914, this building was sold to Hermann Ernest Olle (1871–1953). Businesses located here have included a drugstore, chicken hatchery, skating rink, and café. (E.A. Arnim Archives & Museum/Sweet and Betty Mueller collection.)

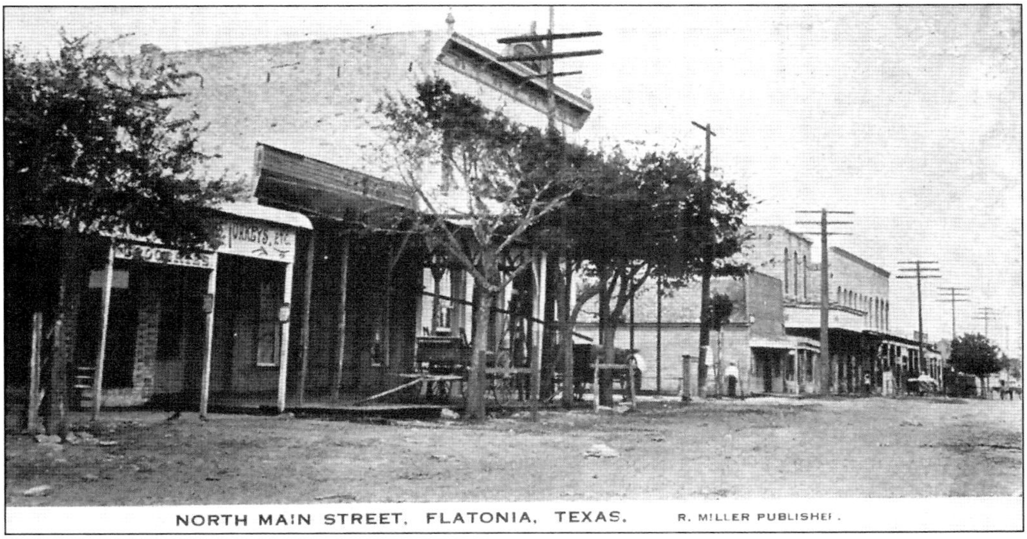

NORTH MAIN STREET, FLATONIA, TEXAS. Shown is a view of Flatonia's North Main Street from about 1910. The break in the buildings in the center is the intersection of North Main and Penn Streets. The building in the foreground is the Armin & Lane Building, constructed in 1886, from which the merchandising firm of Armin & Lane operated. This firm (which served as an insurance agency among other things) was founded in 1886 as a partnership between E.A. Armin (1855–1942), originally of Moulton, Texas, and Jonathan Lane (1853–1916), who served as a state senator from 1886 to 1890. Lane was also a great-nephew of Davy Crockett. (E.A. Arnim Archives & Museum/Felix and Nettie Brunner collection.)

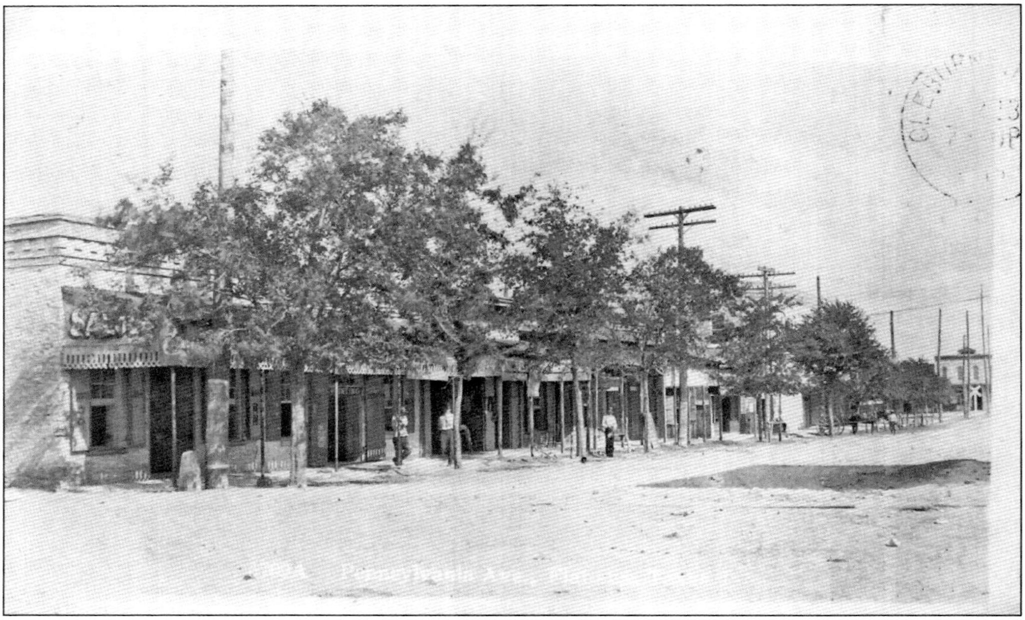

PENNSYLVANIA AVE., FLATONIA, TEXAS. This postcard is a view down Pennsylvania Avenue, looking north toward the center of town from the intersection of what is now called Penn Street and Sixth Street. The Armin & Lane Building is visible in the distance, just across the marked railroad crossing. (E.A. Arnim Archives & Museum/Sweet and Betty Mueller collection.)

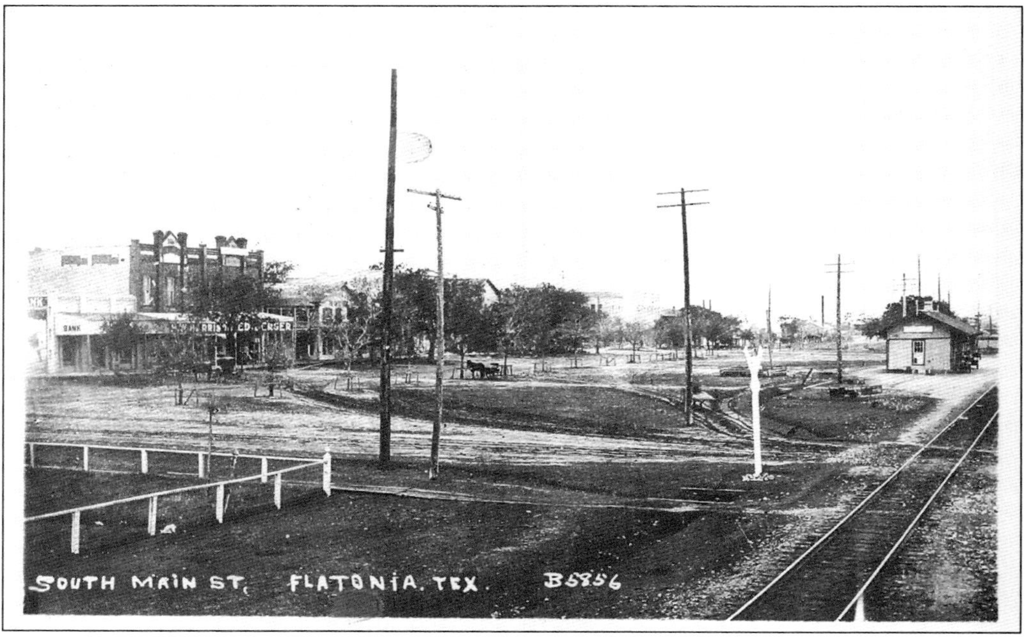

SOUTH MAIN ST., FLATONIA, TEXAS. Shown is a view of Flatonia's South Main Street from about 1910. South Main sits opposite from North Main Street across a grass- and mud-filled esplanade through which the Galveston, Harrisburg & San Antonio Railroad ran. (E.A. Arnim Archives & Museum/Sweet and Betty Mueller collection.)

North Side Front Street, South Side Front Street, Flatonia, Texas. Depicted in a double view is the bifurcated North and South Main Streets, which sit opposite each other and make up the central commercial district of Flatonia. The use of the indicators *North Side Front Street* and *South Side Front Street* is anomalous, given that the streets were and are in fact named North and South Main Street. (E.A. Arnim Archives & Museum.)

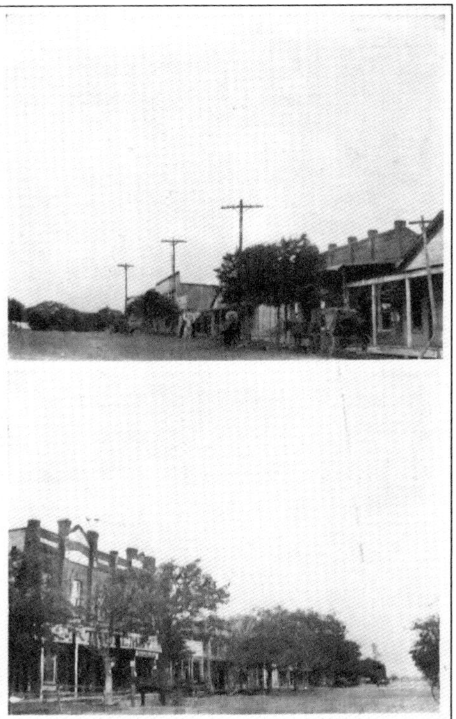

NORTH SIDE FRONT STREET (UPPER).
SOUTH SIDE FRONT STREET (LOWER), FLATONIA, TEXAS

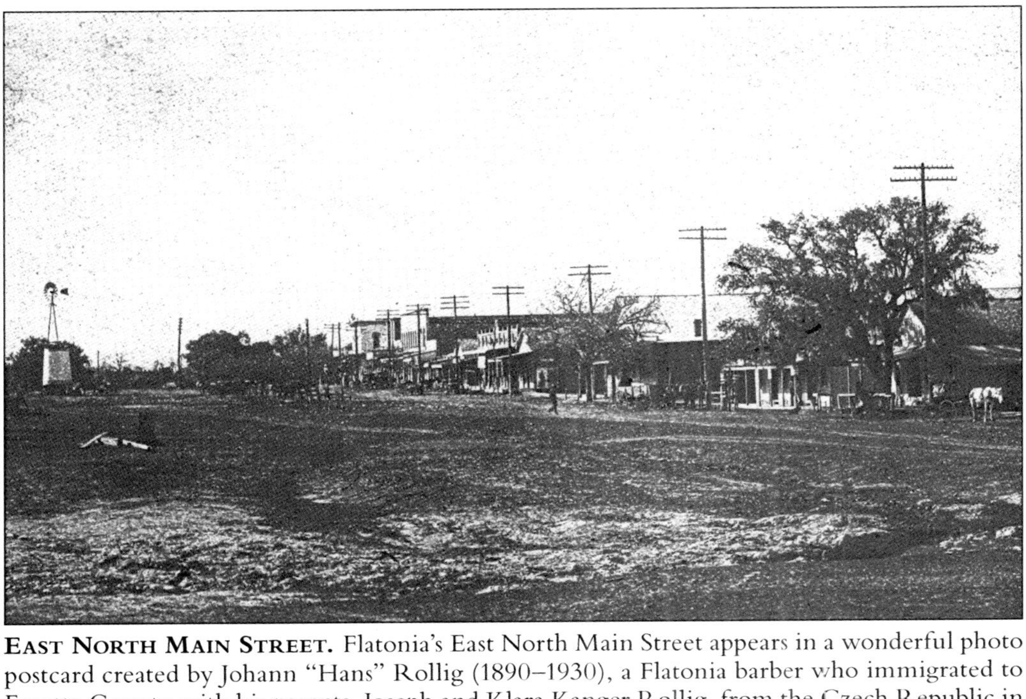

East North Main Street. Flatonia's East North Main Street appears in a wonderful photo postcard created by Johann "Hans" Rollig (1890–1930), a Flatonia barber who immigrated to Fayette County with his parents, Joseph and Klara Kanger Rollig, from the Czech Republic in 1907. (Rollig/Freytag family collection.)

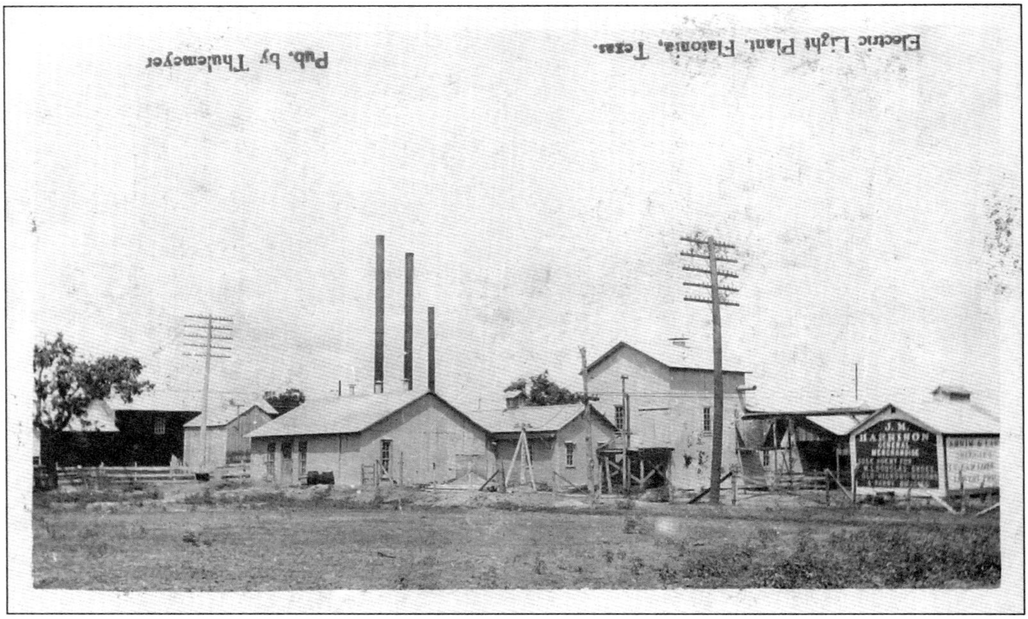

Electric Light Plant, Flatonia, Texas. In 1910, electricity came to stay in Flatonia. Its earlier electric plant was destroyed by fire. In 1910, T.M. Spinks, of Mississippi A&M College, and F.C. Bolton, of Texas A&M College, came to take charge of the enterprise and were given a 50-year franchise. By 1924, the Flatonia Ice and Electric Light Company had secured a franchise to furnish light for Waelder, 12 miles from Flatonia. (E.A. Arnim Archives & Museum/Sweet and Betty Mueller collection.)

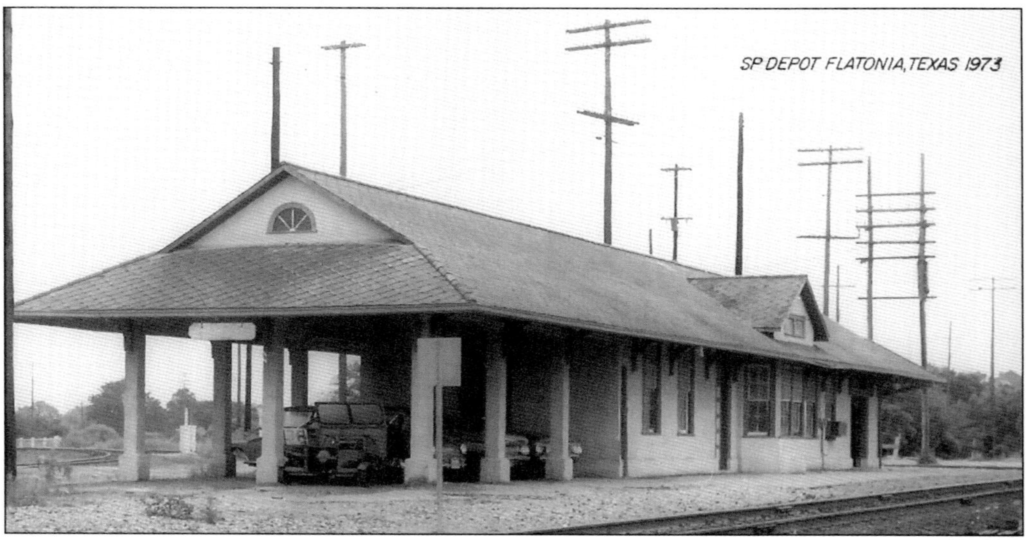

SP Depot, Flatonia, Texas, 1973. This depot was built in 1926 as a Union depot, serving both the east-west Galveston, Harrisburg & San Antonio line and the north-south San Antonio & Aransas Pass line that came through Flatonia. Originally, each had their own small passenger depots. Switching tower No. 3, which still stands today in downtown Flatonia, was located nearby to operate the rail interlocker. This Union depot building was razed in the 1970s. (Author's collection.)

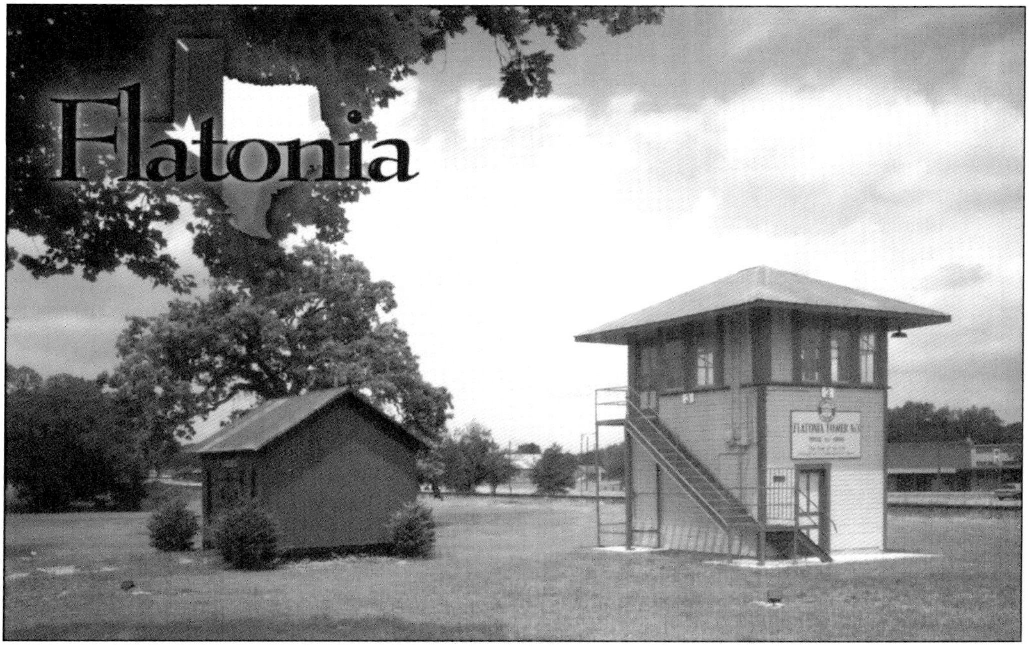

FLATONIA, TOWER NO. 3. Flatonia's Switching Tower No. 3 opened in 1902 because of state law. All Texas interlocking towers were designated by numbers assigned by the Texas Railroad Commission. This tower was built by the Galveston, Harrisburg & San Antonio Railroad to protect the crossing of the north-south San Antonio & Aransas Pass Railway main line and the east-west Galveston, Harrisburg & San Antonio Railroad main line, both of which later became part of the lines of the Southern Pacific Railroad. The tower was manually operated, and parts of its interlocking mechanisms remained in use until its closure on September 30, 1996. The tower is now in downtown Flatonia. (Author's collection.)

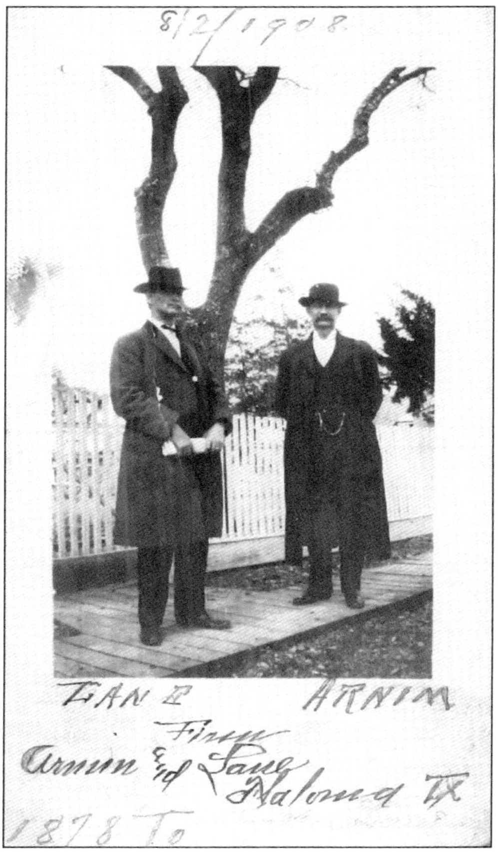

ARNIM AND LANE, FLATONIA, TEXAS. Pictured are E.A. Armin and Jonathan Lane. Arnim was the son of Alexander Augustus Arnim (1821–1896), of Friesack, Germany, and served Flatonia in many roles and functions. His collection forms the basis of the E.A. Arnim Archives & Museum. (E.A. Arnim Archives & Museum/Sam and Ann Arnim collection.)

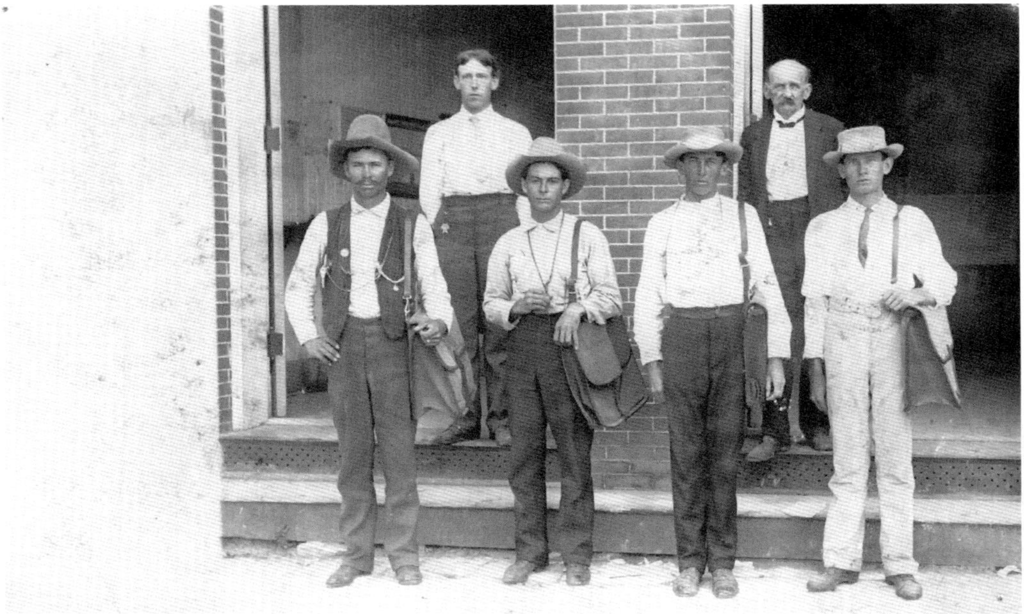

Rural Mail Carriers. Pictured are the rural mail carriers for the Flatonia area. From left to right are (first row) Harry Wiedemann, Frank Pechacek, Hermann Schutz, and Harry Foitek; (second row) incoming postmaster Freddy Laux and his father, retiring postmaster Julius Laux. (E.A. Arnim Archives & Museum/Henry and Jeanne Nikel collection.)

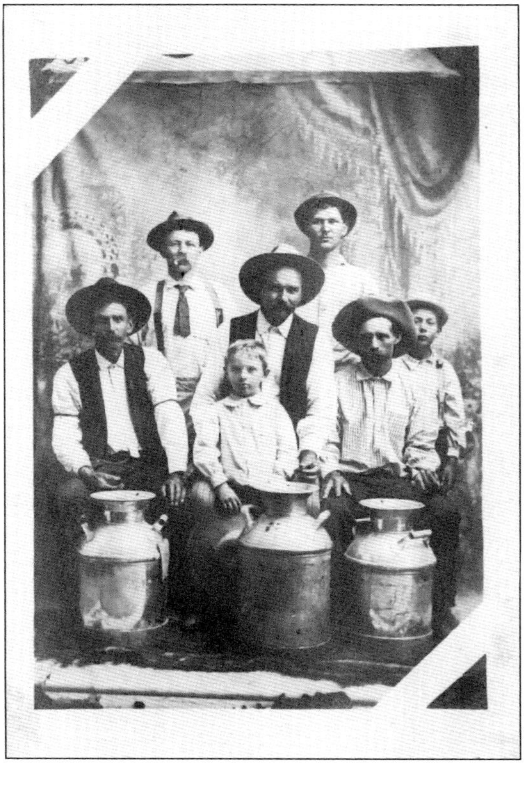

Creamery. In 1912, Flatonia's creamery was the most productive in Texas, shipping more than 27,000 pounds of butter to customers. Founded in 1909, it was shortly thereafter the largest in Texas, being managed by Rasmus "Richard" Boe (1875–1965), who had managed creameries in Germany, where he learned to run an efficient and highly successful operation. Boe was originally from Helanes, Denmark. Pictured from left to right are (seated) Carl Rietz, Killian Brunner (with Boe's son Olaf in front of him), and Gus Doehring; (standing) Boe and August Brunner, who later became a constable and Fayette County deputy sheriff. (E.A. Arnim Archives & Museum/Max and Anita Steinhauser collection.)

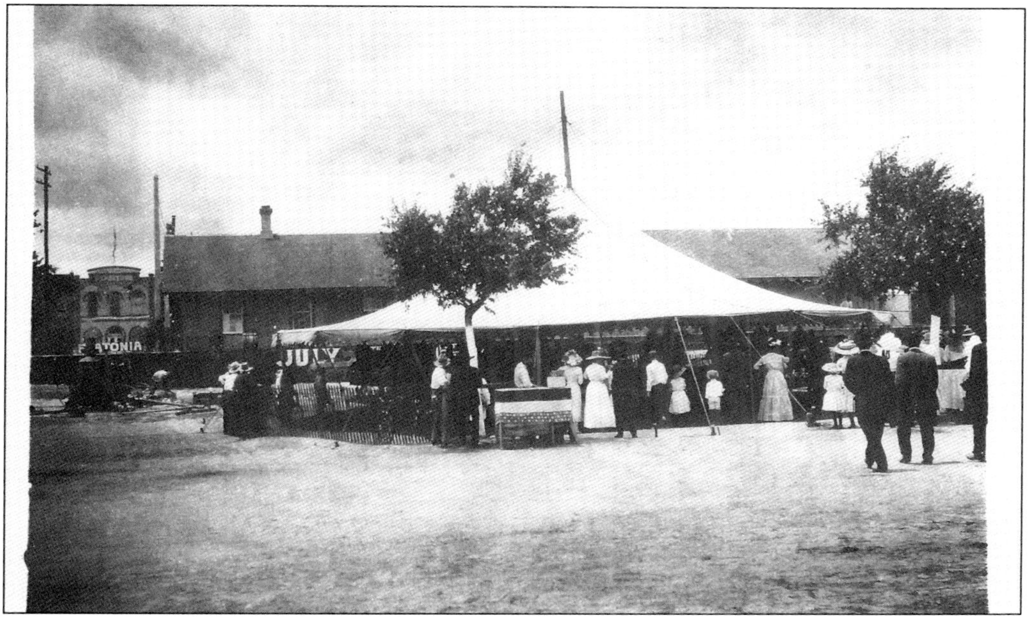

FOURTH OF JULY. Flatonia's residents are celebrating Independence Day on July 4–6, 1912, during an event described by the *Flatonia Argus* as one of the biggest of its kind. The town's name appears along the rail platform. Also visible in the background to the left of the freight depot is the Fernau Furniture Store. (Rollig/Freytag family collection.)

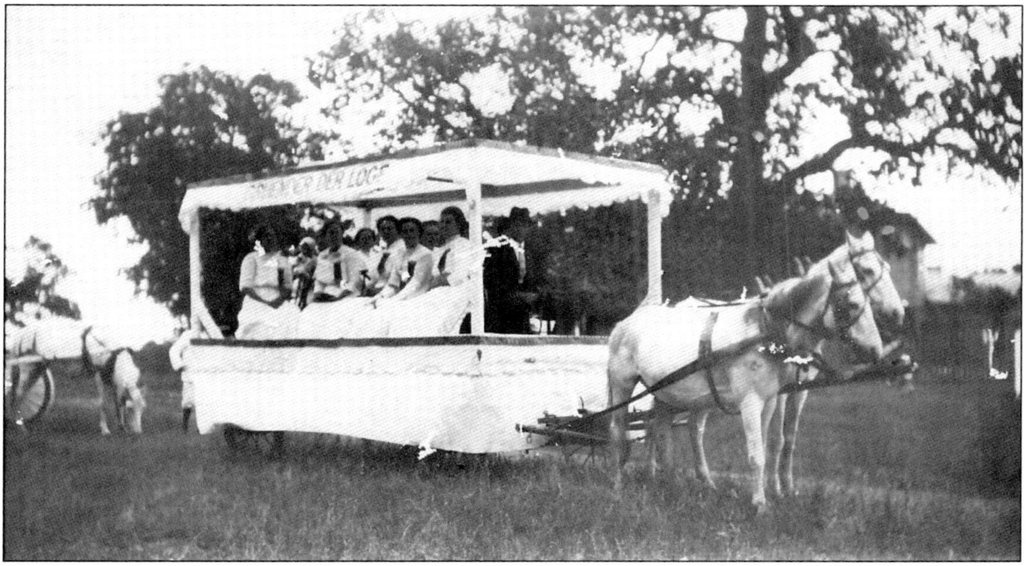

HERMANN SONS FLOAT. Pictured is a parade float carrying members of Flatonia's Hermann Sons Lodge. The Sons of Hermann (or Hermann Sohns Verein) is a German fraternal organization. The Flatonia Sons of Hermann welcomed everyone, not just Germans. In 1912, they started an initiative to create a city park and meeting hall facility, which ultimately grew into a full-fledged fair. The Flatonia Fair attracted people from all over the state and was attended by governors, statesmen, and other dignitaries from 1913 until 1936. (E.A. Arnim Archives & Museum/Max and Anita Steinhauser collection.)

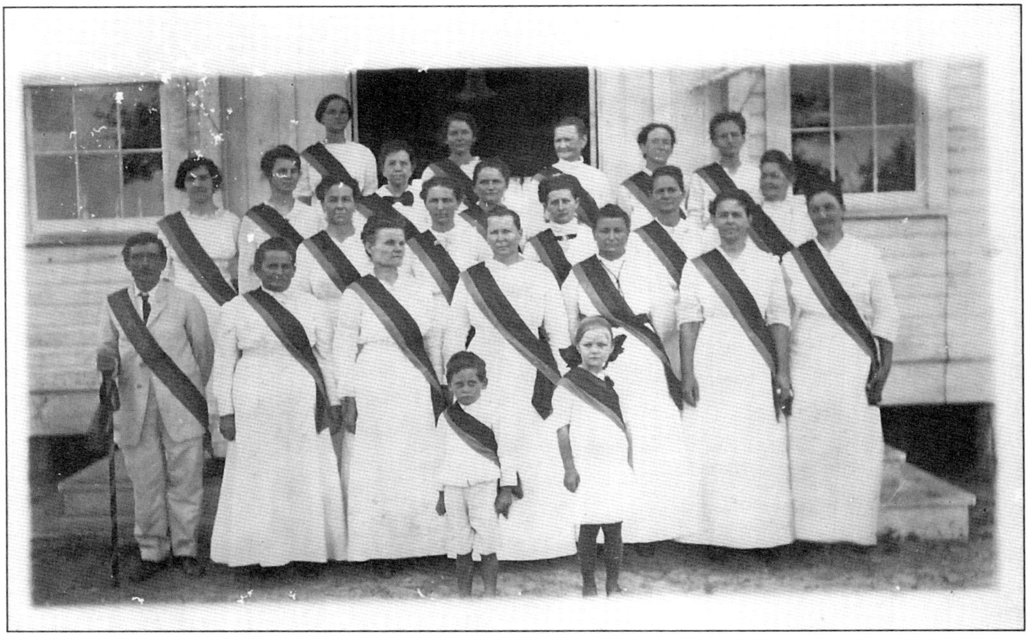

HERMANN SONS LADIES AUXILIARY. Here is Flatonia's Hermann Sons Ladies Auxiliary showing off their gold, red, and black sashes, which honor their German heritage. (E.A. Arnim Archives & Museum/Max and Anita Steinhauser collection.)

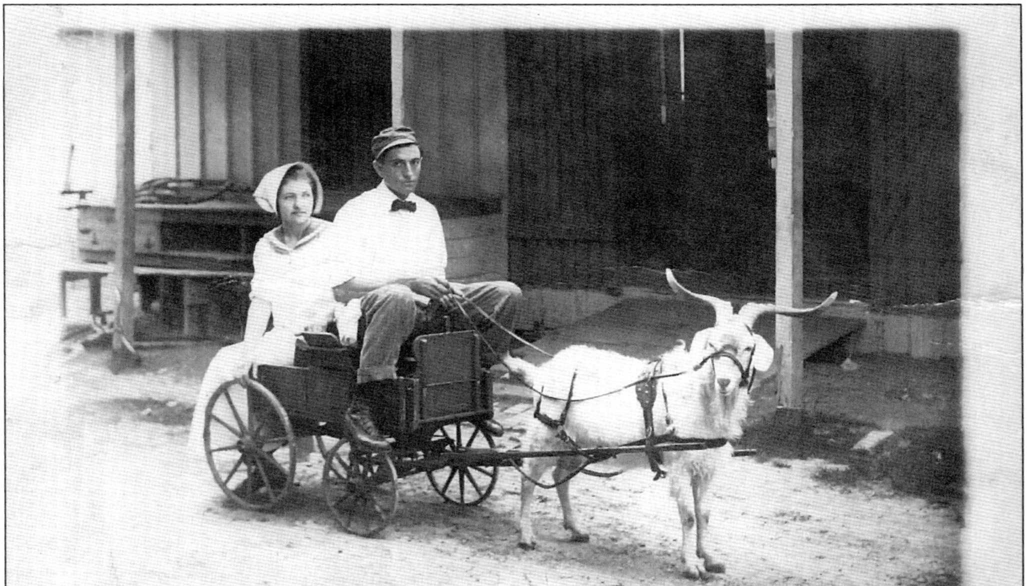

GOAT CART. Siblings Mollie Brueggemann Hodanek (1895–1985) and Leopold "Paul" Brueggemann (1893–1973) are shown here in an amusement of the day—a goat cart. Paul was a butcher at the City Market in Flatonia for many years. (E.A. Arnim Archives & Museum/Greive family.)

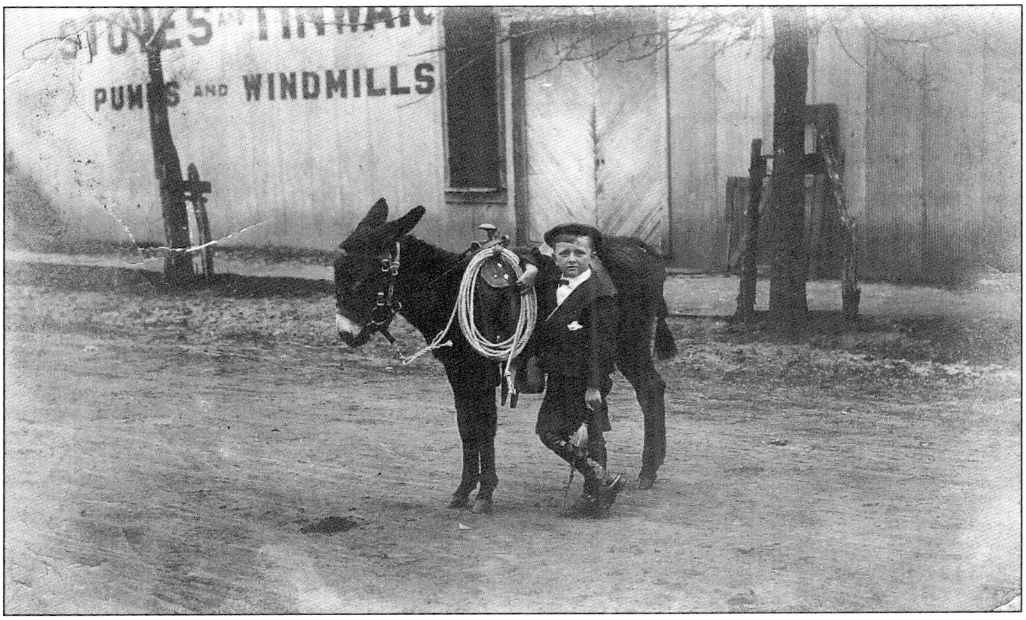

LITTLE EMMETT AND HIS RIG IN 1908. Here is a delightful photo postcard showing a young boy named Emmett and his donkey. Wilhelm Mueller and Alwine Mewes Mueller, Emmett's grandparents, came to Texas from Germany as children and married in Fayette County. Emmett writes to his aunt Selma Mueller (1877–1912) that he had the measles and had to stay indoors, but was later able to go outside. He asks, "How do you like my rig?" (E.A. Arnim Archives & Museum/Rolla Mueller collection.)

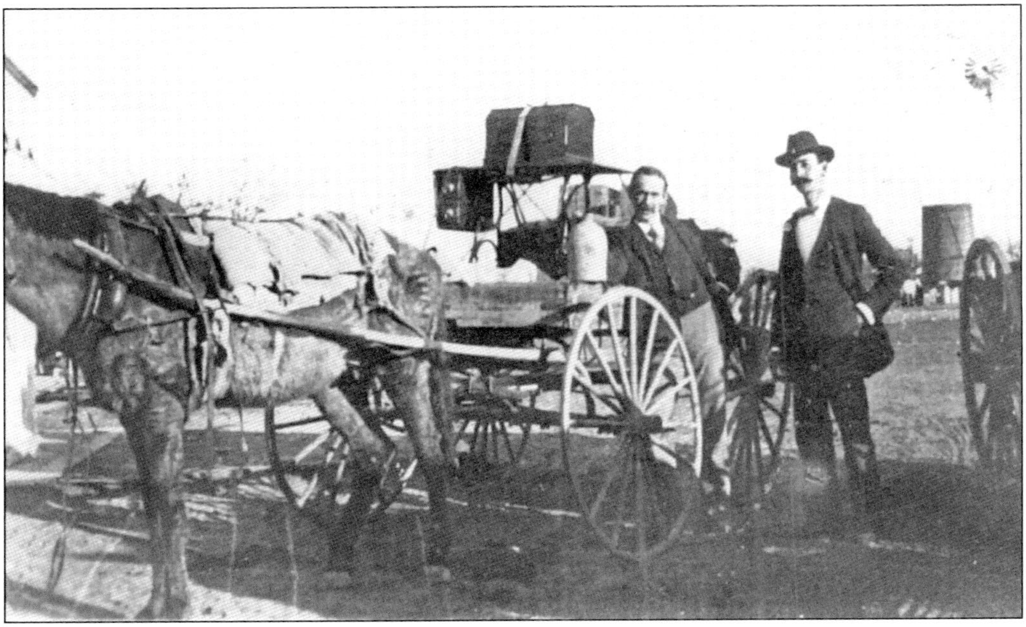

HENRY MILLER AND SEWING MACHINE SALESMAN. Pictured here is Flatonia native Henry Miller standing beside a traveling sewing machine salesman selling his wares. (E.A. Arnim Archives & Museum.)

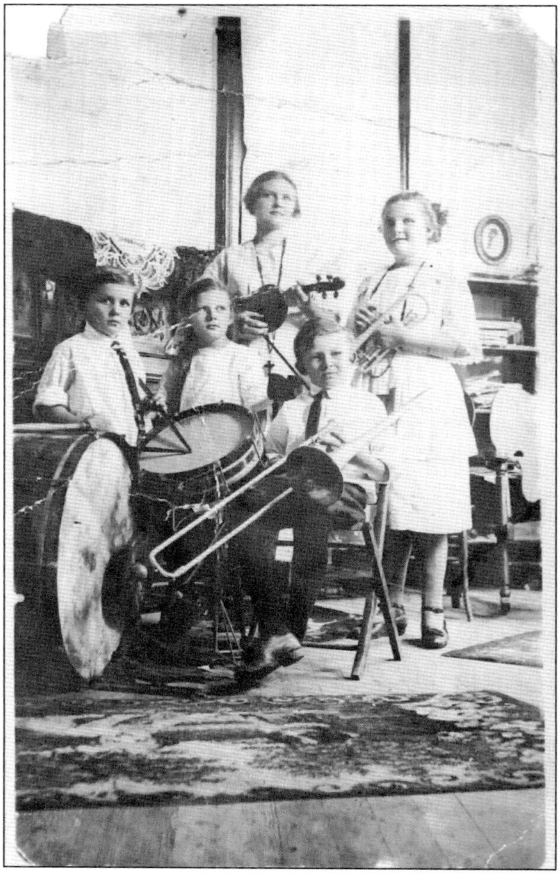

NESRSTA ORCHESTRA. The Nesrsta Orchestra was a family musical group from Flatonia. It had six players, including the father, "Judge" Charles E. Nesrsta, and five of his children, ranging in ages from 8 to 15 years old. The father played violin, and the five children played the instruments pictured here. From left to right are (seated) George, Marie, and Charles Nesrsta; (standing) Annie and Olga Nesrsta. (E.A. Arnim Archives & Museum/Frank Marcie collection.)

CHILDREN'S PARTY ON NORTH MAIN STREET. Taken about 1908, this image shows, in no particular order, Emma Allen, Maggie and Mamie Thulemeyer, Killough Faires, Jaromir Michael, Leon Kotzebue, Leo McAnally, Eva Morris, Nellie and Willie Brown, Lucy Bloodworth, Eulalie and Anita Foitik, Gertrude Brunnemann, Otto Melcher, Louise Meyer, Ruth Paulus, Tinnie Chalk, Allen Baugh, Alma Harrison, and teacher Wilma Cromwell. (E.A. Arnim Archives & Museum/Emma Allen Bailey collection.)

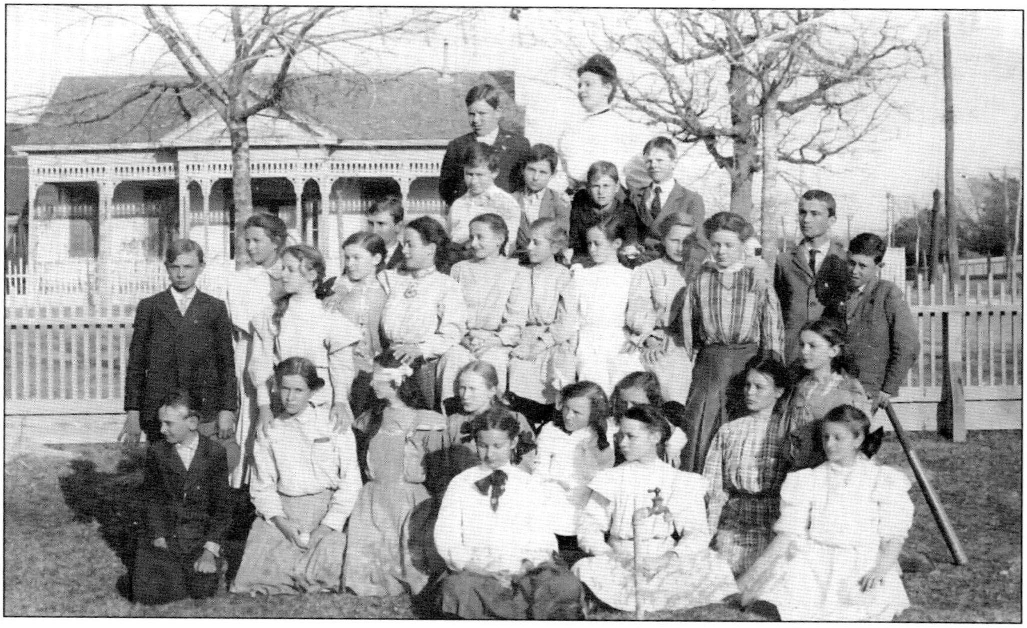

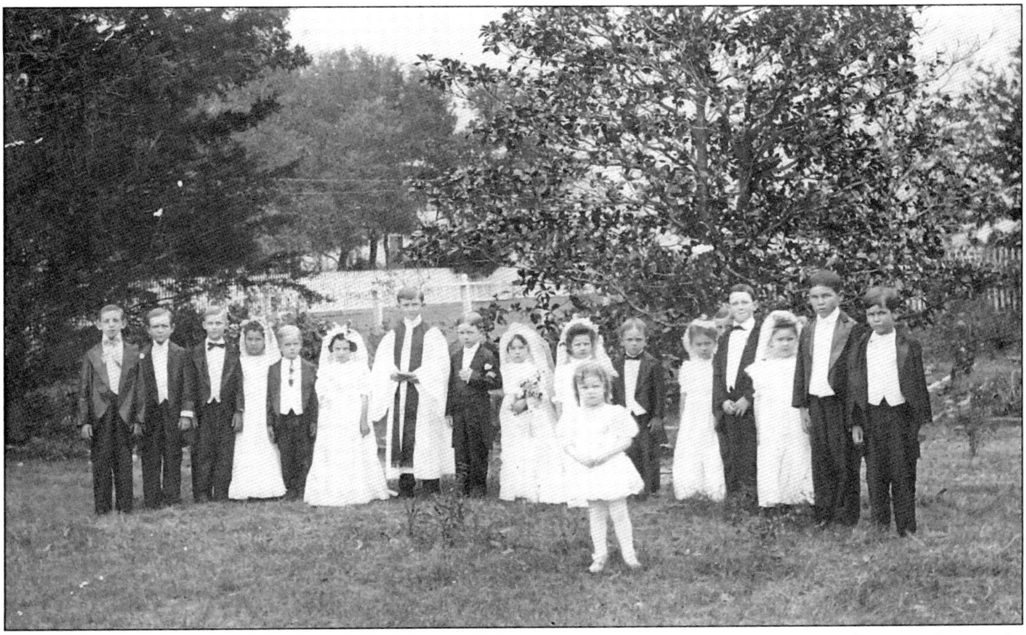

Tom Thumb Wedding Party. Tom Thumb wedding parties were popular in the early 1900s. They involve youngsters dressing up as members of the wedding party. This party in Flatonia took place in about 1908. Several of these events took place in Flatonia over the years, staged for both entertainment and fundraising purposes. (E.A. Arnim Archives & Museum/Richard and Hildegard Wheeler collection.)

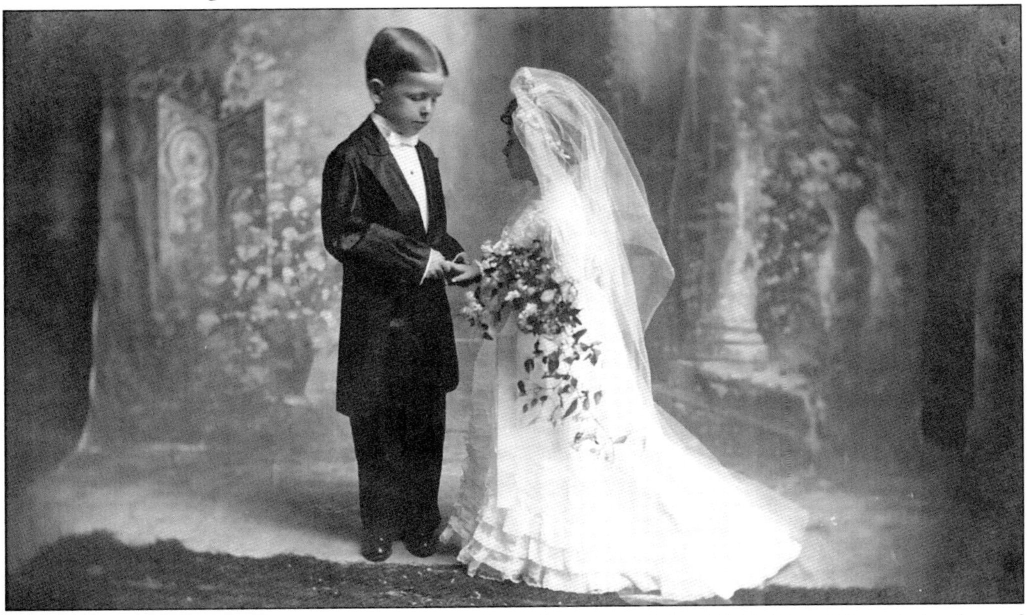

Tom Thumb Bride and Groom. Here is a close-up of the 1908 Tom Thumb bride and groom. Richard Alfred Wheeler Jr. (1902–1969), son of Richard and Mamie Burns Wheeler and great-grandson of E.A. Arnim, is the groom. (E.A. Arnim Archives & Museum/Richard and Hildegard Wheeler collection.)

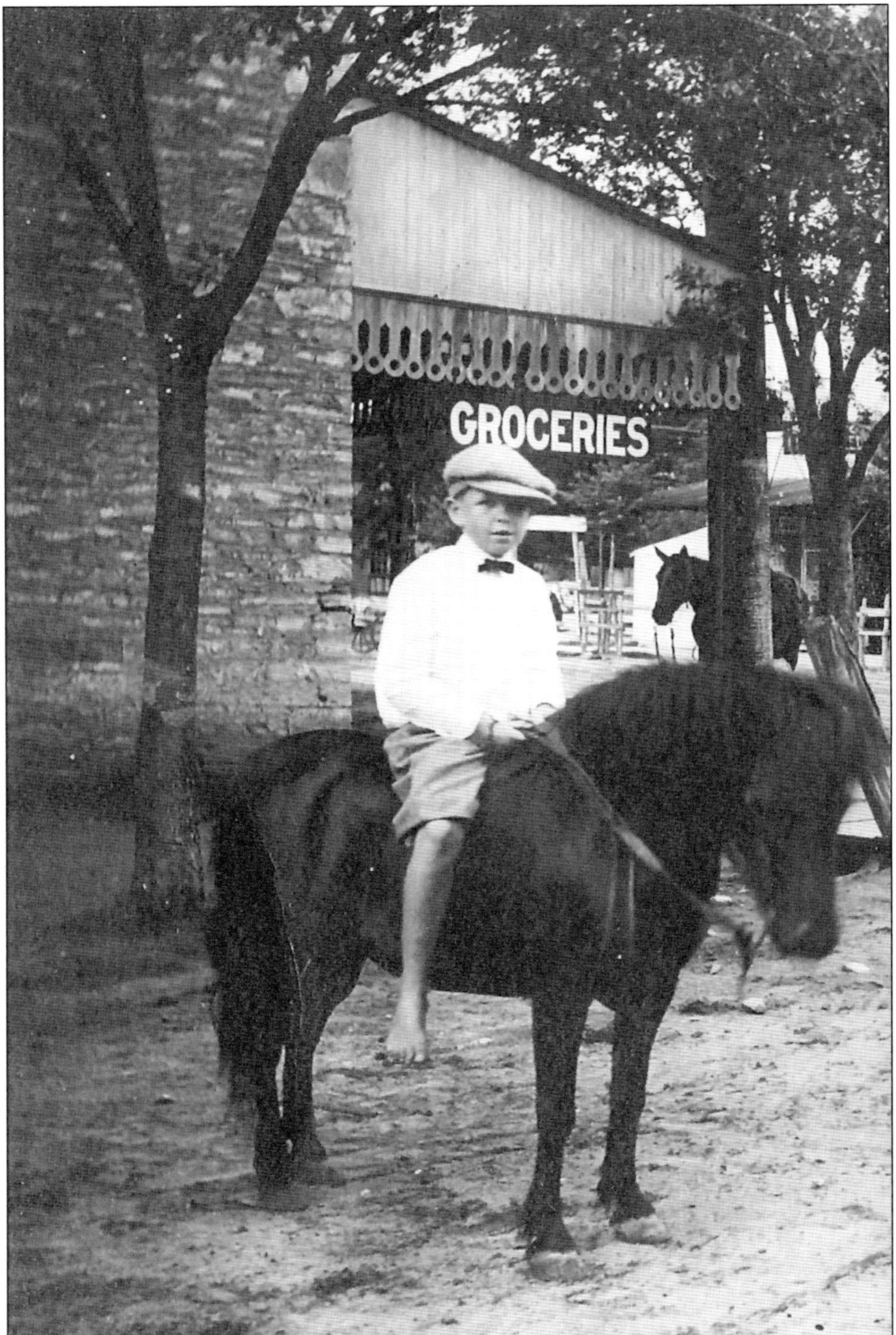

GREETINGS FROM FLATONIA. Richard Wheeler Jr. appears on his miniature horse in downtown Flatonia. (E.A. Arnim Archives & Museum)

Five

Northern Fayette County
Round Top, Carmine, and Others

The northern section of Fayette County, which can be defined roughly as lying north of a line drawn from Willow Springs in the east to Winchester in the west, is a diverse and inviting landscape. It is rich in both culture and history, as well as in natural beauty. The area is known as being the ember of German immigration to Texas as well as home to some of the earliest Anglo settlements in the county, both groups being attracted to the abundant flora and fauna and general productivity of the Cummins Creek watershed, which was named for early pioneer James Cummins.

The primary population center in this part of the county is Round Top, named for an octagonal tower atop the once-prominent home of early German settler and immigration champion Alwin Heinrich Soergel (1815–1875). Round Top was originally known as Townsend's Settlement, after the Robert Townsend family who migrated from Florida to the high-topped hill beside Cummins Creek in 1826. Situated on the La Bahia Road between Washington-on-the-Brazos and Goliad, the town became a thriving commercial center in the very earliest days of the county.

In 1843, a group of German noblemen known as the Adelsverein came into northern Fayette County to further their stated aim of directing German immigrants to the Republic of Texas. Originally wanting large land grants on the then far west frontier of Texas, but not being able to procure such from the Texas Congress, Count Ludwig Joseph von Boos-Waldeck (1798–1880) instead purchased the W.H. Jack league, roughly five miles west of Round Top. Boos-Waldeck named the 4,428-acre parcel Nassau Plantation in honor of the Adelsverein's patron, Duke Adolph I of Nassau, with plans for a hierarchical settlement for immigrant Germans in the image of the Southern plantation economy prevalent in Texas then.

While the plantation did not fulfill its original goal of becoming the heart of a new German colony, it did find success as a way station and supplier for the thousands of German immigrants who came to Texas during the 1840s and 1850s. Ultimately, Nassau Plantation was sold off in parts to pay debts, first to Otto von Roeder, then to Peter Carl von Rosenberg, and finally after a lengthy title lawsuit, to Georg Weyand, all three of whom made names for themselves in Fayette County's history.

The other major settlement in the north is Carmine, situated on Fayette County's border with Washington County. Carmine, like Flatonia and Schulenburg, owes its existence to the railroad, specifically the Houston & Texas Central Railway. In 1871, the line from Austin only extended as far as Ledbetter, located to Carmine's west. When the line needed to proceed to Houston, Carmine was born, named for Newt Carmean, who owned much of the land upon which the town site was planned. The town was at first known as Sylvan. But the name was changed to *Carmean* when the name *Sylvan* was determined to be confusing. The US Post Office changed the town name's spelling to *Carmine* in 1892.

Because of its prime location on the railroad, Carmine thrived as a commercial center well into the 20th century and attracted numerous settlers, the earliest of whom included Dr. Benjamin Jackson Thigpen, Heinrich August Weyand, Ernest Wilhelm Hoppe, and Hoppe's father-in-law Wilhelm Johann Umland, earlier of Round Top.

Other communities in northern Fayette County include Waldeck and Walhalla, early German settlements south of Ledbetter; Warda, a sister settlement of the Wendish colony of Serbin in Lee County; Warrenton, an early trading center south of Round Top that was once called Neese's Store; Winedale, an early stagecoach stop near the Nassau Plantation; Winchester, an early Anglo settlement laid out in 1851; and Oldenburg, settled late by Germans in 1886.

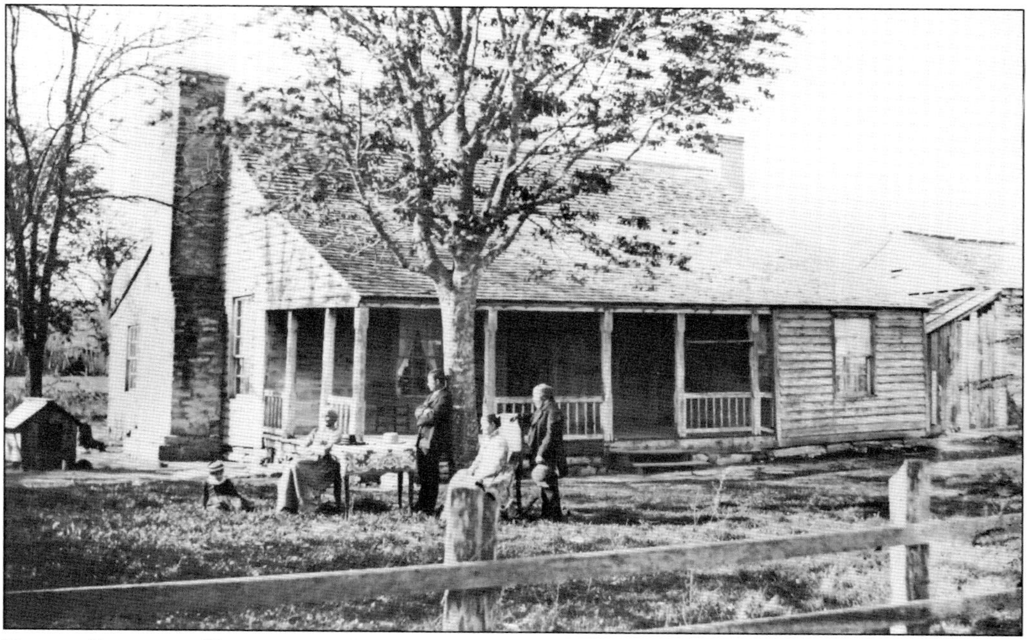

PETER CARL VON ROSENBERG HOME, ROUND TOP. The building pictured here was the second home of Baron Peter Carl Johann von Rosenberg (1794–1866) and his second wife, Amanda. It is not known precisely when this home was built, or who constructed it, as the Robert Zapp family also resided there. Von Rosenberg's son Carl Eugen von Rosenberg (1830–1913) and his wife, Theodore "Dorchen" Sack von Roeder von Rosenberg (1829–1904), also lived here. Dorchen was a pianist and music teacher and taught classes in this home, having studied music herself in her hometown of Dusseldorf, Germany. (Von Rosenberg family collection.)

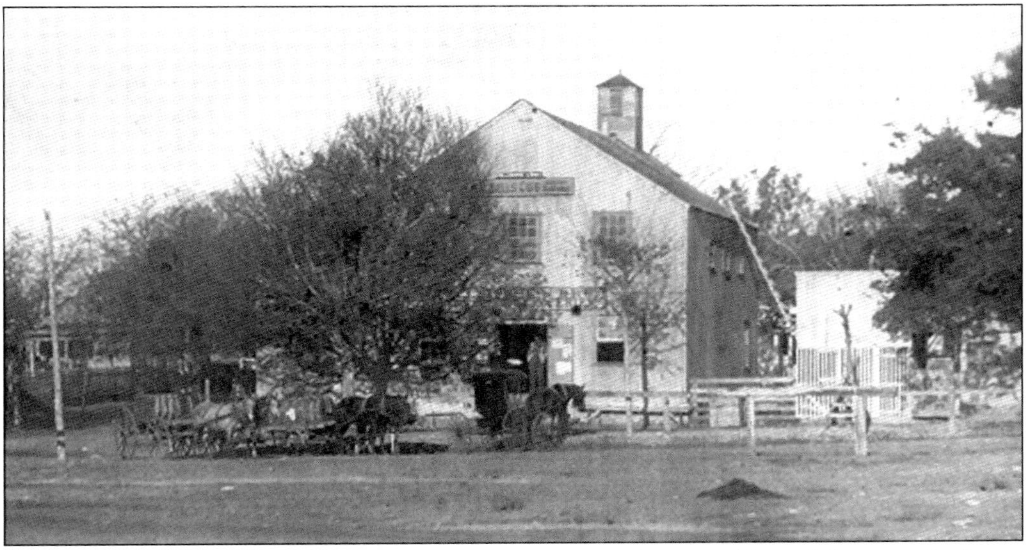

JOHANNES VON ROSENBERG STORE AND HOTEL, ROUND TOP. Johannes Carl von Rosenberg (1826–1906) was the third son of Peter Carl von Rosenberg. This was his store. The von Rosenberg family immigrated to Texas in 1849, after Johannes's brother Carl Wilhelm was deemed a *freidenker* (a freethinker) by the Prussian government and his future in Prussia was put in doubt. To escape the reactionary events of that time, the entire von Rosenberg family chose to leave the Old World behind. (Von Rosenberg family collection.)

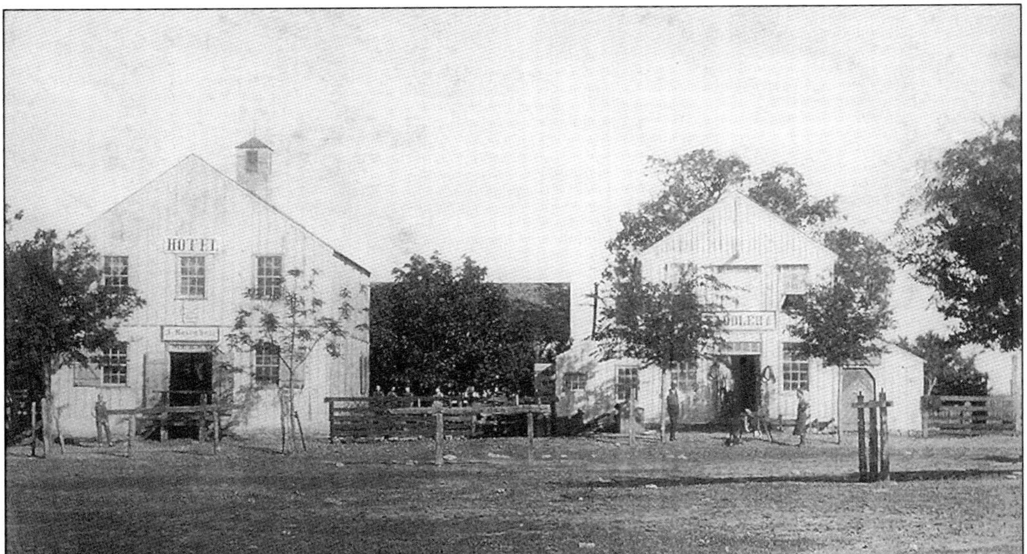

JOHANNES VON ROSENBERG HOTEL AND SADDLERY, ROUND TOP. Upon arriving in Texas, Johannes's father sought a home for his wife, Amanda Fallier von Rosenberg (1806–1864), and eight children. In 1850, he purchased 800 acres and the *herrenhaus* (manor house) of the Nassau Plantation from Otto von Roeder (1807–1875), who held title to the plantation in satisfaction of debts owed to him by the Adelsverein. Johannes lived near the plantation on his own farm after marrying Julie Wilhelmina Groos (1829–1894), but he later moved to Round Top and ran the store, grocery, and hotel pictured here. (Von Rosenberg family collection.)

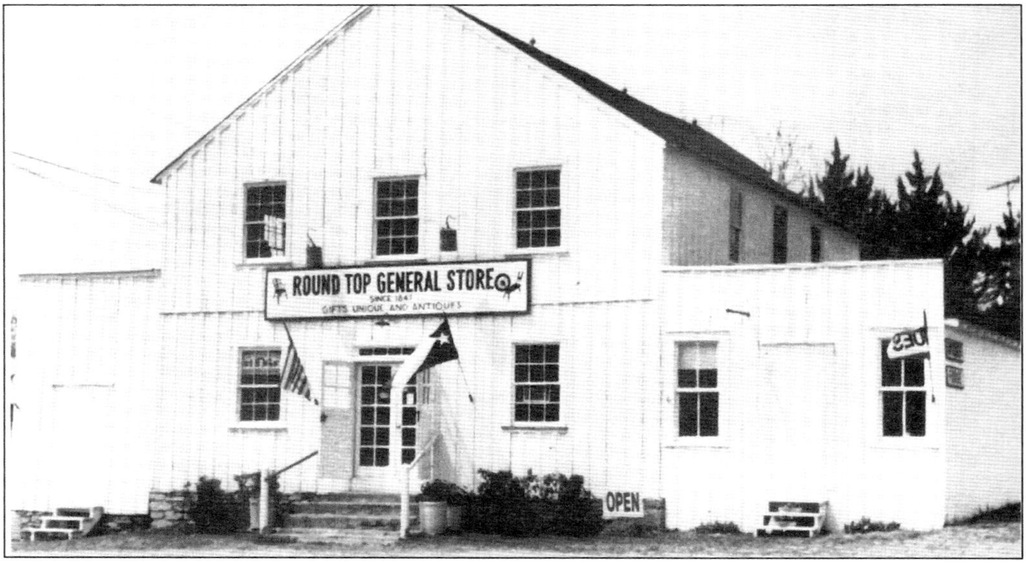

ROUND TOP GENERAL STORE. Johannes von Rosenberg's hotel depicted here is located on the square at the intersection of Washington and Mill Streets. A saddlery was operated by several of Johannes's sons next door, as well as a photographer's studio run by Gustav Froelich (1841–1922), who was von Rosenberg's cousin. Froelich came to Texas in 1860 at the behest of his brother Adolph Froelich (1834–1864), who came shortly after the von Rosenbergs in 1850. (Gary E. McKee.)

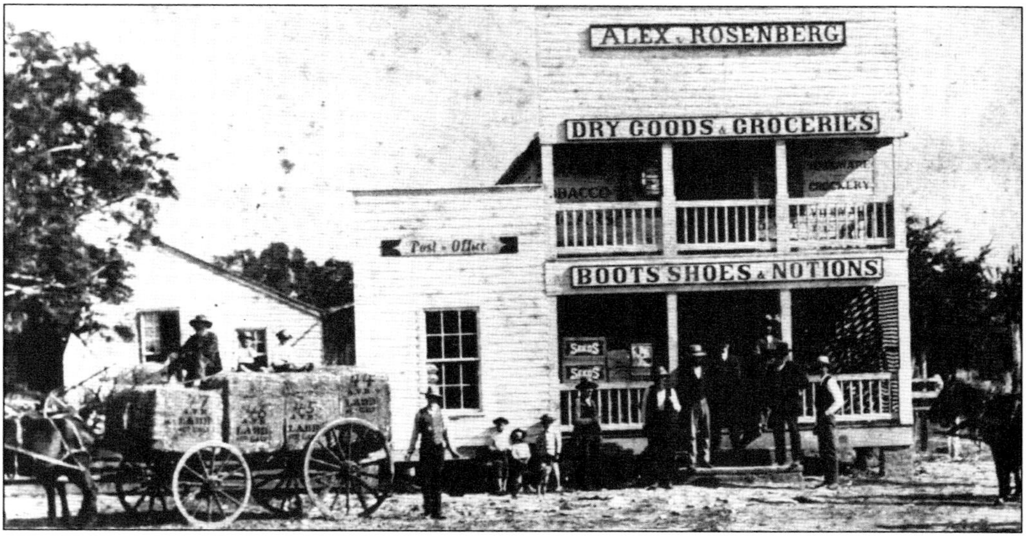

ALEX V ROSENBERG DRY GOODS & GROCERIES. Alexander Eugen "Alex" von Rosenberg (1857–1930), the author's great-great-grandfather, was the son of Carl Eugen and Dorchen von Rosenberg. After working in the general store of Georg Weyand (1825–1896), located on the old Nassau Plantation, he married the boss's daughter, Emma "Emmie" Weyand (1858–1943). They later moved to Round Top and took over the pictured store, which still exists and was originally located across the street from its present location. Following a shooting in 1901 involving Alex's son George and Justice of the Peace Adolph Becker (who was also a cousin), von Rosenberg and his family moved to La Grange. (Von Rosenberg family collection.)

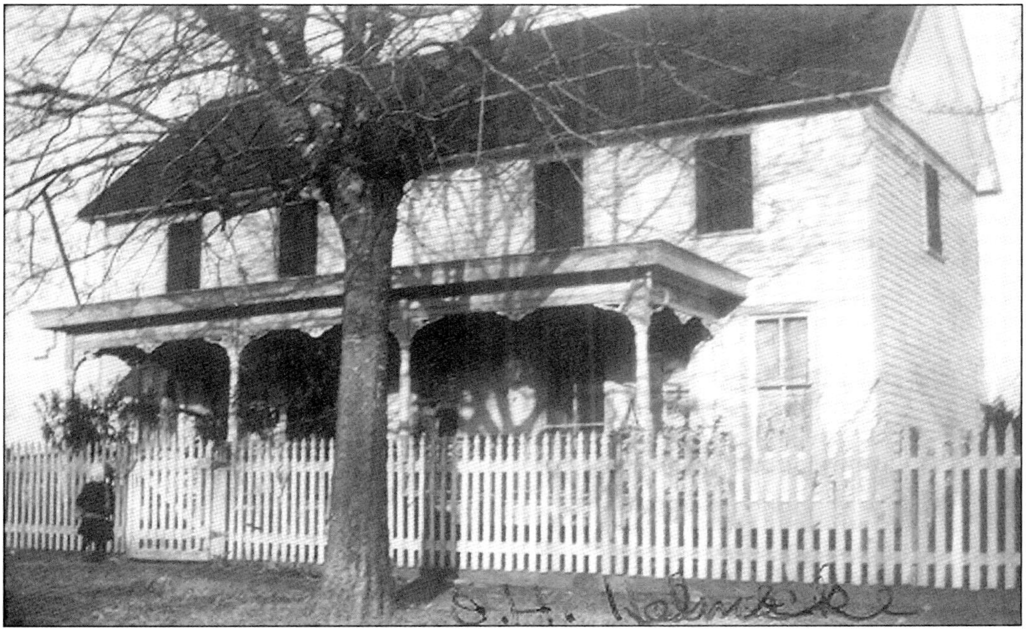

OTTO HEINRICH HELMECKE HOME, ROUND TOP. Shown is the Round Top home of Otto Heinrich Helmecke (1854–1907). Helmecke married Johannes von Rosenberg's daughter, Johanna Caroline von Rosenberg (1859–1935), and ran a general store in Round Top in addition to raising two sons. (Von Rosenberg family collection.)

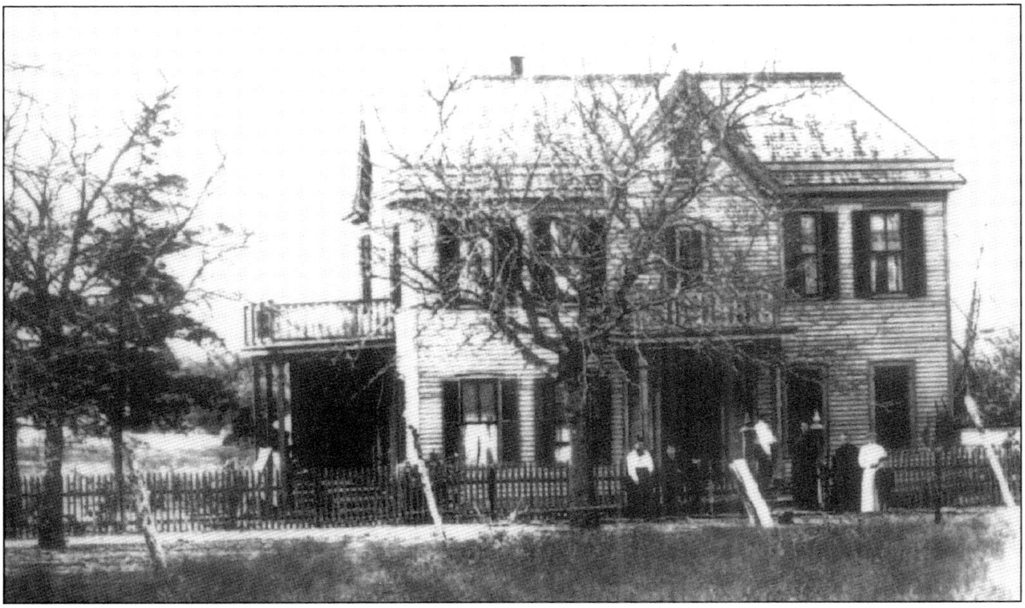

ALEX VON ROSENBERG HOME, ROUND TOP. The home pictured was built around 1875 by Wilhelm Johann Umland, an early Round Top merchant who relocated to Carmine. After Umland left Round Top, Alex von Rosenberg moved into the residence located at the corner of Mill and Von Rosenberg Streets. The Bender, Sacks, and Diers families also lived there. (Von Rosenberg family collection.)

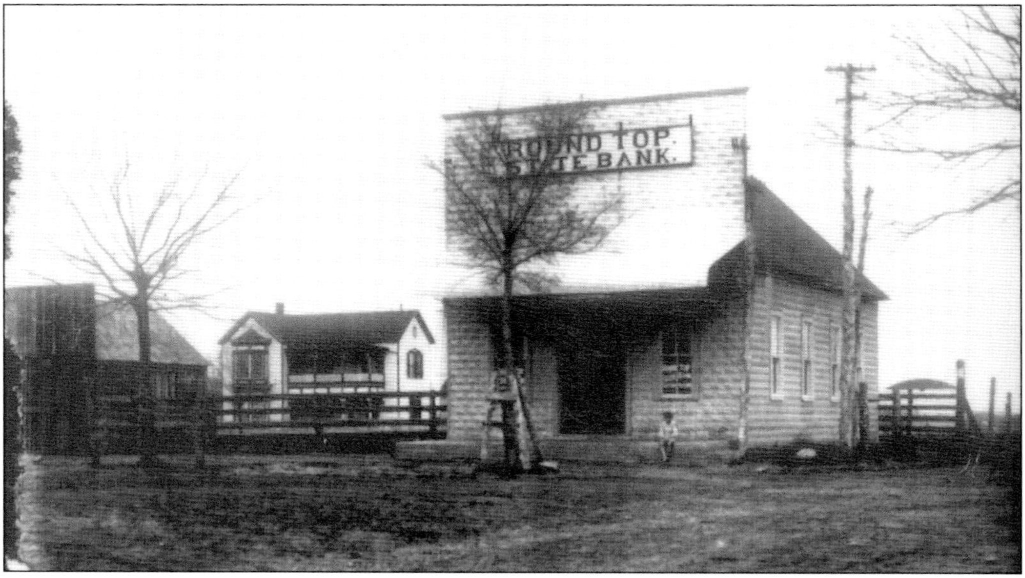

ROUND TOP STATE BANK. The Round Top State Bank was chartered in 1912 and is still in operation today. In the background is the home of Herman Eugen von Rosenberg (1854–1906) and his wife, Lucy Marie Levien (1862–1950). Herman was the son of Carl Eugen and Dorchen von Rosenberg. He ran a cigar factory and a dry goods store in Round Top and was president of the Round Top Schuetzen Verein (shooting club). (Von Rosenberg family collection.)

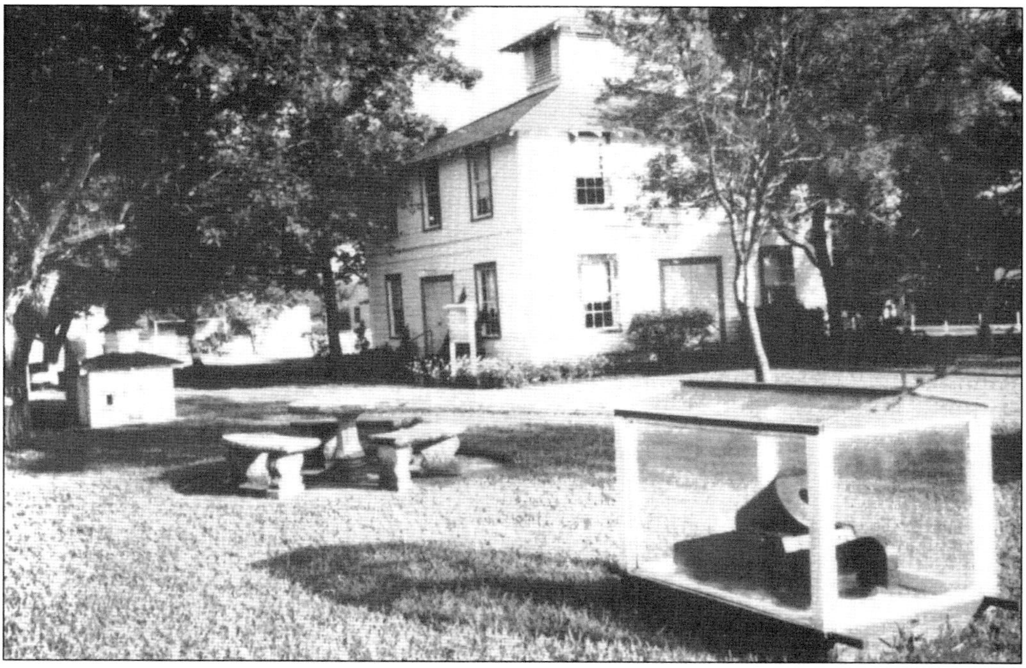

CANNON IN ROUND TOP TOWN SQUARE. Each Independence Day, a cannon is fired to signify the official start of the festivities in Round Top. The cannon pictured lies on the town square grounds. In the background is Round Top's restored Justice Precinct Courthouse, which was built in 1924 to replace an earlier one constructed in the 1880s. (Gary E. McKee.)

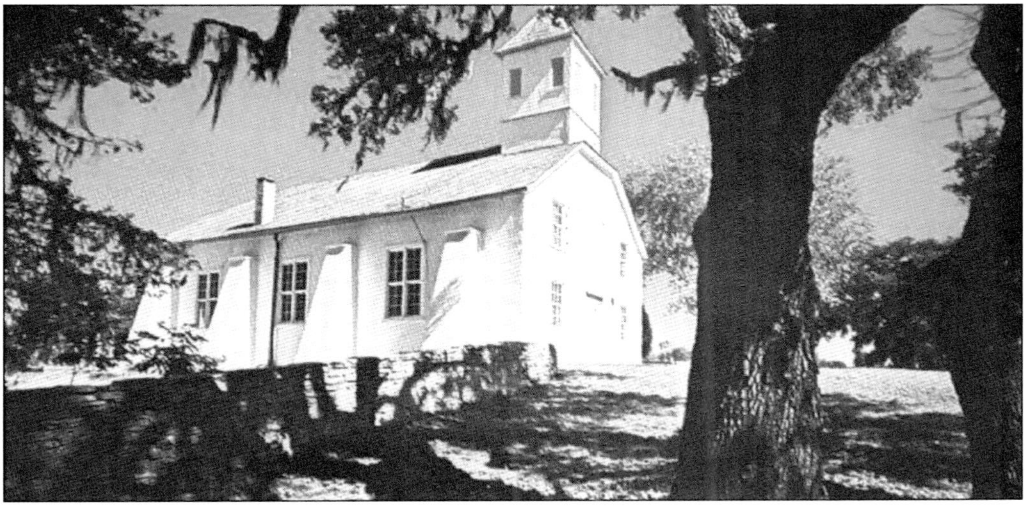

BETHLEHEM LUTHERAN CHURCH, ROUND TOP. This church was dedicated October 28, 1866, at the directive of Rev. Adam Neuthard (1828–1902), who was instrumental in bringing an organized Lutheran faith to northern Fayette County. The stone used came from the hill upon which the church overlooking Cummins Creek still stands, as did the cedar timbers used to frame the building. The builder was Carl Siegismund Bauer (1792–1873), Neuthard's grandfather. (Author's collection.)

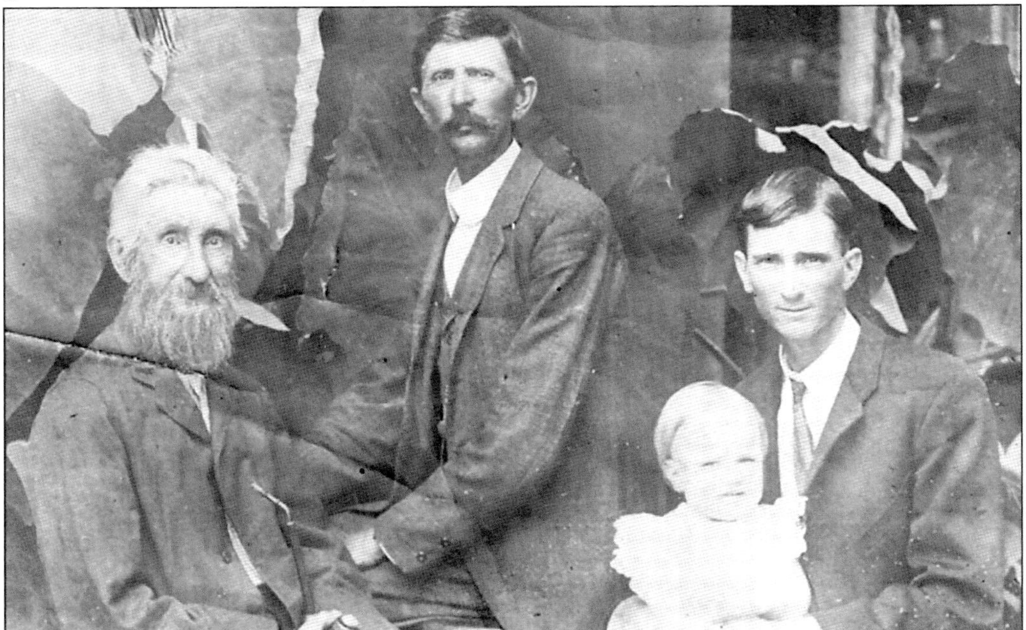

FOUR GENERATIONS. Here are four generations of the von Rosenberg family. From left to right are Eugen, his son Alex, grandson George, and baby Edgar. Eugen von Rosenberg is the author's great-great-great-grandfather and Alex is his great-great-grandfather. Eugen was instrumental in establishing the Bethlehem Lutheran Church along with his brother Johannes Carl von Rosenberg, as well as the Bauers, Scheuddemagens, and Weyands, among others. (Von Rosenberg family collection.)

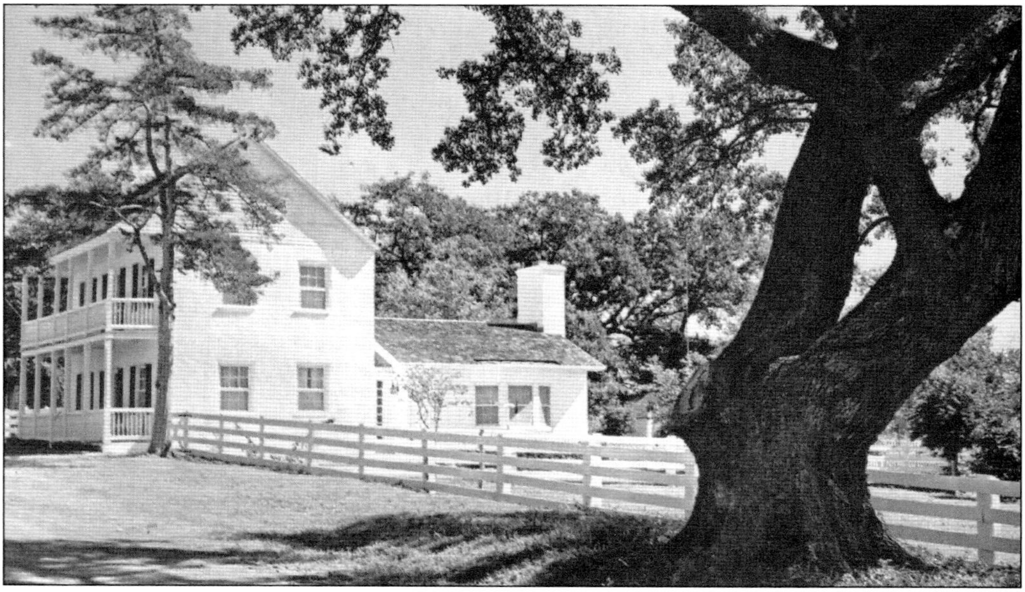

Bauer Scheuddemagen Home, Round Top. The home of Conrad Scheuddemagen (1811–1900) and his wife, Wilhelmine Bauer Scheuddemagen (1825–1897), was built in 1852 by Scheuddemagen's father-in-law Carl Bauer. The building is a replica of the Bauer family's home in Saxony, Germany, and was designated a Texas Historic Site in 1965. (Gary E. McKee.)

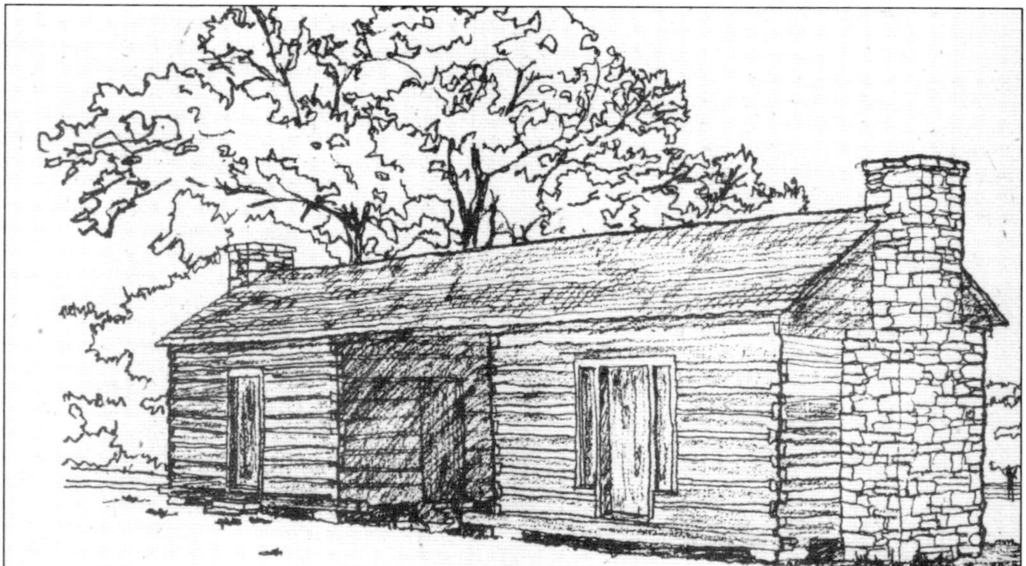

Moore's Fort, Round Top. The early home of Col. John Henry Moore was built in 1828 on land that would later become North Main Street in La Grange. It is purported to be the oldest existing building in Fayette County. The fort was dismantled and moved from La Grange at an unknown time, and it eventually came into the ownership of the Schott family, who donated it and assisted in having it moved to the Texas Pioneer Arts Foundation in Round Top in 1977, where it still stands today. This postcard rendering is from a drawing by Lennie Brown. (Gary E. McKee.)

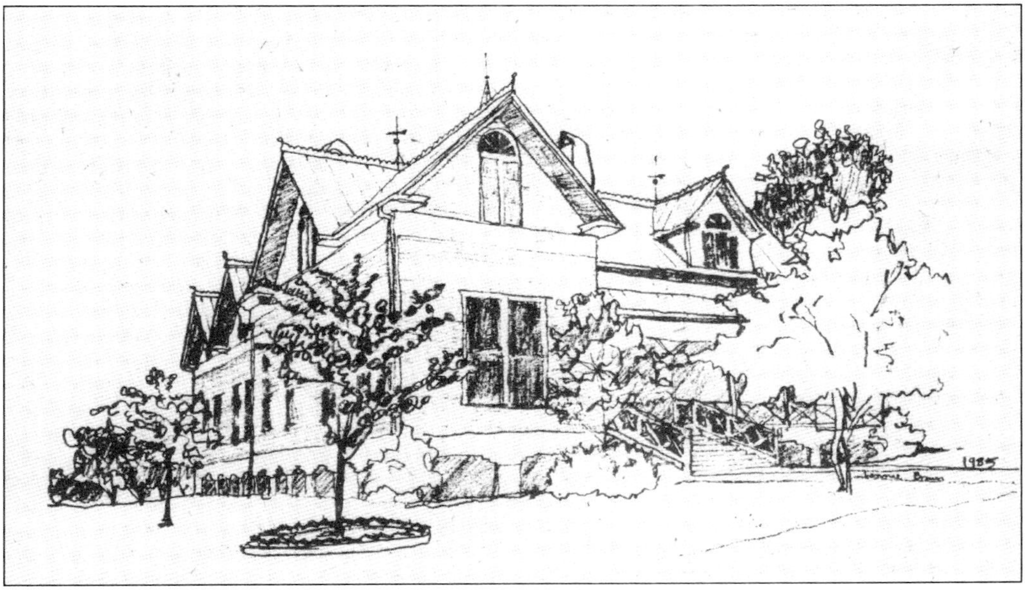

William Lockhart Clayton House, Festival Hill. The home depicted in this postcard illustration by Lennie Brown was the first structure moved in 1976 to the Round Top Festival Institute, begun in 1971 by pianist James Dick. The home, built in 1885, originally was in La Grange. It is named in honor of Texas statesman William Lockhart Clayton (1880–1966). (Gary E. McKee.)

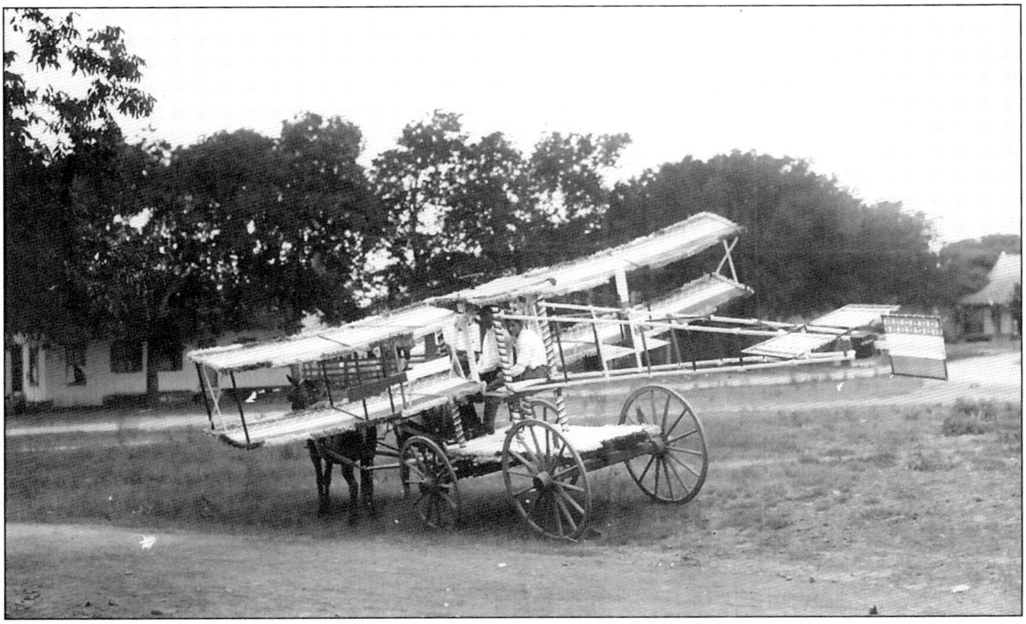

Float in Round Top Fourth of July Parade. Round Top has the distinction of having the oldest continuous Fourth of July parade west of the Mississippi. The first recorded festivities occurred on July 4, 1851, the nation's 75th anniversary. This float celebrating what was then the new technology of flight was built by Willie Giese (1896–1922), son of Henry and Bertha Spies Giese. (Carolyn Heinsohn.)

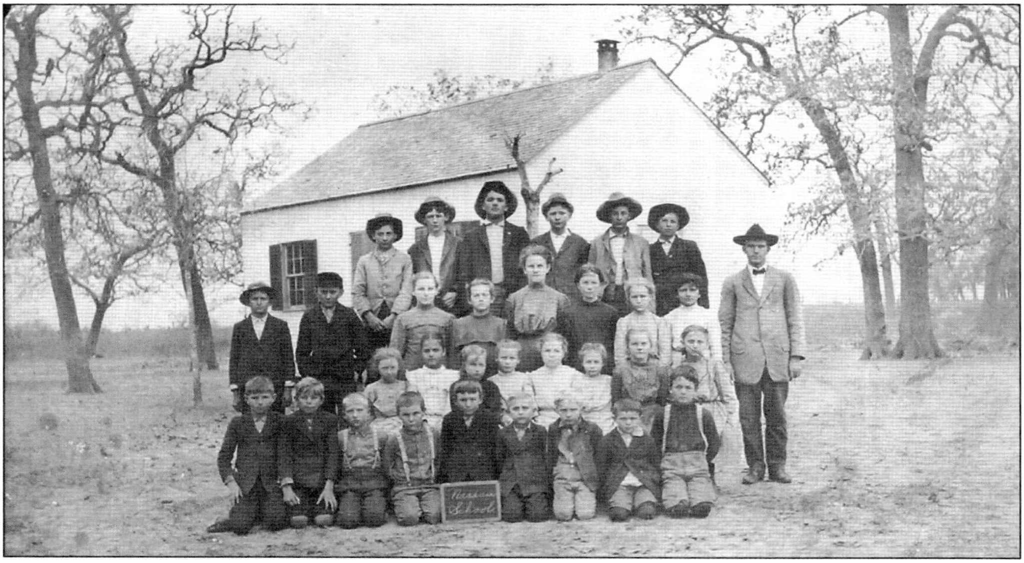

NASSAU SCHOOL, ROUND TOP. The Nassau School operated from 1890 to 1943 and served those who lived near the former Nassau Plantation, five miles southeast of Round Top. The teacher here is Armin Giese, son of Henry and Bertha Spies Giese. The area surrounding the former Nassau Plantation was home to numerous African American families after the Civil War. The children of these families attended the Nassau Colored School, which was located close to the school depicted here about 1910. (Carolyn Heinsohn.)

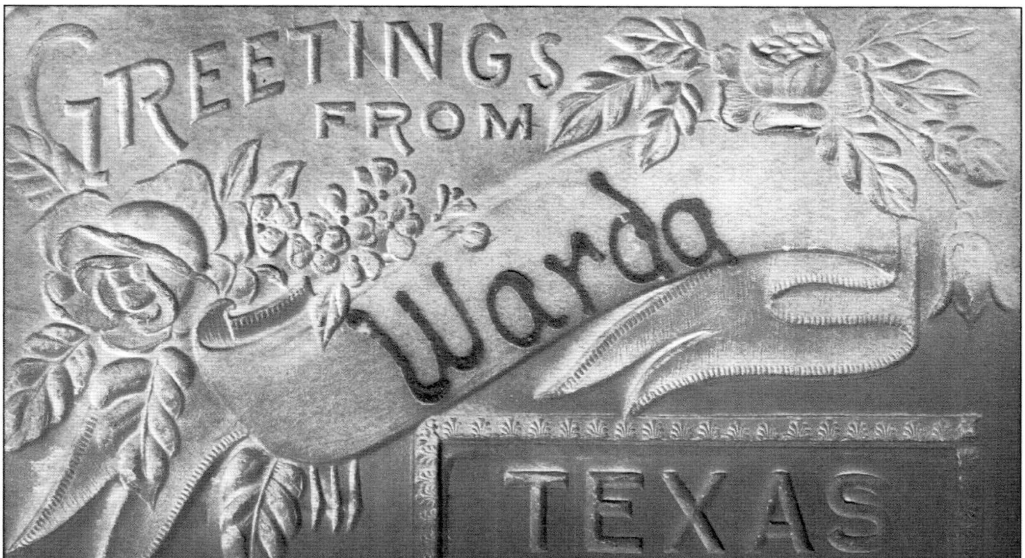

GREETINGS FROM WARDA, TEXAS. Warda is approximately 11 miles north of La Grange and 16 miles west of Round Top on Highway 77. The town's name is derived from a community in Germany named Wartha and was founded by Wendish families in 1873, as a satellite colony to the larger and more prominent Wendish community of Serbin, eight miles to the northwest. The Wends were a religiously devout minority community that came to Texas as a group in 1854 to practice their brand of Lutheranism without interference or prejudice. (Gary E. McKee.)

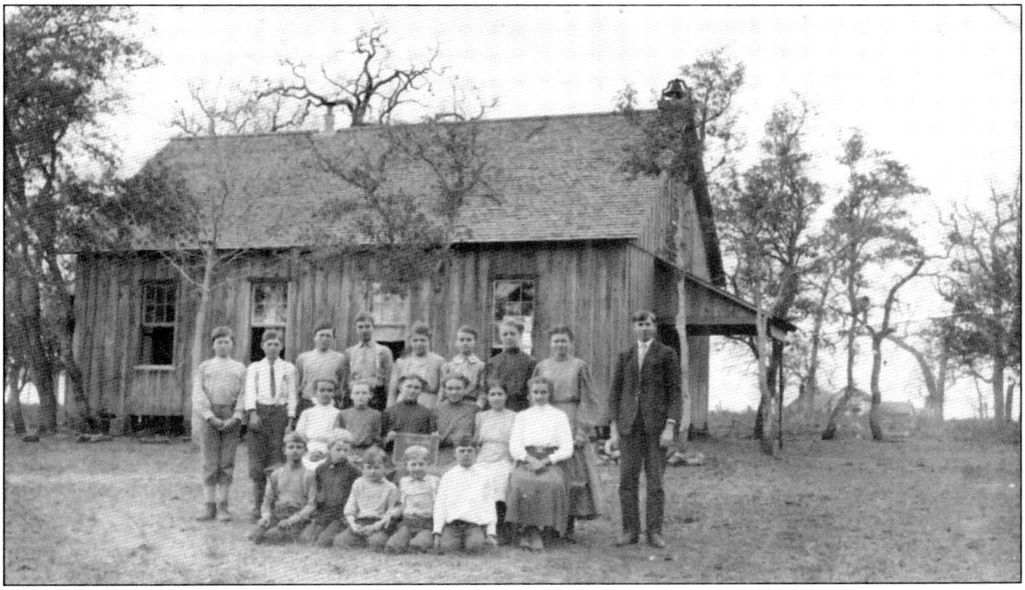

Urwald School, Walhalla, Texas. The community of Walhalla is located approximately 14 miles north of La Grange and two miles southwest of Round Top. It was founded by settlers from northern Germany. The school shown here was in operation until 1944, when it was incorporated into the Round Top-Carmine School District. (Fayette Heritage Museum & Archives.)

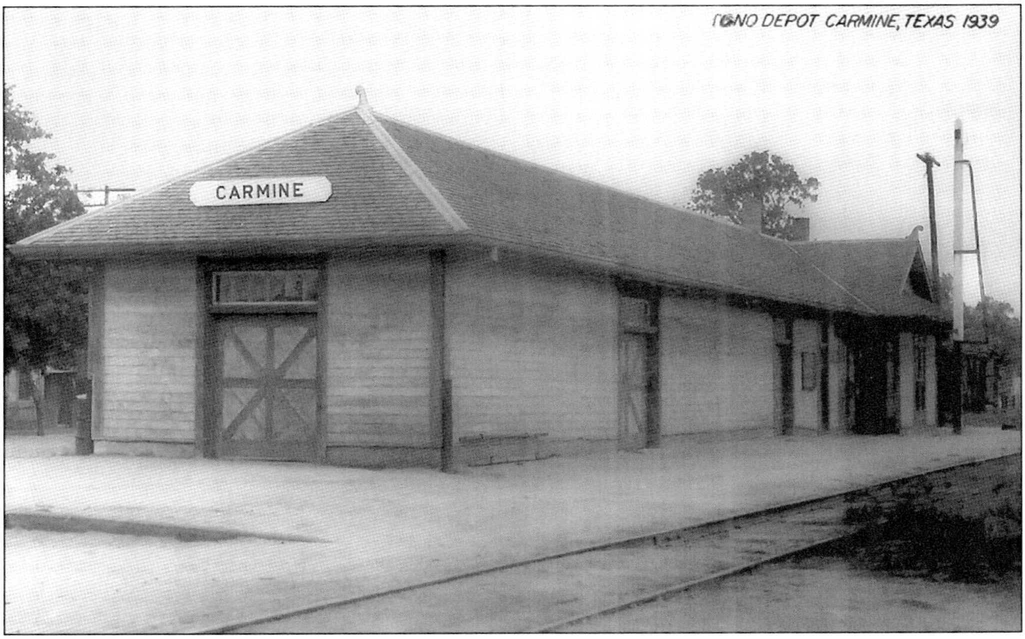

T&NO Depot, Carmine, Texas, 1939. Shown in this photo postcard is the railroad depot of Carmine as it appeared in 1939. The rail line noted on the postcard is the Texas & New Orleans Railroad, the successor to the Houston & Texas Central Railway, the initial rail line going through Carmine, built in 1871. This depot still stands today. (Author's collection.)

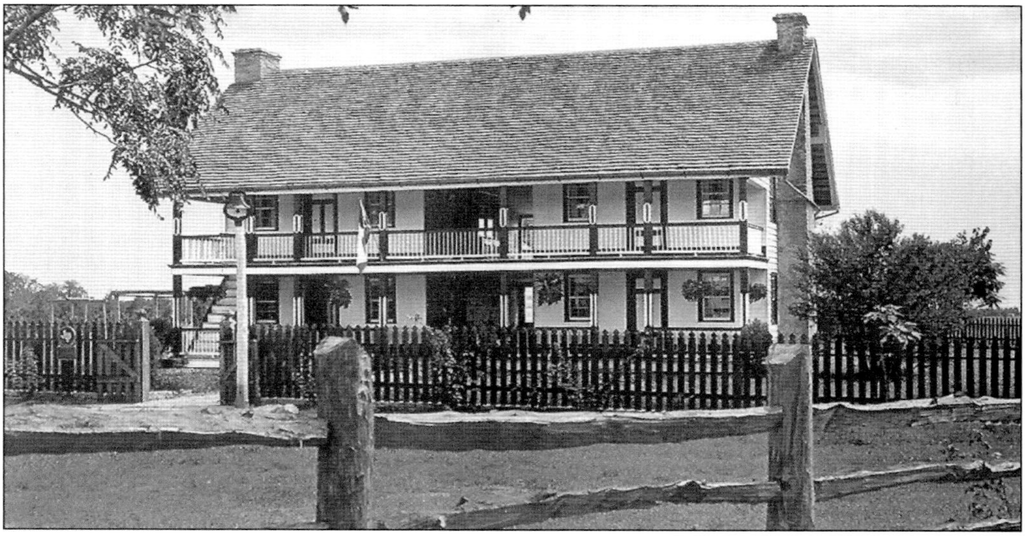

Winedale Inn, Winedale, Texas. Pictured here is a building known intermittently as the Winedale Inn, the Stagecoach Inn, and the Sam Lewis Stopping Place. It was built by William Stapleton Townsend (1807–1848) and his wife, Mary Burnam Townsend (1816–1846), around 1834 as a one-room frame structure with a fireplace and loft above. In 1840, Townsend sold the property to his brother John, who then sold it to John York. York sold it in 1848 to Samuel Knight Lewis (1807–1867), who enlarged it. The structure was sold again in 1887 by Lewis's heirs to Joseph Georg Wagner, a German who came to Texas in 1853. Philanthropist Ima Hogg purchased it in 1963 and underwrote its preservation, giving it to the University of Texas in 1965. (Author's collection.)

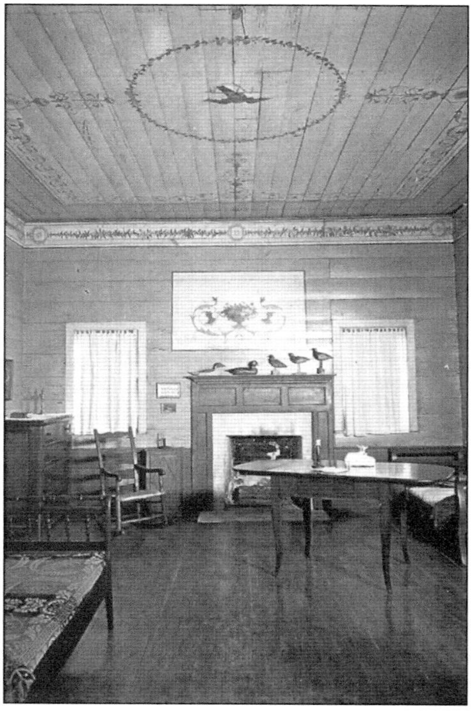

Melchior Room, Stagecoach Inn, Winedale, Texas. The Stagecoach Inn's Melchior Room was named after German artist Rudolph Melchior (1836–1870), who painted the room's eaves, ceiling, and walls. Melchior, who came with his brother to Texas from Burg, Germany, in 1853, was a trained decorative artist. While he was related to later owner Joseph Wagner, it is believed that Samuel Lewis hired Melchior to do the work in the 1860s, bridging the dominant cultures in Fayette County at that time. (Author's collection.)

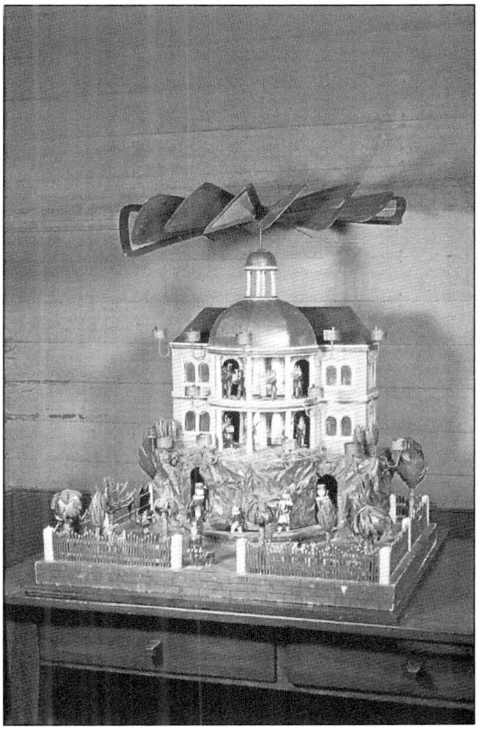

EMIL SCHUHMANN TOY. This postcard details a toy known as a baromet or pyramid, which has movable figures and a propeller that turns when the heat from built-in oil lamps rises. It is similar to the wooden Christmas windmills and pyramids that are so often identified with German Christmas traditions. This particular toy was carved by Emil Schuhmann (1856–1937), a German musician and talented carver from the Waldeck community, and was purchased from Schuhmann by Ima Hogg for $500. (Author's collection.)

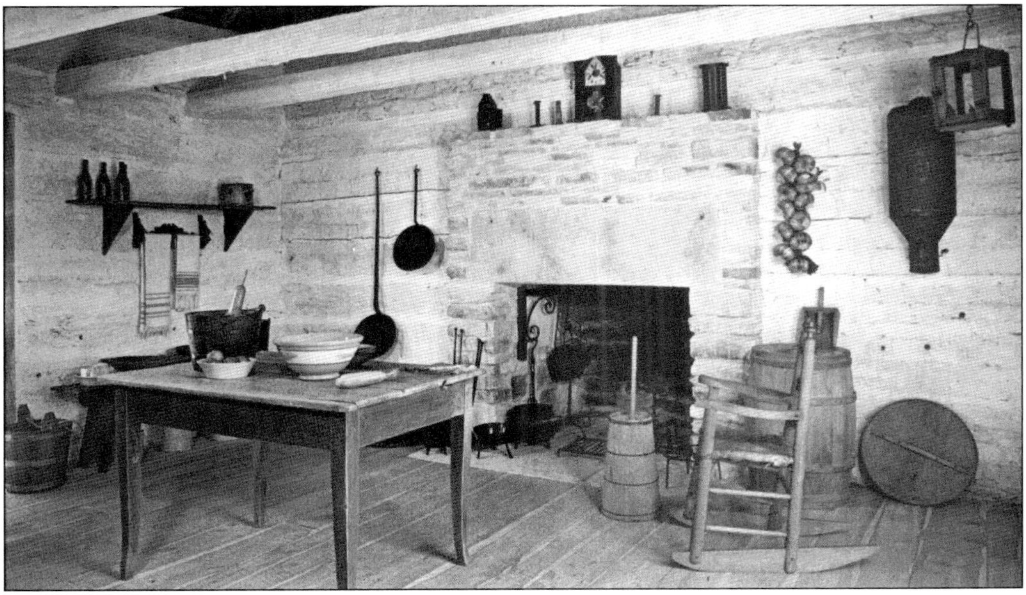

STAGECOACH INN KITCHEN, WINEDALE, TEXAS. Ima Hogg, daughter of Gov. James Hogg, had a fondness for all things primitive, especially early-American and early-Texan primitive structures and furnishings. Hogg acquired properties and artifacts, such as those depicted in the Stagecoach Inn's kitchen, which was located behind the main house. Hogg's initial plan was to move the building to Bayou Bend, her home in Houston. Luckily, she changed her mind and decided to restore the landmark at its original site. (Author's collection.)

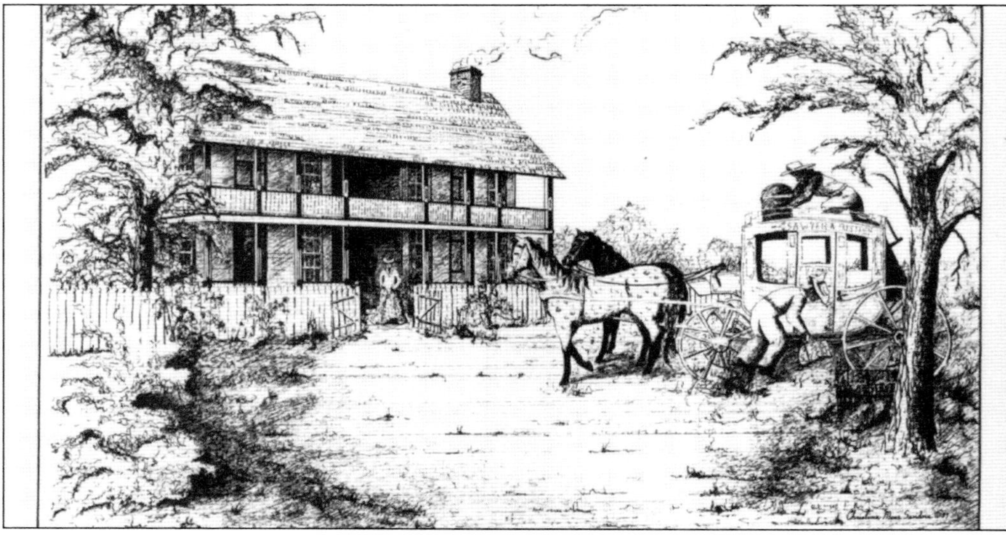

LEWIS HOUSE. This postcard by Christine Sanders features the "inn" in Winedale near Round Top. The home was occupied by the Lewis family from 1848 to 1867. During Lewis's life, it was a plantation that used slave labor to produce cotton. The home was located near the road between Bastrop and San Felipe (Gotier's Trace), which is likely why it was considered an inn. (Gary E. McKee.)

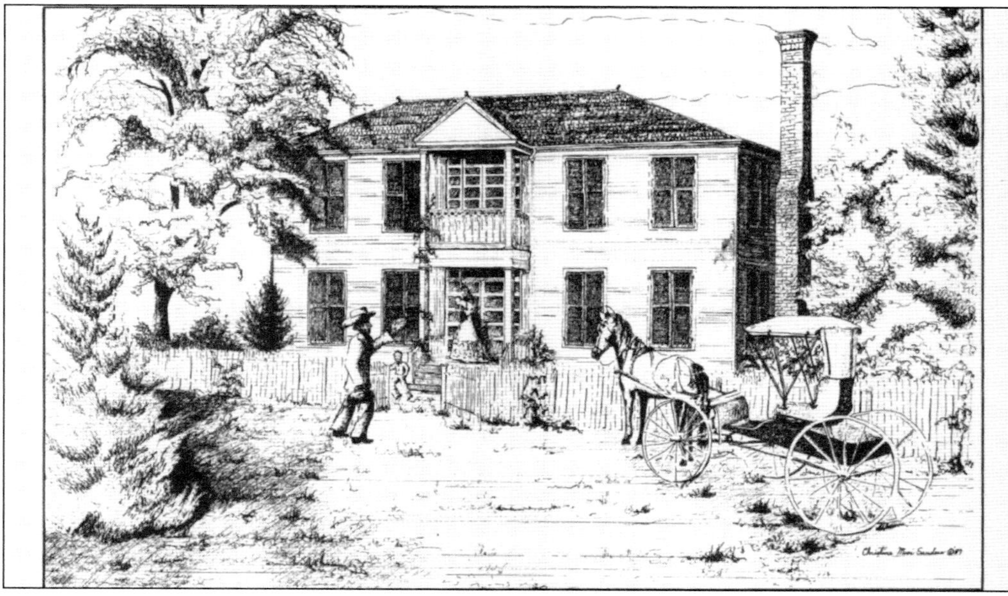

MCGREGOR-GRIMM HOUSE. Built in 1861 by Dr. Gregor Carmichael McGregor (1824–1892), a land speculator who came to Texas in 1852, the home illustrated here by Christine Sanders was originally on Mill Creek in Washington County. Upon moving his family to Waco, McGregor sold the home to neighbors, and it eventually came into the possession of Charles Grimm. Grimm's heirs sold it to Ima Hogg in 1968, and she moved it to Winedale. McGregor married Anna Fordtran (1838–1919), daughter of Fayette County pioneer Charles Fordtran (1801–1900). Charles was instrumental in assisting the Adelsverein in establishing the nearby Nassau Plantation. (Gary E. McKee.)

Six

Central Fayette County

Ellinger, Fayetteville, and Others

The communities around the county seat of La Grange and the central portion of the county are some of the most charming in Texas. Among these varied locales are Halsted, a once active, but now abandoned railroad station; Hostyn, once known as Bluff, a center of Czech Catholic culture; Kirtley, a railroad stop once known as Primm; Plum, another rail station settlement created in 1889 by the Bastrop & Houston Railway; Rutersville, the former site of Rutersville College, which was chartered in 1840 and one of the earliest higher learning institutions in Texas; and West Point, another early Anglo town site settled in the 1840s by immigrants from the southern United States.

The largest of these central Fayette County communities is Fayetteville, which was not named after the Marquis de la Fayette but for the birthplace of the town's founder, Phillip James Shaver (1814–1875), who platted the town in 1850 after migrating to Texas from North Carolina.

Even before formally becoming a town site, Fayetteville was a center of activity for the early Anglo settlers in the area, as it was a stagecoach stop on the road between San Felipe and Bastrop. Several of Stephen F. Austin's Old Three Hundred made their homes in or around the site that would become Fayetteville, including John Crier, James Cummins, and James J. Ross, who gave his name to the same area that was then known as Ross Prairie.

Fayetteville, like Round Top, is unusual in Texas for having its own precinct courthouse. Located on the town square, the town's populace takes great pride in the courthouse, which has been restored to its fine early appearance, including its 1934 Seth Thomas clock.

While being settled early on by Anglos, by the 1840s and 1850s, many German settlers called Fayetteville home, and in 1853, the Germans were followed by the first Czech settlers. The first Czech Protestant religious services in Texas were held in Fayetteville in 1856. Afterwards, Catholic Czech pioneers came and found a home in Fayetteville. By the 1870s, most of the early Anglo settlers had moved out and Fayetteville became predominantly Czech and German. In 1872, Fr. Joseph Chromcik came to Fayetteville from Moravia and held the first service performed in the native Czech tongue in Texas. Texas's first Czech insurance and fraternal organizations, the Katolická Jednota Texaská (KJT), or the Catholic Union of Texas, and the Slovanska Podporujici Jednota Statu Texas (SPJST), or the Slavonic Benevolent Order of the State of Texas, were formed in Fayetteville, which is why the city is often referred to as the "Cradle of Czech Immigration to Texas."

Some six miles to the south of Fayetteville lies the town of Ellinger, a town that, like Flatonia in the southern part of the county, was a reincarnation of an earlier settlement caused by the ever-present impetus of the railroad. In 1873, a rail line was extended from Columbus to La Grange, and the nearby community of Live Oak Hill was moved closer to the tracks and renamed Ellinger, after the locale's earliest pioneer, Franciscus Joseph Ehlinger. He was an Alsatian German who had immigrated to Texas very early on in 1835 and participated in the

Battle of San Jacinto under Gen. Sam Houston. Ellinger grew as a commercial center buoyed by the surrounding cotton, corn, and later tomato farming enterprises; however, this growth ebbed when train service ended in the early 1940s.

Of special note in this part of the county is a settlement that is now lost—Biegel. The community, which now lies under Lake Fayette (created when the Fayette Power Plant was built in 1975), was founded in 1836 by Joseph Biegel, who was of German ancestry but hailed from the Alsace region of present-day France. Biegel grew as its founder invited friends and relations to join him, many of whom were also of Alsatian German descent, including Jean Baptiste December, Otto Phillip de Lassaulx, and Johann Placidus Heller.

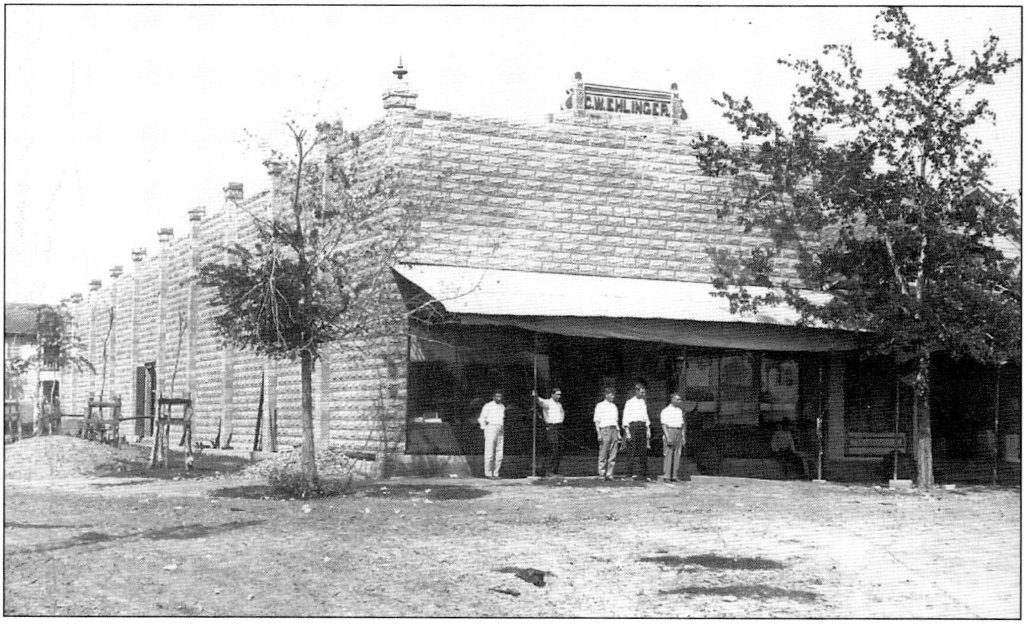

C.W. Ehlinger Store, Ellinger. Charles W. Ehlinger (1823–1872) was born in Saint Amarin, in the Alsace region of France, and came to Texas in 1835 with parents, Franciscus Joseph Ehlinger (1792–1845) and Marie Anne Koehl (1793–1873). Like many Alsatian Germans after them, the Ehlingers immigrated to central Fayette County, settling close to Live Oak Hill, near the present community of Ellinger. Charles Ehlinger ran the pictured store on Main Street in Ellinger. (Carolyn Heinsohn.)

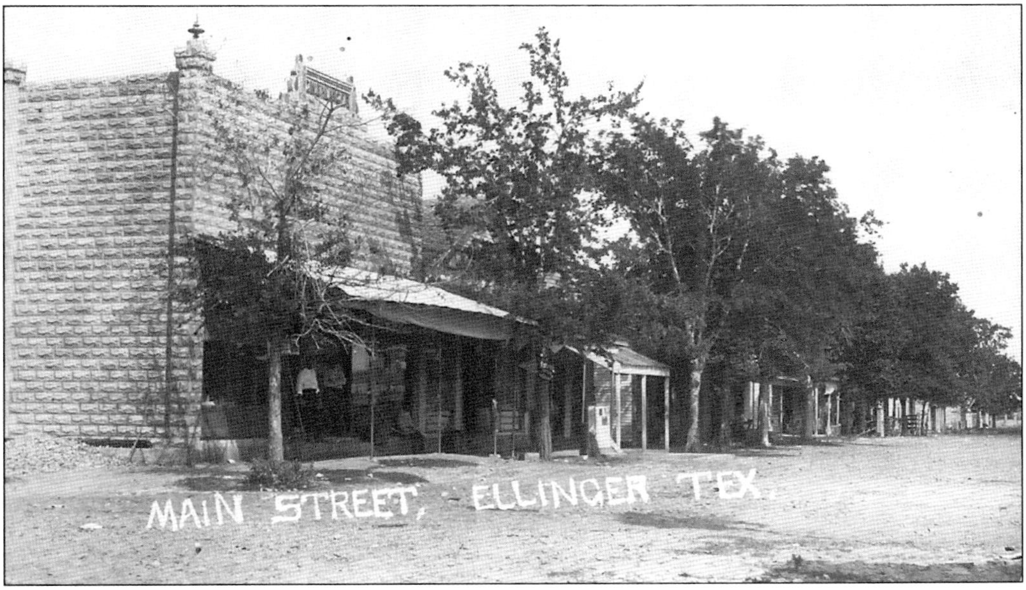

Main Street, Ellinger, Tex. Ellinger was founded in 1873 after a spur rail line was built from Glidden, near Columbus, to La Grange. The depot between these stations was dubbed *Ellinger* to honor Franciscus Joseph Ehlinger, a veteran of San Jacinto. Ehlinger's son Charles ran the store prominent in this postcard. (Carolyn Heinsohn.)

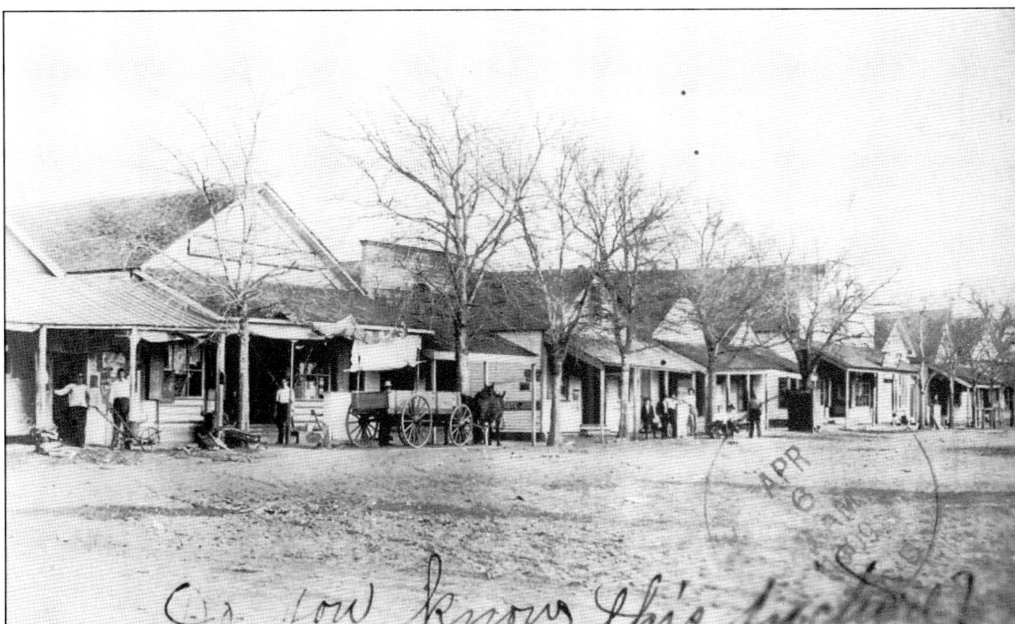

Ellinger's Main Street. This view of Ellinger's Main Street was taken about a block from Train Street in the middle of town. Ellinger was a thriving commercial center after the railroad came in 1873, but it was significantly dependent upon the surrounding cotton farms for its economy. (Fayette Heritage Museum & Archives.)

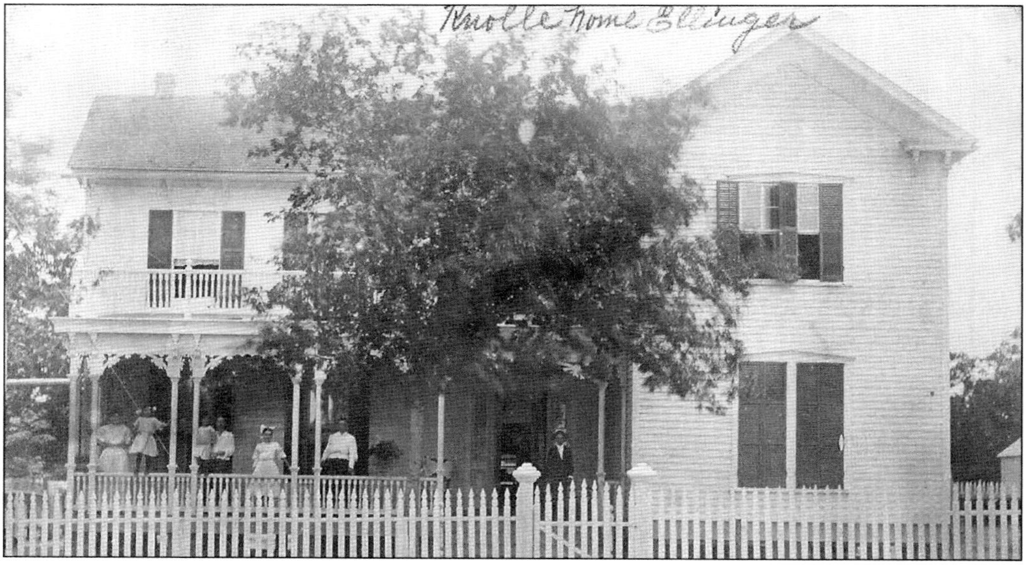

KNOLLE HOME, ELLINGER. Dr. Albert P. Knolle (1870–1931), whose Ellinger home is pictured here, was one of three physicians serving the Ellinger community in the 1890s and 1900s. Knolle was originally from Industry in Austin County and the son of Hermann Knolle and Caroline Scherrer Knolle. He came to Fayette County in the 1880s to live with his Scherrer grandparents, after which he went to Tulane University in New Orleans to earn his medical degree. (Author's collection.)

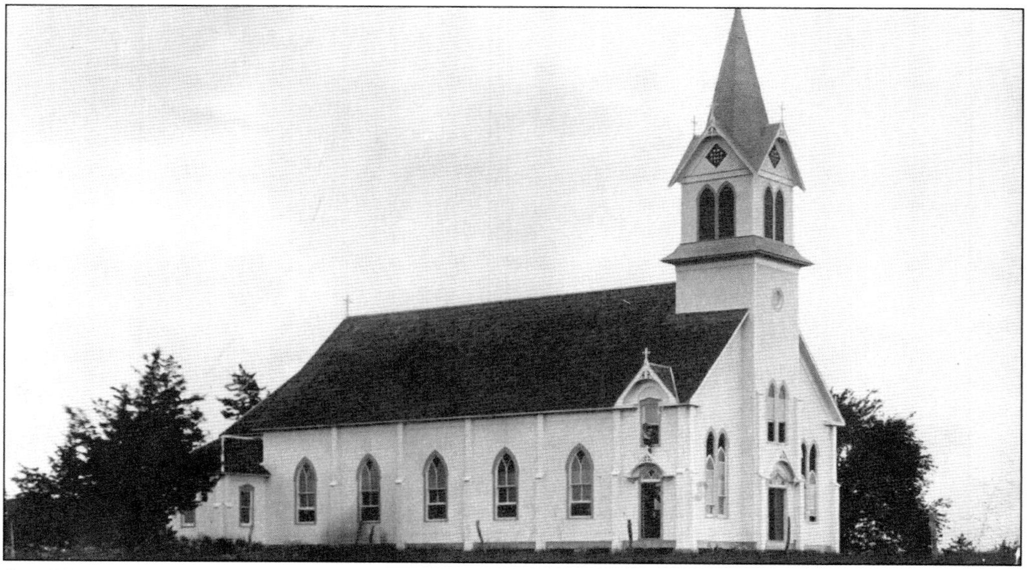

ST. MARY CHURCH, LIVE OAK HILL, NEAR ELLINGER. St. Mary Catholic Church in Live Oak Hill, near Ellinger, is the oldest Catholic congregation in Fayette County, having been established in 1855 as St. Joseph Catholic Church in Ross Prairie. The church was relocated to Live Oak Hill in 1861. The early church was replaced by the one pictured in 1879 and renamed Immaculate Conception Catholic Church. On Easter Sunday 1905, this new church burned and was replaced again; however, that same year a storm demolished the new structure, which was again rebuilt. (Fayette Heritage Museum & Archives.)

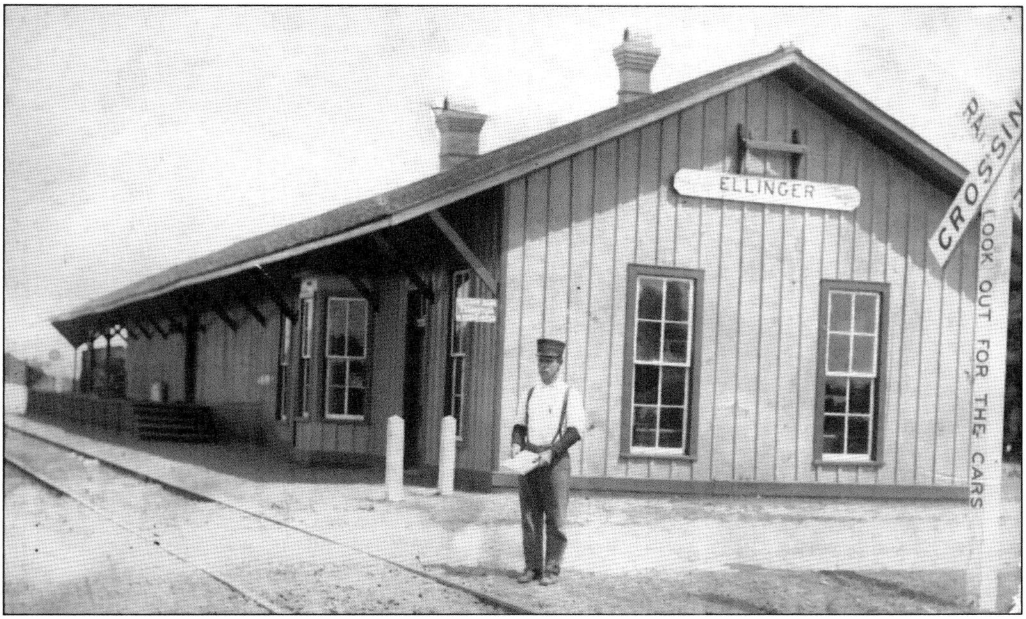

LOOK OUT FOR THE CARS. This depot served Ellinger in 1873 when the La Grange Tap was built between La Grange and Glidden to link the Galveston, Harrisburg & San Antonio Railroad and the Taylor, Bastrop & Houston Railway. (Fayette Heritage Museum & Archives.)

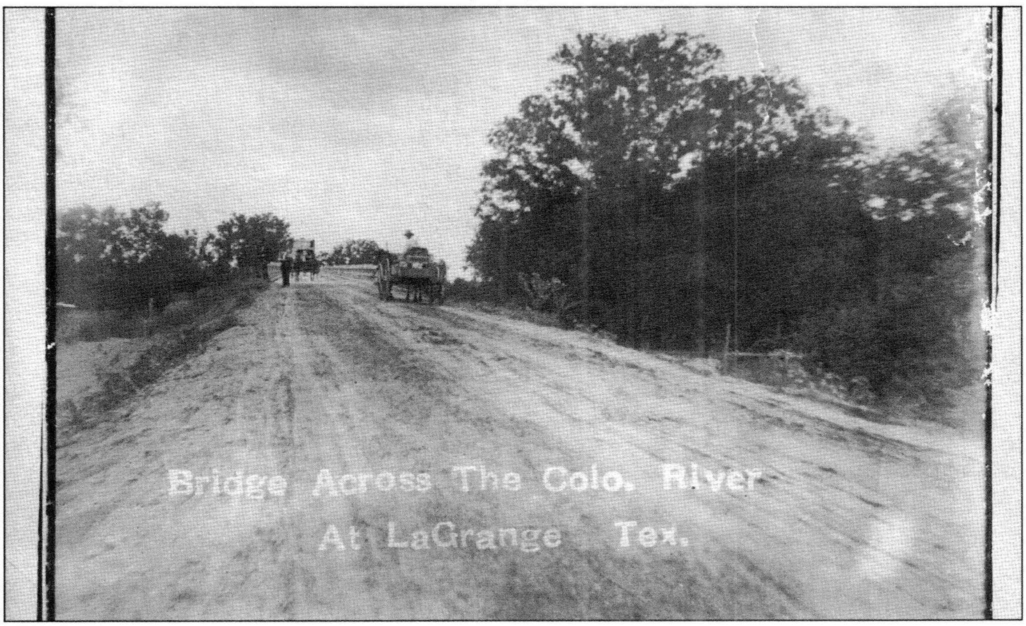

BRIDGE ACROSS THE COLO. RIVER AT LA GRANGE, TEX. Shown is the approach to the bridge across the Colorado River at La Grange. This seems to be the early wooden bridge that crossed the river, just west of La Grange. It was built in 1883 under private subscription, linked to the Bluff road that crossed over Buckner's Creek, and connected to the Schulenburg road. This bridge was later replaced by a steel structure in 1899 and then again by a more modern steel truss bridge in 1941. (Gary E. McKee.)

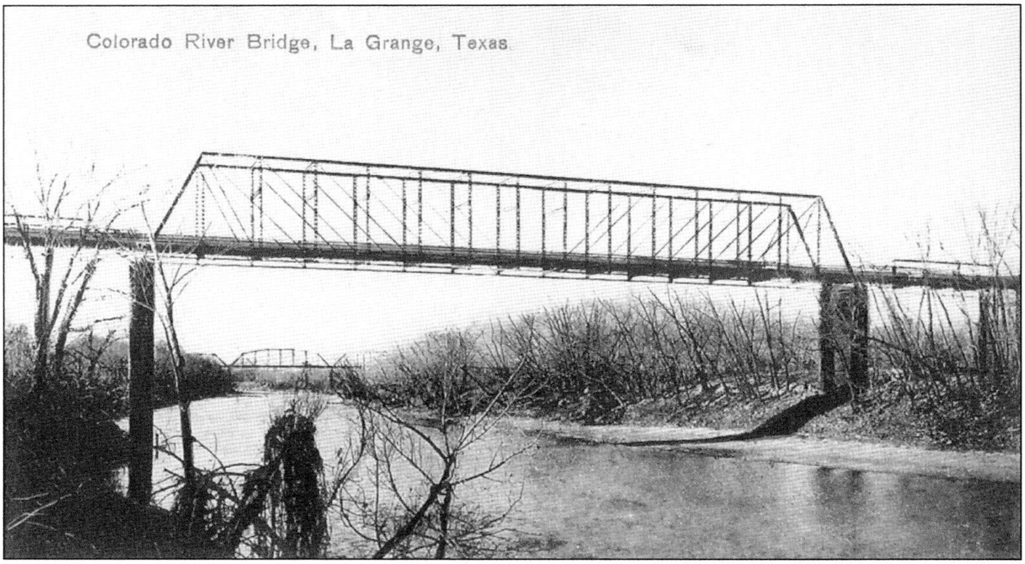

COLORADO RIVER BRIDGE, LA GRANGE, TEXAS. In 1883, the city's first bridge, a wooden one, was built at La Fayette Street across the Colorado River, replacing a ferry. La Fayette Street was known as Ferry Road until the late 1840s. The bridge pictured is the 1899 steel replacement bridge. In the background, the railroad bridge built in 1906 by the King Bridge Company of Cleveland, Ohio, is visible. Train service first came to La Grange on December 31, 1880, with the arrival of the Galveston, Harrisburg & San Antonio Railroad. (Author's collection.)

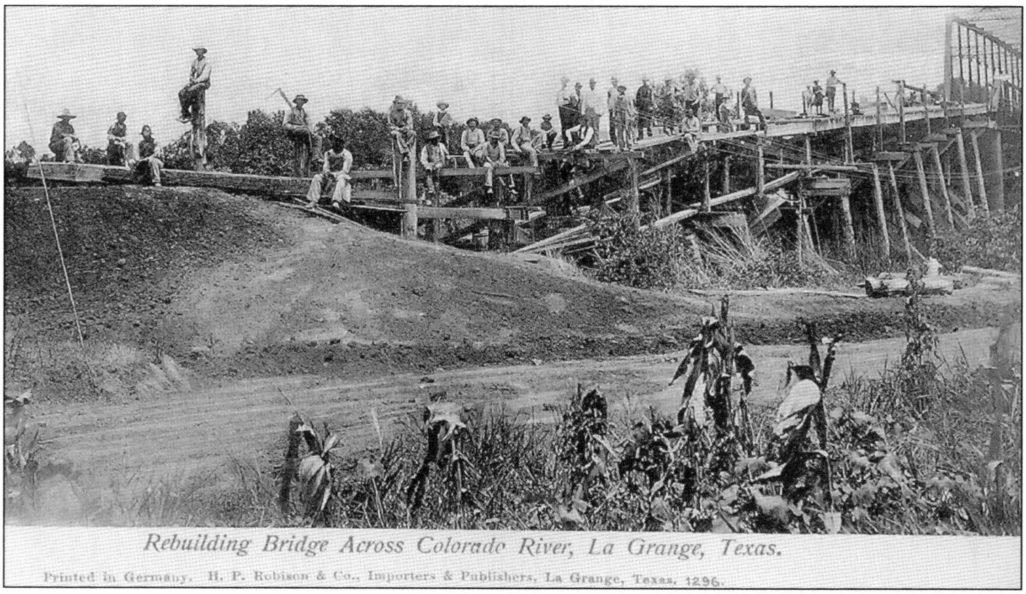

REBUILDING BRIDGE ACROSS COLORADO RIVER, LA GRANGE, TEXAS. The bridge at La Grange was first a wooden bridge, and a toll was paid to cross it. The Commissioner's Court purchased this bridge in 1887 for $41,500; La Grange appropriated $8,000 so that crossing the bridge would be free. The wooden bridge was replaced by a steel single-truss span, visible in the background to the right. Here, workers refurbish the earthen approach to the bridge, which was damaged by the 1913 flood. (Author's collection.)

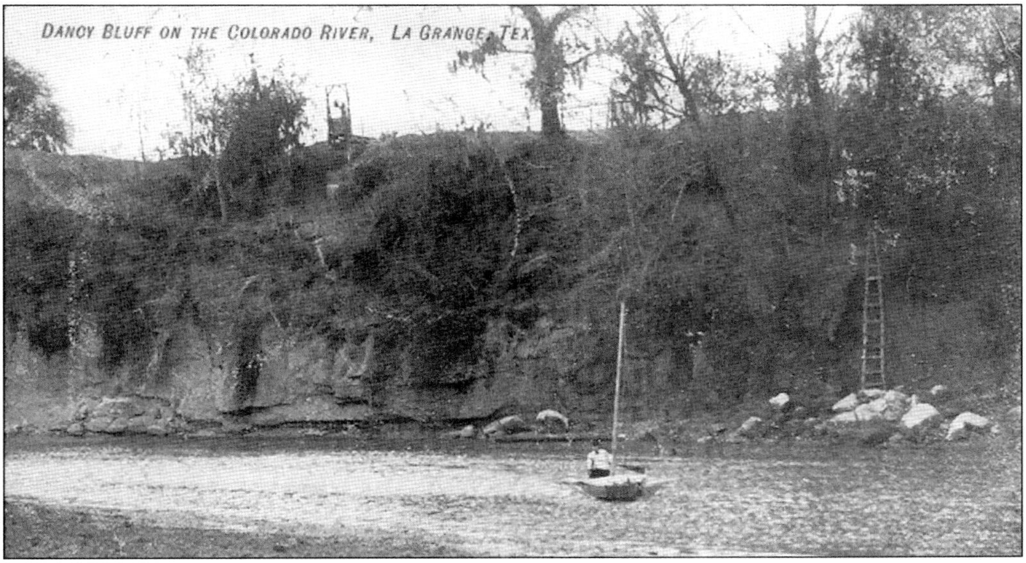

DANCY BLUFF ON THE COLORADO RIVER, LA GRANGE, TEX. John Winfield Scott Dancy (1810–1866) was a planter from Virginia who came to Fayette County in 1836 following the death of his first wife. He purchased 640 acres of bottomland along the Colorado River near La Grange, where he grew cotton and raised a family with his second wife, Lucy Ann Nowlin. Dancy was a lawyer, legislator, railroad promoter, and erstwhile land speculator, contriving a plan for Colorado City, envisioned across from La Grange, but which never came to fruition. Dancy ran unsuccessfully for governor in 1853. The high banks bordering the Dancy Plantation's are pictured here. (Author's collection.)

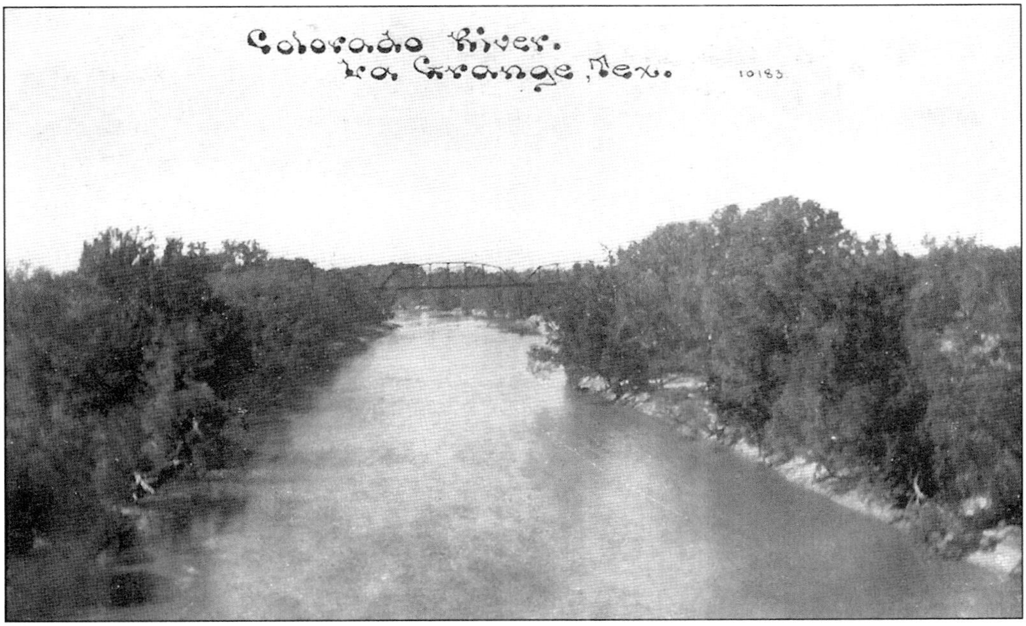

COLORADO RIVER, LA GRANGE, TEX. This view of the Colorado River is most likely taken from the 1899 steel bridge, looking north at the 1906 iron train trestle bridge, which crosses the river just north of La Fayette Street in La Grange. (Author's collection.)

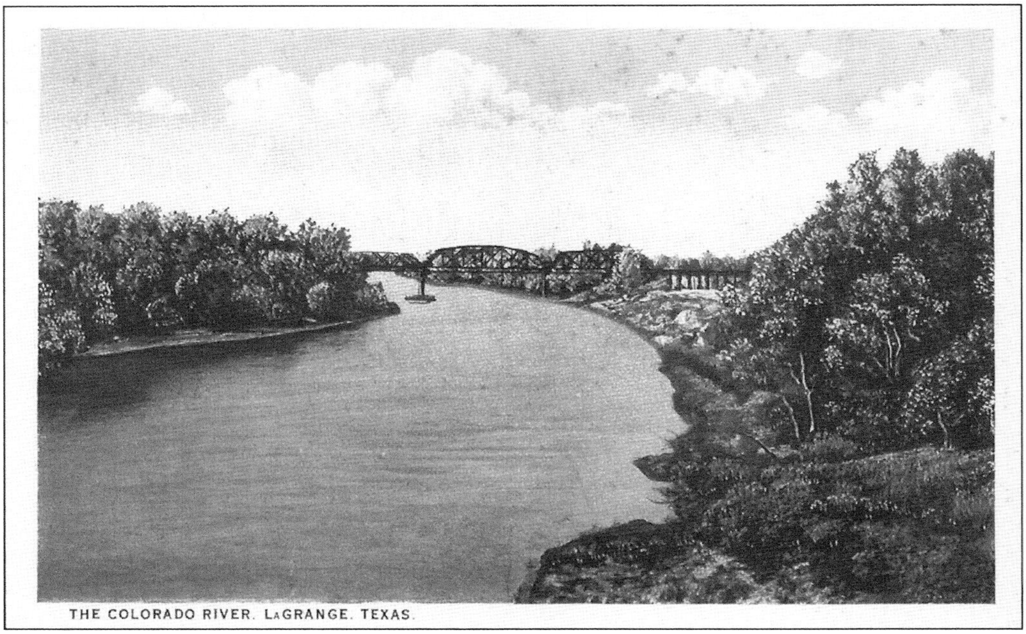

The Colorado River, La Grange, Texas. This depiction of the 1906 iron train trestle bridge crossing over the Colorado River at La Grange is drawn from a photograph and appears to show the train trestle bridge from the north, looking south when factoring in the leftward curve of the river. (Author's collection.)

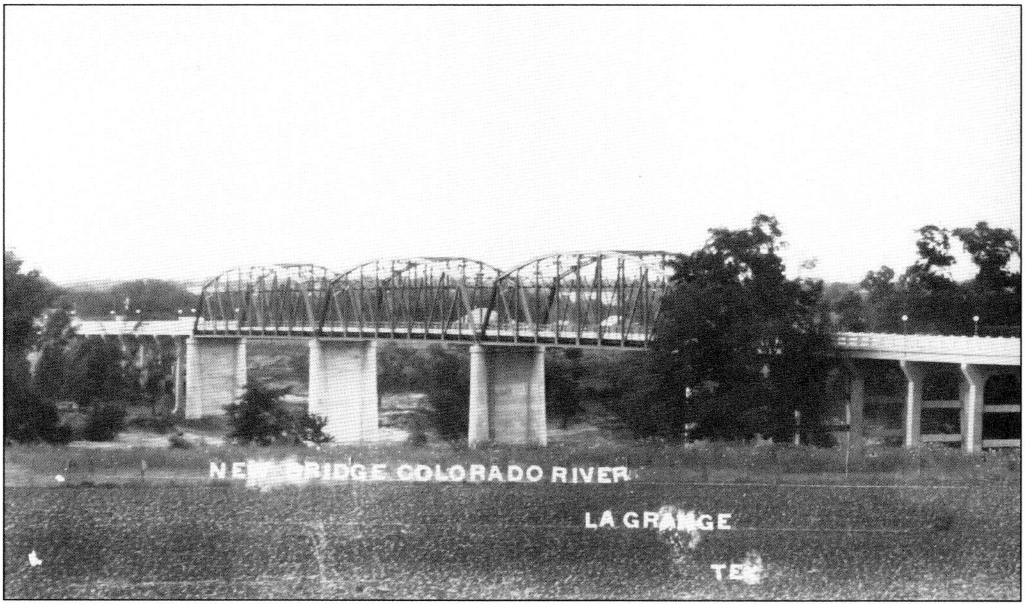

New Bridge, Colorado River, La Grange, Tex. In the mid-1920s, it was determined that having only one bridge over the Colorado River was insufficient. In 1926, a second bridge to the south of La Grange was built, along with a winding drive up the Bluff. The steel and concrete bridge pictured was built with three truss spans and concrete approaches. This bridge was recently demolished and replaced with a flat concrete span. (Fayette Heritage Museum & Archives.)

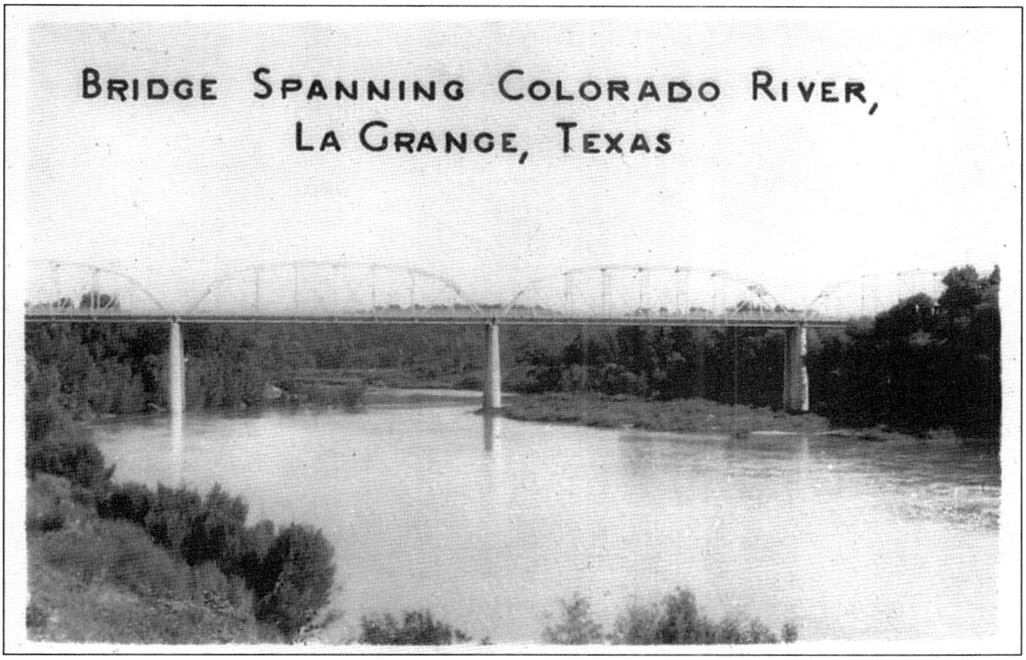

BRIDGE SPANNING COLORADO RIVER, LA GRANGE, TEXAS. The Highway 71 Bridge across the Colorado River at La Grange was built in 1941 by the Austin Bridge Company, of Dallas, Texas, after the 1899 bridge was damaged by a flood on July 27, 1938. It was registered as a National Historic Place in 1996. (Gary E. McKee.)

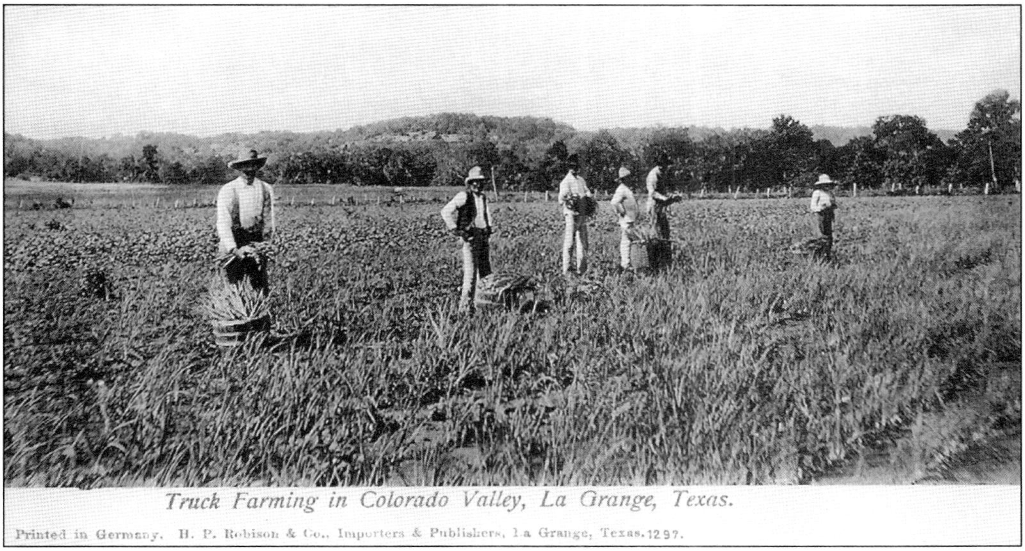

TRUCK FARMING IN COLORADO VALLEY, LA GRANGE, TEXAS. Prior to truck farming, local farmers typically grew only enough to satisfy their own needs plus a little to sell. However, with the advent of transportation networks, such as trains and highways, truck farming began to take hold, allowing farmers to grow more produce for distant markets. Here, farmers in the Colorado River valley surrounding La Grange are packing their crops for delivery to such far away markets as Houston and San Antonio. (Author's collection.)

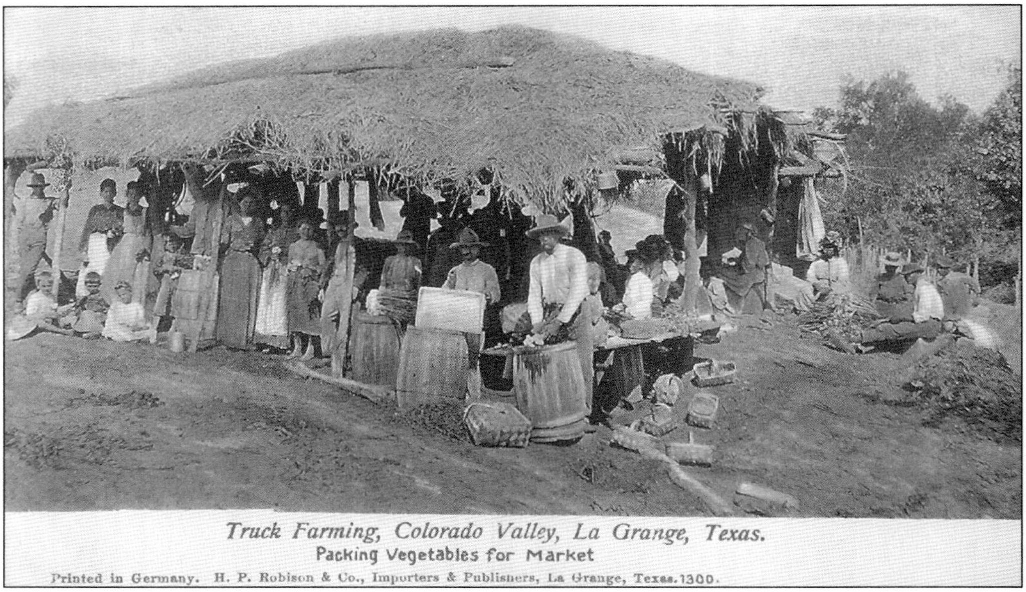

PACKING VEGETABLES FOR MARKET. With the expansion of the railroads and larger motorized vehicles, truck farms popped up in the growing regions of the American West and South; from there, seasonal crops could be shipped to markets where cultivation was more limited by climate. Fayette County was a truck-farming area for tomatoes, melons, beans, cucumbers, radishes, onions, and cabbage. (Author's collection.)

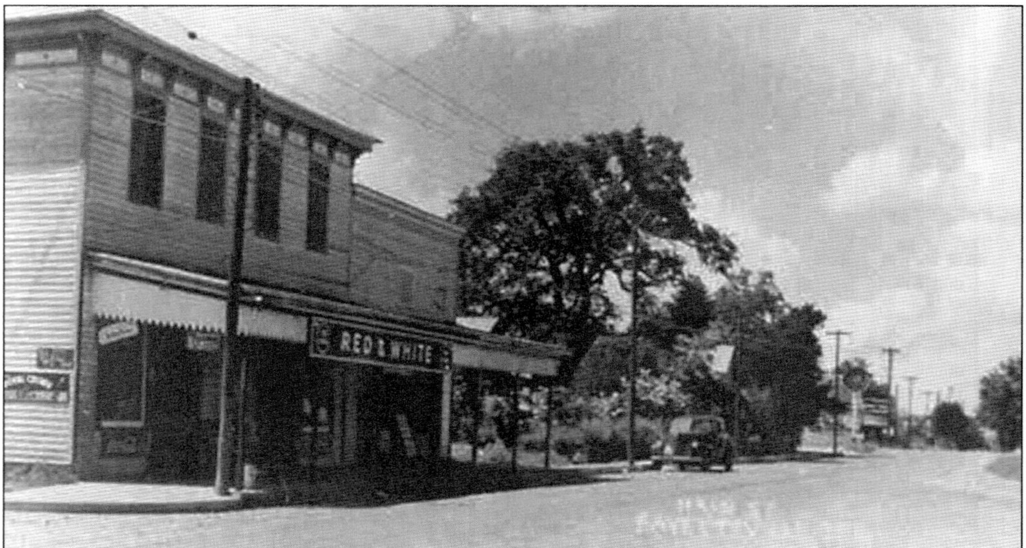

MAIN STREET, FAYETTEVILLE. The Red and White grocery store is located at the corner of Live Oak and Main Streets, on Fayetteville's square. It is believed to have been built around 1835 by Sylvester Stansbury Munger and is thought to be one of the oldest commercial structures in the area. For many years, the store and its companion Dawn Theater were operated by brothers Rudolph "Rudy" Mynar (1896–1973) and Joseph "Joe" Mynar (1887–1973). Rudy and Joe's father, Ignac Mynar, came to Texas late in 1880 from Bordovice, Czech Republic. (Fayette Heritage Museum & Archives.)

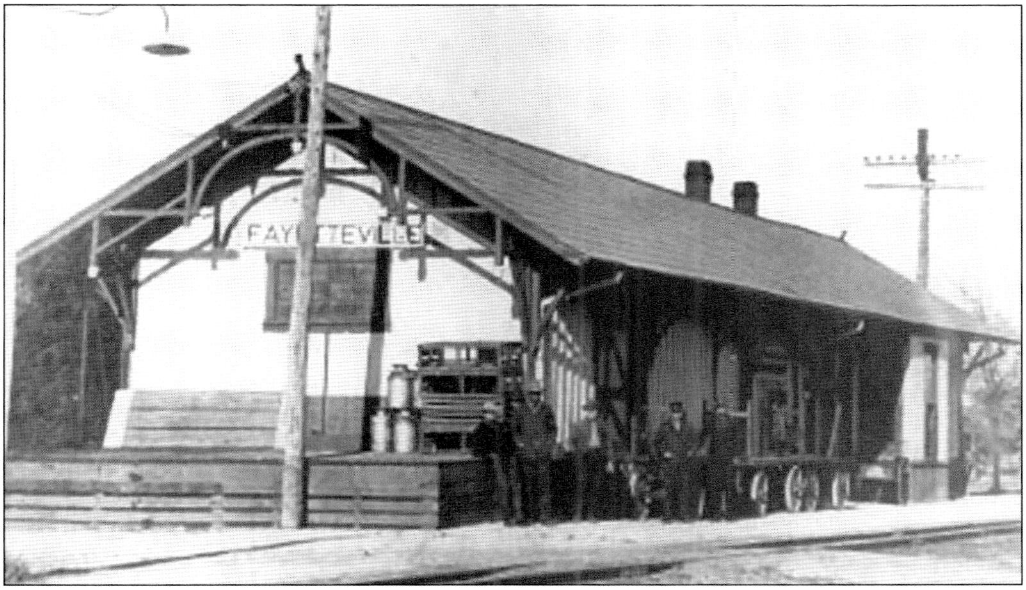

FAYETTEVILLE DEPOT. In 1887, the Taylor, Bastrop & Houston Railway built a line through the town of Fayetteville, adding a depot at the intersection of the railroad and South Scott Street. The land for the rail line and depot was donated by Hugc Carl Zapp (1822–1903), a prominent businessman who immigrated to Texas in 1860 from Elberfeld, Germany. (Fayette Heritage Museum & Archives.)

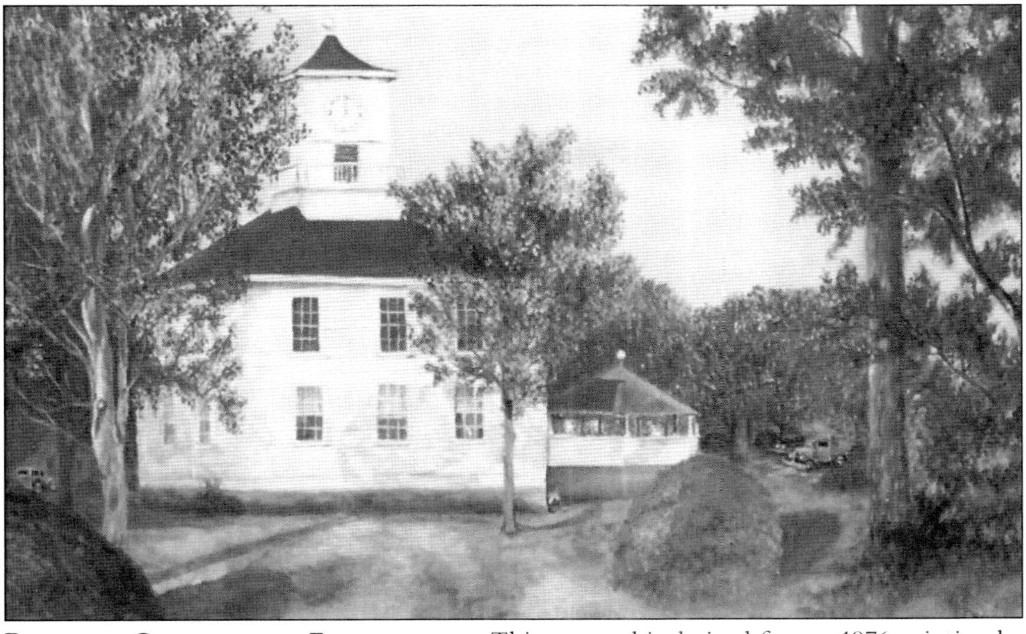

PRECINCT COURTHOUSE, FAYETTEVILLE. This postcard is derived from a 1976 painting by Evelika Drizga Chitwood. It is Fayetteville's Justice Precinct Courthouse with its 1934 four-faced Seth Thomas clock, which still keeps good time today. The Fayetteville courthouse was built in 1880, and two jail cells were added in 1887. The gazebo in the background was erected in 1932. (Author's collection.)

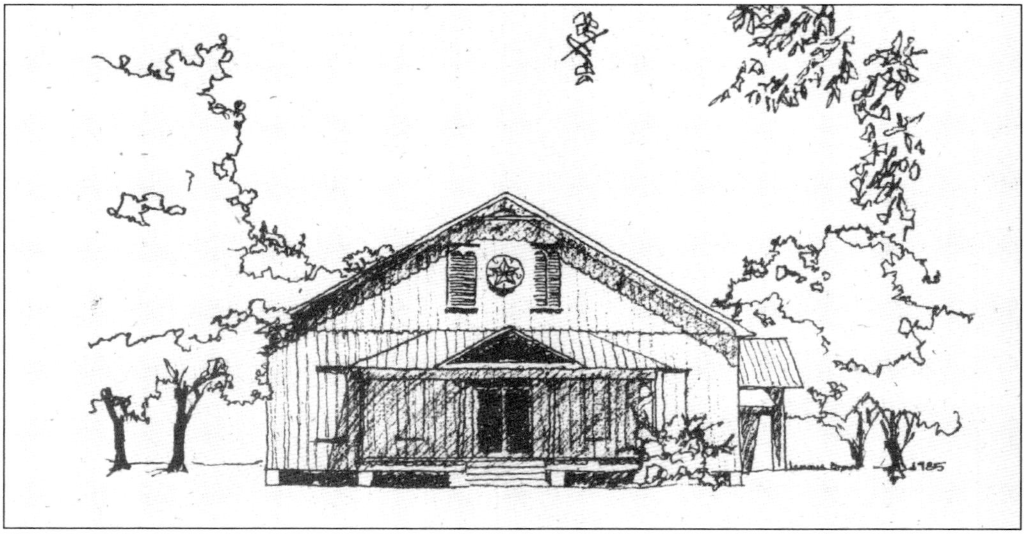

SPJST HALL, FAYETTEVILLE. The SPJST Lodge No. 1, depicted in a hand-drawn postcard by Lennie Brown, was the first such hall built in Texas. It is located just outside Fayetteville on State Road 159. The SPJST is a fraternal beneficial insurance society created in 1897 under the direction and guidance of John Rudolph Kubena (1868–1938), originally from Lichnov, Czech Republic. (Gary E. McKee.)

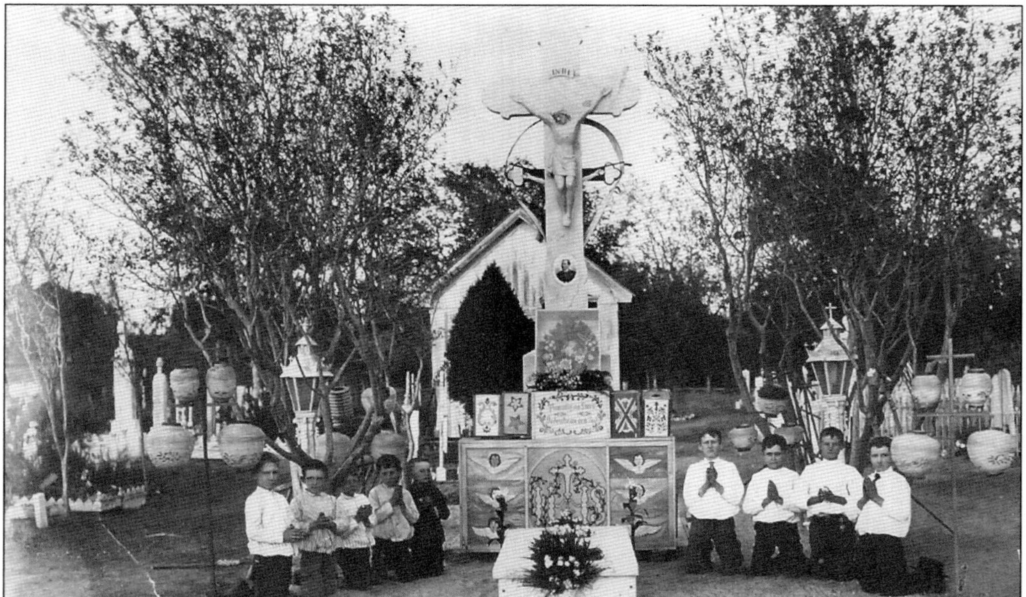

GRAVE OF REV. JOSEF CHROMCIK, FAYETTEVILLE CATHOLIC CEMETERY. Fayetteville boys are kneeling at the grave of Rev. Josef Chromcik (1845–1910), a Czech Catholic priest who came to Texas in 1872 from Zenklebeu Stramberka, Czech Republic, at the request of the Czech Catholic community of Fayetteville. He celebrated his first Mass in Fayetteville on December 25, 1872. He encouraged many Czechs to come to Texas, and when he died April 7, 1910, many bid farewells to their *taticek* (dear loving father). He is buried in the Fayetteville Catholic Cemetery, and the monument shown was erected. (Carolyn Heinsohn.)

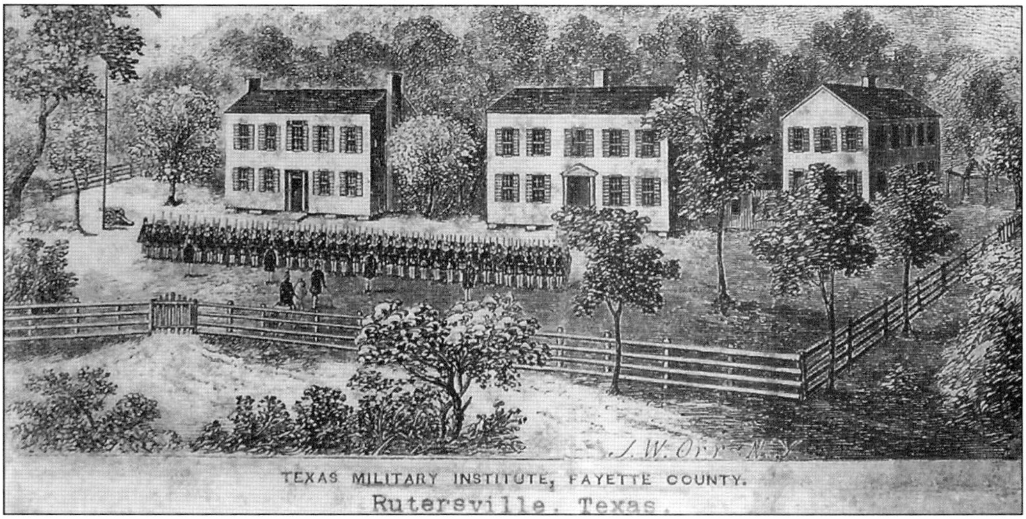

TEXAS MILITARY INSTITUTE, FAYETTE COUNTY, RUTERSVILLE, TEXAS. Rutersville was home to the first chartered college in Texas, when the Republic of Texas granted one in 1840 for the Rutersville College, named for Rev. Martin Ruter (1785–1838), an early Methodist missionary to Texas from Massachusetts. The college opened in 1842, flourished through the remainder of the Texas Republic, and was merged with the Texas Military Institute of Galveston and the Texas Monumental Committee of La Grange in 1856. Sam Houston's son was a student. After the Civil War, the school ceased operations, and none of its facilities survive today. (Author's collection.)

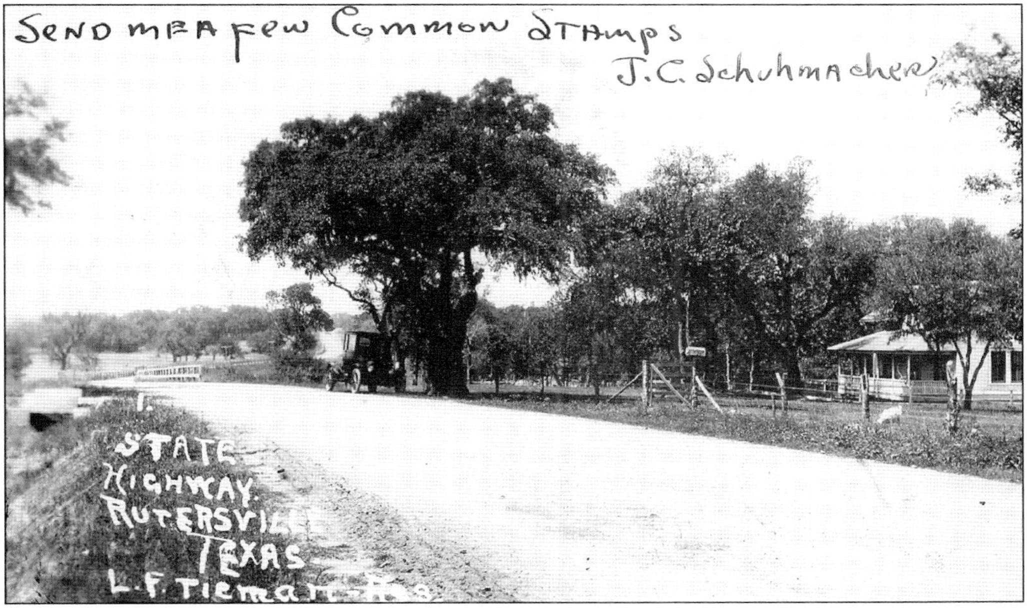

STATE HIGHWAY, RUTERSVILLE, TEXAS, L.F. TIEMANN RES. Sent by John Charles Schumacher (1887–1952), whose wife, Leonida Amberg (1887–1973), grew up in Rutersville, this postcard was written to a pen pal and a fellow stamp collector in New Zealand. John's parents were John Schumacher Sr., a banker and merchant in La Grange, and Louise Frede. The home pictured in the postcard is Louis Fred Tiemann's (1858–1929). (Author's collection.)

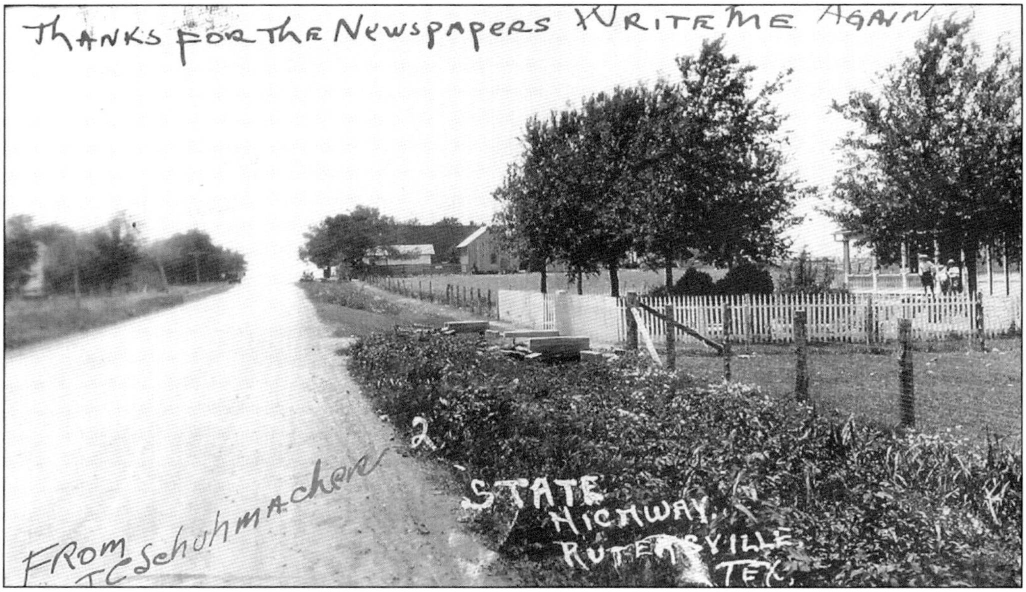

STATE HIGHWAY, RUTERSVILLE, TEX. Attracted by Rutersville College, a number of German families moved to Rutersville, including the Amberg, Fritsch, Tietjen, Struve, Pohl, Brendle, Luecke, Tiemann, and Schulz families. (Author's collection.)

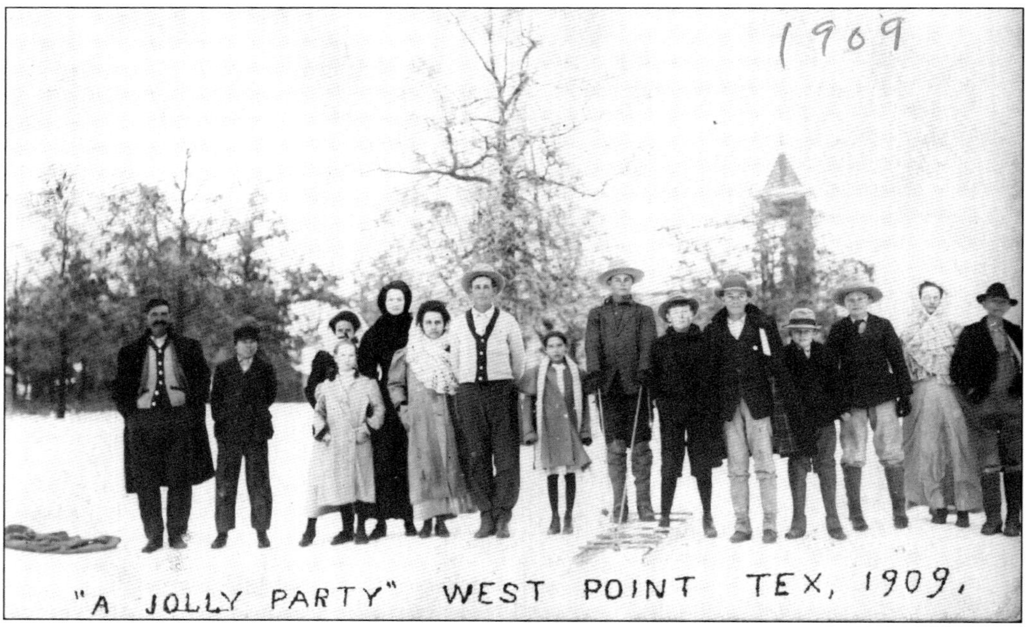

"A JOLLY PARTY," WEST POINT, TEX., 1909. West Point, established in the 1840s by American settlers, is one of the oldest communities in Fayette County. It was named after West Point, Mississippi, the home of early pioneer Samuel Armstrong Young (1788–1867), who came to Texas around 1840 with his wife, Jane Kerr Young (1794–1851). Their son William Young (1814–1873) is credited with naming the town. (Fayette Heritage Museum & Archives.)

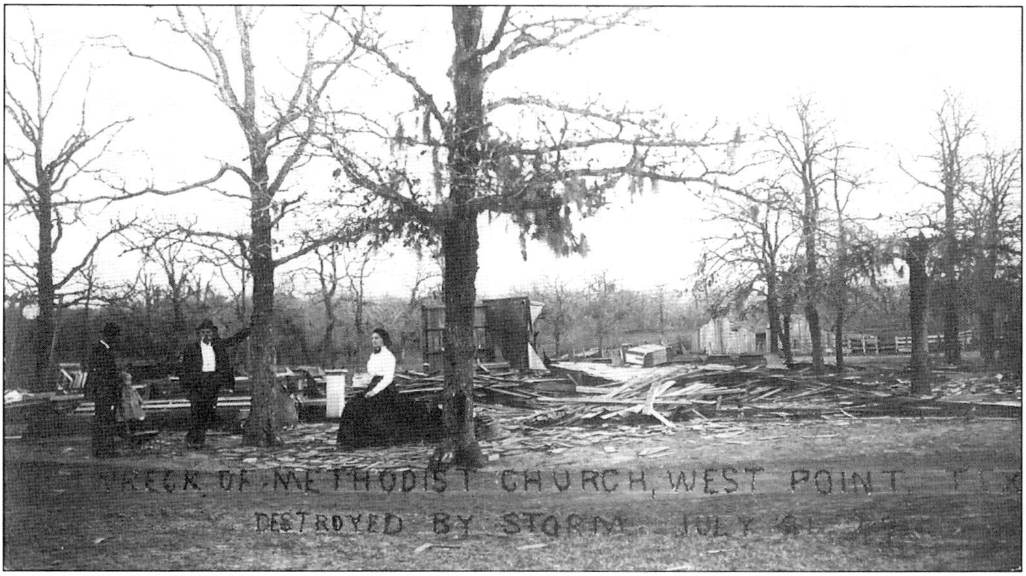

Wreck of Methodist Church, West Point, Tex. West Point was founded by American pioneers whose interests were primarily agricultural, especially in cotton, given the rich river bottom nearby. The initial settlers were the Young, Moore, and Woods families—the latter was associated with Zadock Woods (1773–1842), who died at the Dawson Massacre at Salado Creek. The church referenced here was the Methodist Church in West Point, which was destroyed by a storm on July 21, 1909. (Author's collection.)

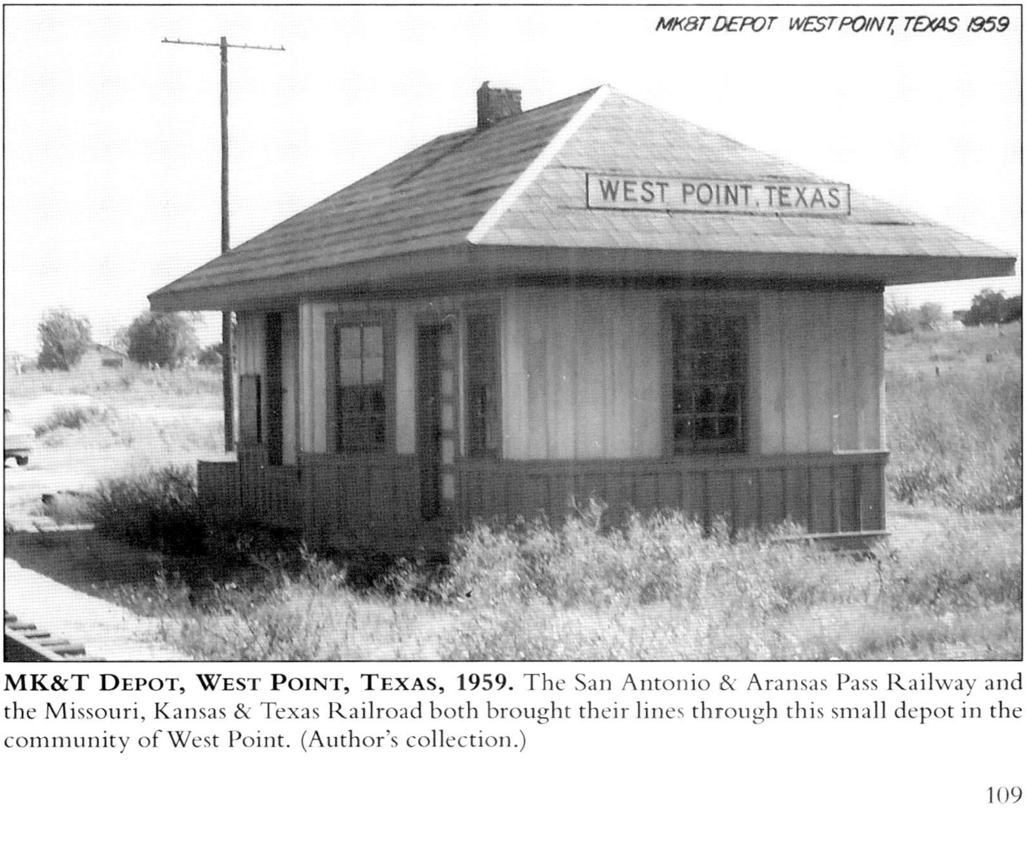

MK&T Depot, West Point, Texas, 1959. The San Antonio & Aransas Pass Railway and the Missouri, Kansas & Texas Railroad both brought their lines through this small depot in the community of West Point. (Author's collection.)

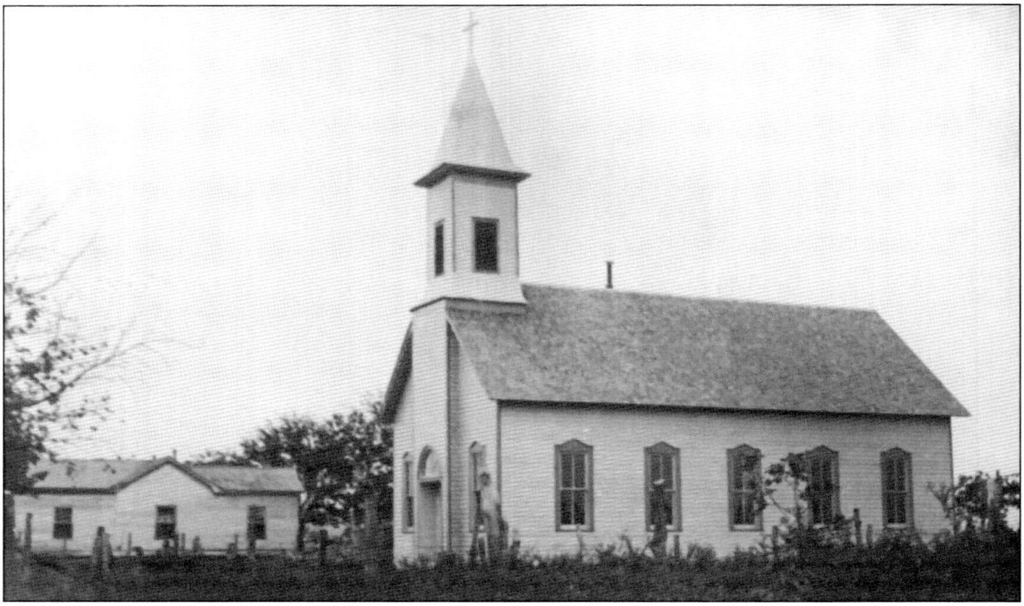

TRINITY HILL LUTHERAN CHURCH. Trinity Hill Evangelical Lutheran Church was located at the intersection of Old Plum Highway and Golden Valley Lane, three miles outside of La Grange, near Plum. This church organized in 1892 and built its first chapel in 1893. The church pictured was built in 1911. In 1962, Trinity Hill Lutheran and Zion Lutheran Church in La Grange merged into Mount Calvary Lutheran Church, within the Missouri Synod. The old Trinity Hill Church building was torn down, and all that is left is the Mount Calvary Lutheran Church Cemetery. (Fayette Heritage Museum & Archives.)

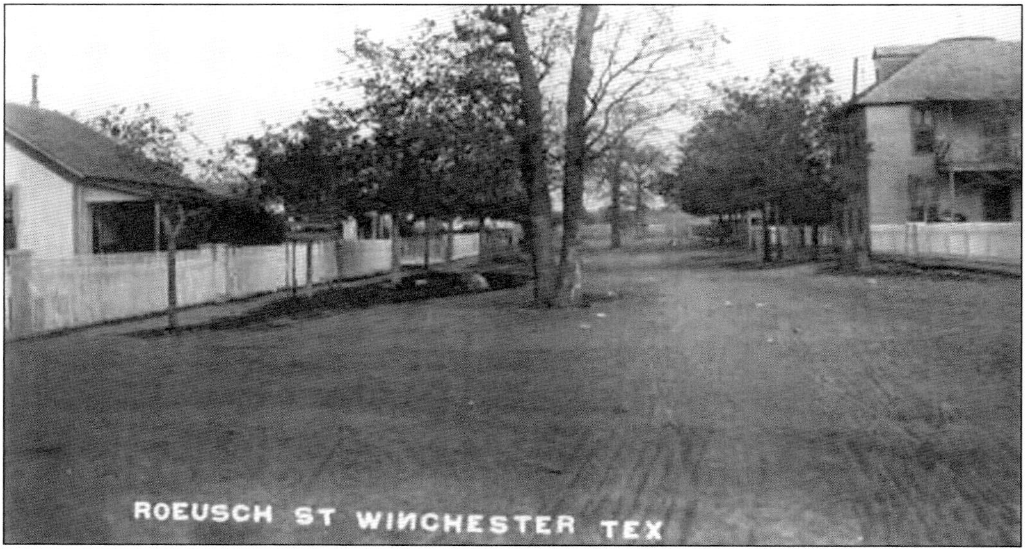

ROENSCH ST., WINCHESTER, TEX. Winchester is 19 miles northwest of La Grange, sitting opposite the Colorado River from West Point. It is one of Fayette's earliest settlements and was first inhabited by John Ingram around 1832. The town site was laid out in 1851 by John Gromme, and named for Winchester, Tennessee. The Waco-Yoakum branch of the San Antonio & Aransas Pass Railway came through the town in 1888. (Fayette Heritage Museum & Archives.)

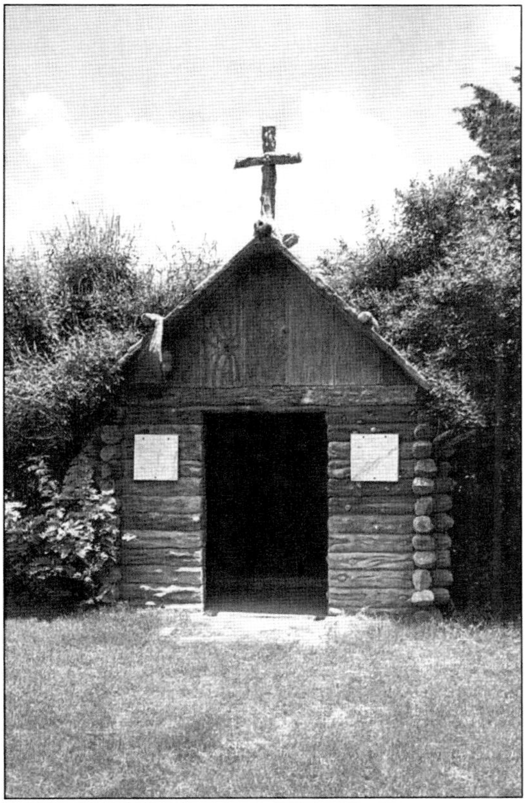

Replica of First Catholic Church at Hostyn. The first church at Hostyn was built in 1856, after the area was settled by early Czech pioneers, including the Adamcik, Janda, Parma, Klimicek, Kolibal, Koza, and Marak families. The log cabin chapel shown is a replica of that first church, built on land donated by Johann A. Laux (1838–1916). In 1845, Laux came to Texas from Elz, Germany, along with his sisters and their parents, Peter Laux (1804–1864) and Rosina Pauli Laux (1796–1870). The Lauxes are the author's great-great-great-great-grandparents. (Author's collection.)

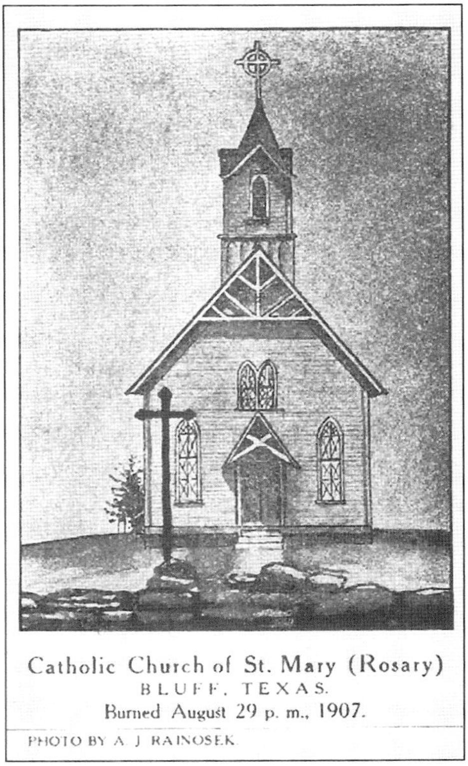

Catholic Church of St. Mary (Rosary), Bluff, Texas. The third Catholic church built at Hostyn (shown) burned August 29, 1907. The old rock wall surrounding the churchyard, visible in this postcard drawing, was later used in 1925 to build the famed Hostyn Grotto. This postcard is based on a photograph taken by A.J. Rainosek. (Author's collection.)

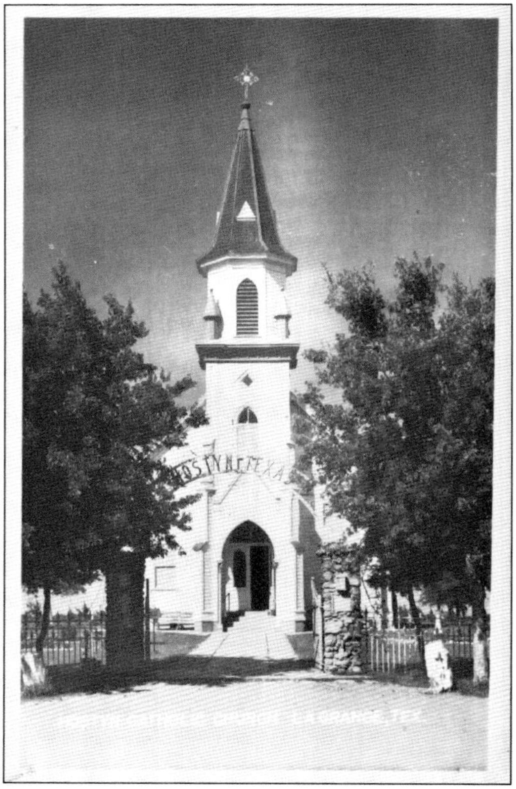

Hostyn, Texas. The first chapel at Hostyn was built in 1856 to serve the Hostyn community's Catholic congregation. At that time, the area was known as Bluff, but as more Czech immigrants came, the hill upon which the church stood was renamed Hostyn, after the Czech pilgrimage site. A larger wood-frame structure was built in 1869, and with growing need, a third edifice was built and the second church was used as a rectory. After this third building burned in 1907, the fourth church (shown) was built. (Fayette Heritage Museum & Archives.)

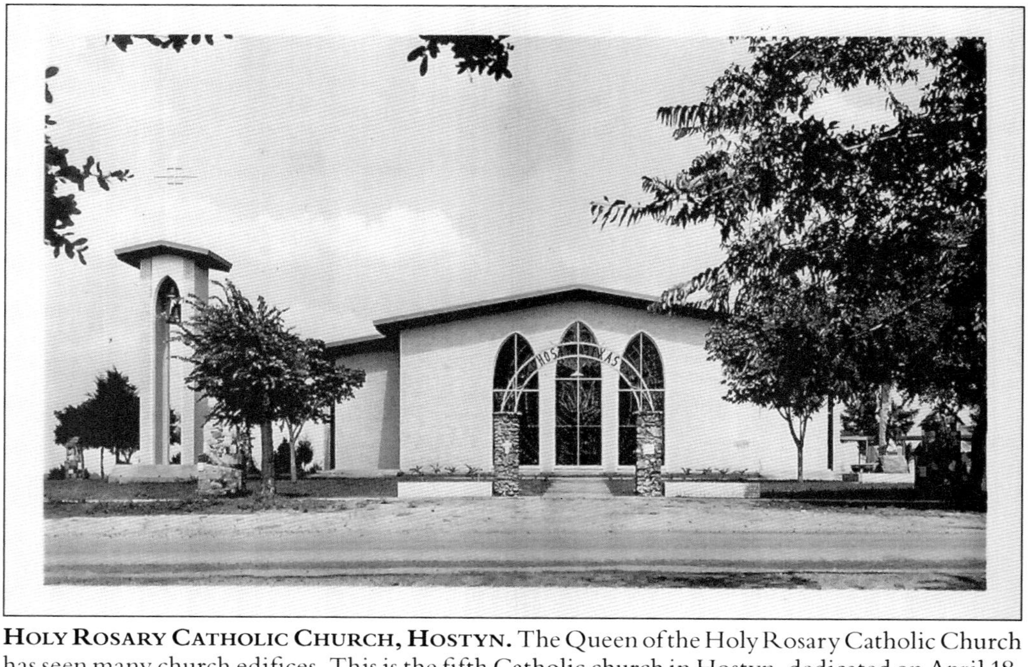

Holy Rosary Catholic Church, Hostyn. The Queen of the Holy Rosary Catholic Church has seen many church edifices. This is the fifth Catholic church in Hostyn, dedicated on April 18, 1966, in the presence of Archbishop Joseph Cardinal Beran, of Prague. (Author's collection.)

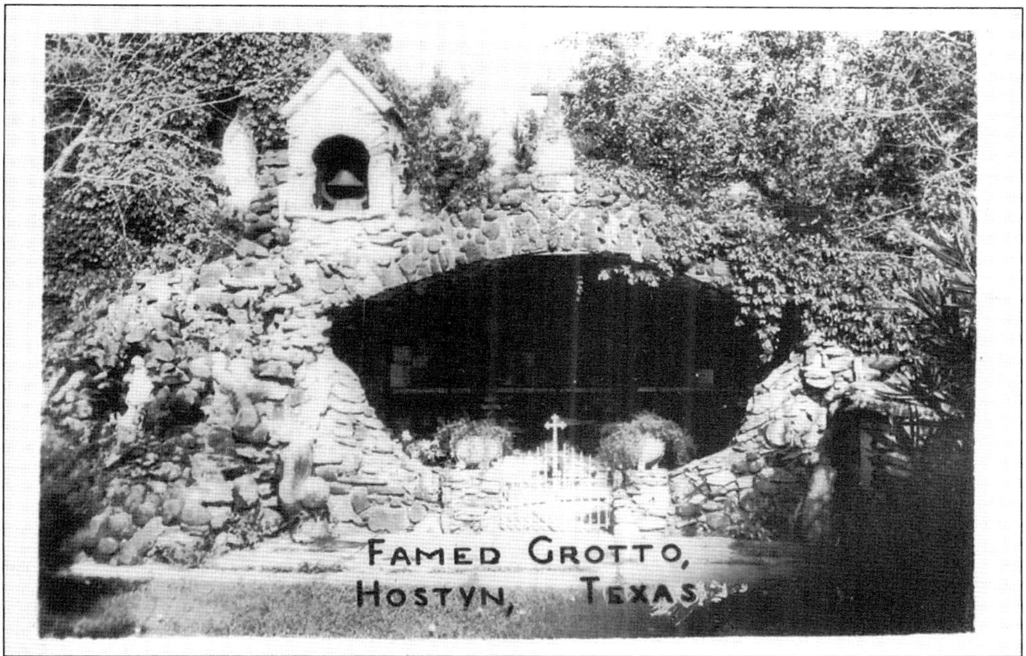

FAMED GROTTO, HOSTYN, TEXAS. The Hostyn Grotto, also known as the Hostyn Chapel to Our Lady of Lourdes, attracts many visitors. It was built in 1925, at the direction of Rev. Paul Kaspar, from the remnants of a rock wall that had surrounded the churchyard. It is modeled on the grotto found at Lourdes, France. (Gary E. McKee.)

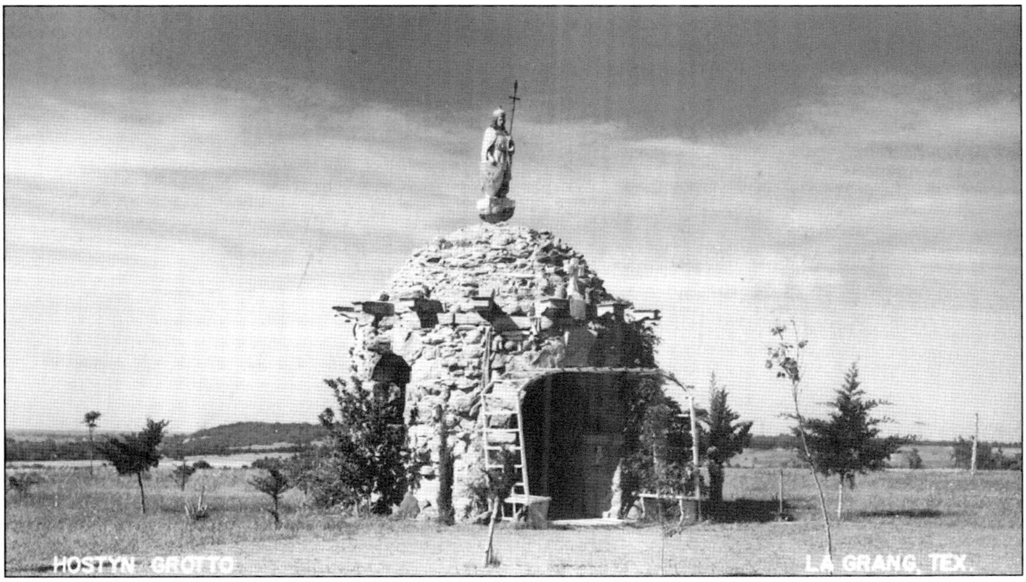

HOSTYN GROTTO, LA GRANGE, TEX. Hostyn's St. Wenceslaus Chapel was built in 1933 by Frank C. Janda (1863–1934) and his wife, Anna Parma Janda (1859–1948), in honor of their parents. Janda's parents were Josef and Anna Kana Janda, who came to Texas from Frenstat, Czech Republic. Anna Kana Janda's parents were Ignac and Terezie Krtsche Parma, also from Frenstat. (Fayette Heritage Museum & Archives.)

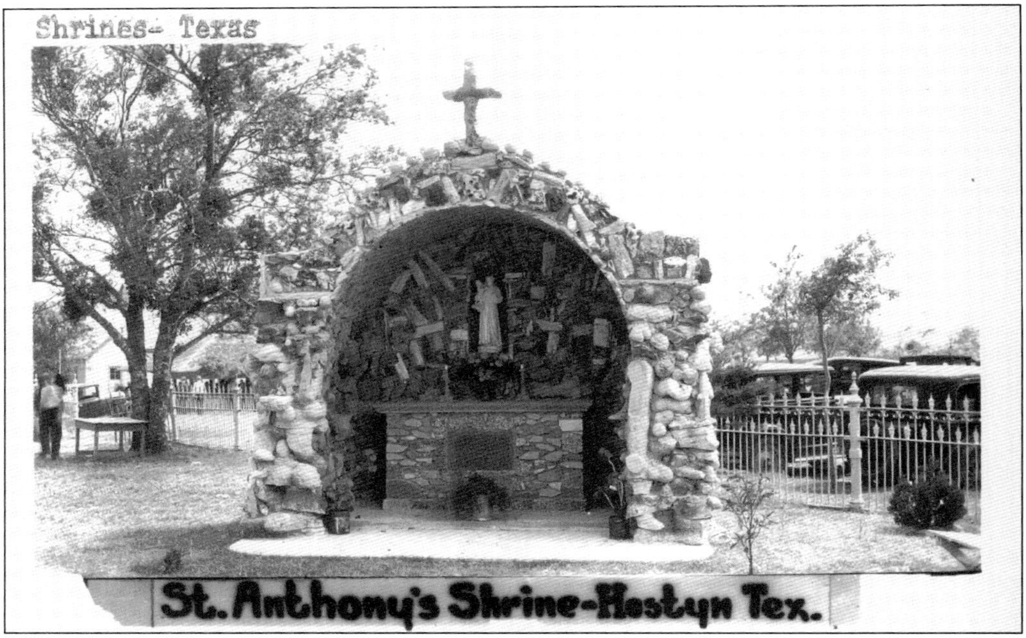

St Anthony's Shrine, Hostyn, Texas. The Hostyn shrine to St. Anthony honors Saint Anthony of Padua, Catholicism's patron saint of lost things and missing persons (and patron saint of San Antonio, Texas). It was built in 1931 to celebrate the 75th anniversary of the local Hostyn parish. (Gary E. McKee.)

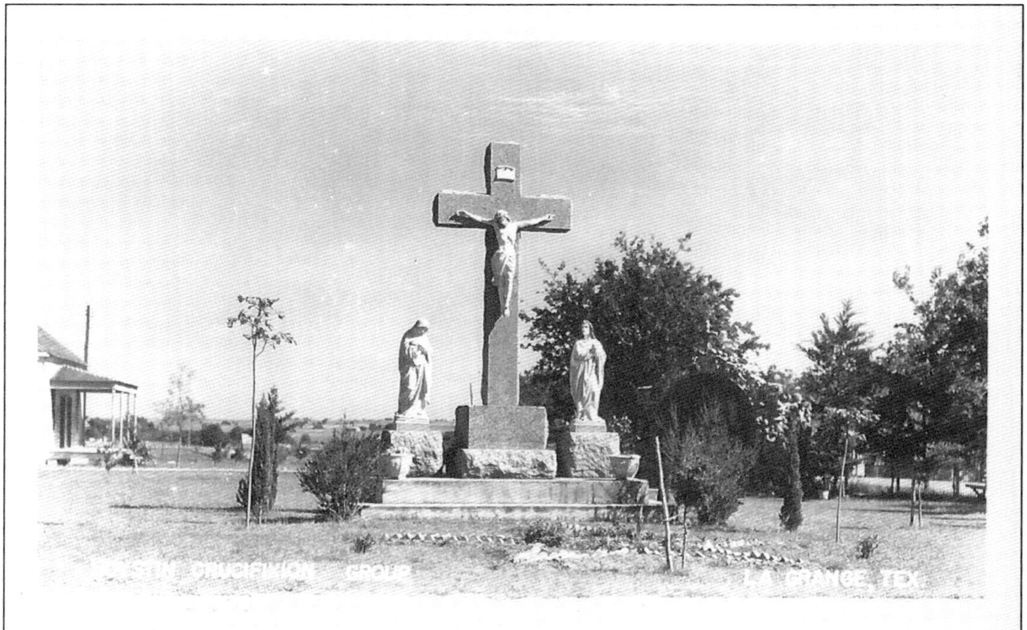

Hostyn Crucifixion Group, La Grange, Tex. The Calvary Group, which depicts the scene of Christ's crucifixion at Calvary, was built at Hostyn in 1929, at the same time the cross was built in the Hostyn Catholic Cemetery. (Author's collection.)

Seven

Southern Fayette County
Praha, Muldoon, and Others

Similarly to Winchester and West Point in the northern part of the county, many early communities of southern Fayette County were predominantly Anglo in makeup and included Black Jack Springs, Cistern, Lyons, O'Quinn, and Pin Oak. Some of the early settlers of this section of the county were James Lyons, who was killed by Comanches in 1837; Jacob Castleman, a veteran of the Battle of San Jacinto; David and Thomas Berry, who came to Texas in the early 1830s from Tennessee and who were sacrificed in Dawson's Massacre; and George Washington Tuttle, another veteran of the Texas Revolution, originally from New York.

Following these early settlers, as elsewhere in Fayette County, were Germans and Czechs, who settled in these same communities. Such was the case with Black Jack Springs, which blossomed as a center of learning and culture under the guidance Johannes Nathanial Romberg (1808–1891) and others. Romberg, a poet and writer in his native Germany, founded the Prairie Blume Society, a literary group that espoused a literate society among Fayette County's German youth of the 1850s and 1860s. These European newcomers also established their own new communities, such as Ammansville, Dubina, Freyburg, Praha, and Swiss Alp.

Ammansville was founded in the early 1870s by an Austrian-Swiss immigrant, J. Andreas Amman (1818–1895), and many Czech and German families joined Amman in creating a thriving business center that boasted cotton gins, a sawmill, a blacksmith shop, and numerous other commercial establishments. Some earlier residents were Alonzo Runnels, Frank Kossa, and Joseph Bartos, followed later by Martin Srubar, Joseph Fietsam, J.J. Munke, and Theophilus Heller. Ammansville was closely tied to Bluff, situated to the north. St. John the Baptist Catholic Church, one of the Painted Churches of Fayette County, first began in 1890 as a mission church to its sister congregation in Hostyn, then known as Bluff.

Many of Fayette County's other Painted Churches are found in its southern section, including St. Mary's Church of the Assumption, in Praha, a Czech community named after Prague, Czech Republic. Another of the famed churches in Dubina, which like Praha was and remains a Czech enclave, is the lovely SS. Cyril and Methodius Catholic Church. Lastly, the community of High Hill, which was the mother of Schulenburg in many ways, lays claim to one the grandest of these architectural gems—the Nativity of Mary, Blessed Virgin Catholic Church.

The remaining locales in this bucolic region, such as Freyburg and Swiss Alp, can best be described as community centers around which the local, mainly German populations gathered to celebrate their religious beliefs, do business, raise families, and carry on their cultural traditions. Freyburg was the location of one of the first German Methodist communities in Texas, having its 1868 beginnings in the home of local resident, Frederich Thulemeyer. Swiss Alp was settled in the 1870s by the Steinmann, Meyer, Franke, and Bolling families, among others, all of whom came to Texas from near Oldenburg, Germany.

One of the other rail stops on the San Antonio & Aransas Pass Railway that caused Flatonia consternation early on was the settlement of Muldoon. As with most of the rest of Fayette County, the earliest residents around what became Muldoon were entirely Anglo. However, after the Civil War, many Czechs and Germans were attracted to this part of the county, and they slowly displaced the Anglo Americans, though not entirely.

The town site of Muldoon was laid out and ultimately settled in the late 1880s, when the railroad completed its line between Yoakum and Waco; Muldoon's first post office was established in 1887 with James Kerr as its first postmaster. The town was named in honor of Fr. Miguel Muldoon, an Irish-born, Spanish-educated Catholic priest. He came to Texas in 1831 and served as the first curate of Stephen F. Austin's colony there, at a time when settlers had to profess their Catholic faith to be considered suitable settlers by the governing Mexican authorities. Many of the early American pioneers who so professed their newly, and perhaps cynically, acquired faith were deemed "Muldoon Catholics," as a result of Father Muldoon's prolific conversions.

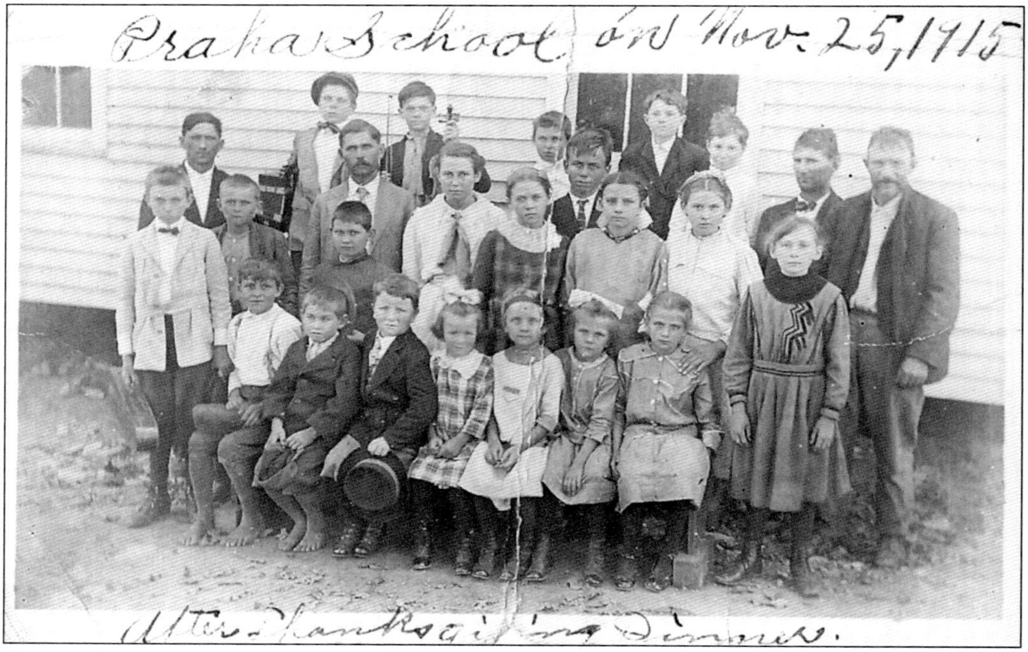

PRAHA SCHOOL ON NOVEMBER 25, 1915. Here is the multiple level class of the Praha School in 1915 after just having had their Thanksgiving dinner. (E.A. Arnim Archives & Museum.)

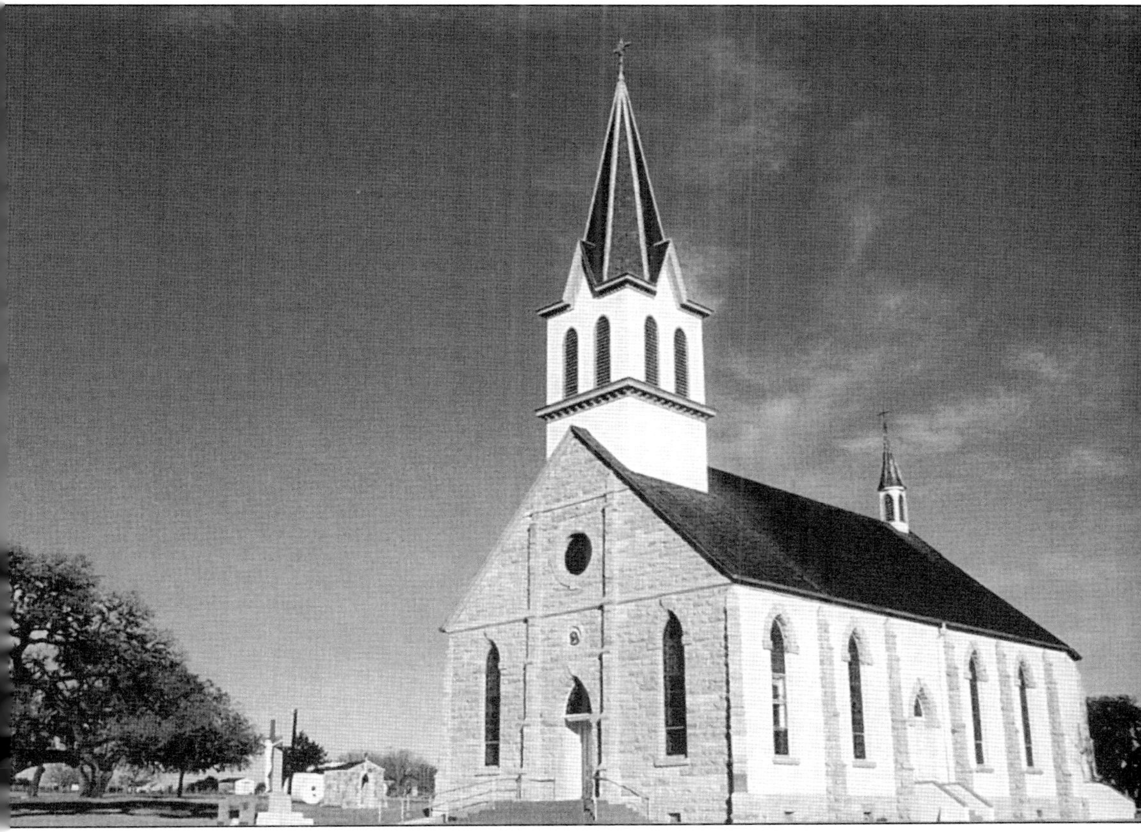

ST. MARY'S CATHOLIC CHURCH, PRAHA. The Assumption of the Blessed Virgin Mary Catholic Church in Praha, also known as St. Mary's Catholic Church, is the center of Praha's cultural, social, and religious community. Originally, the Czech immigrants settling in Praha worshipped in Matej Novak's home; however, Mass soon was said in a stone chapel nearby. A larger timber structure was later built, and it met the settlers' needs until 1876, when a larger church was erected. Finally, given the rapid growth of the Czech community in and around Praha, the present stone church shown was erected in 1895. The church continues to draw many throughout the year, such as during its annual homecoming on August 15, when many parishioners come back to Praha, affectionately called "Maticka Praha," or Mother Praha. (Gary E. McKee.)

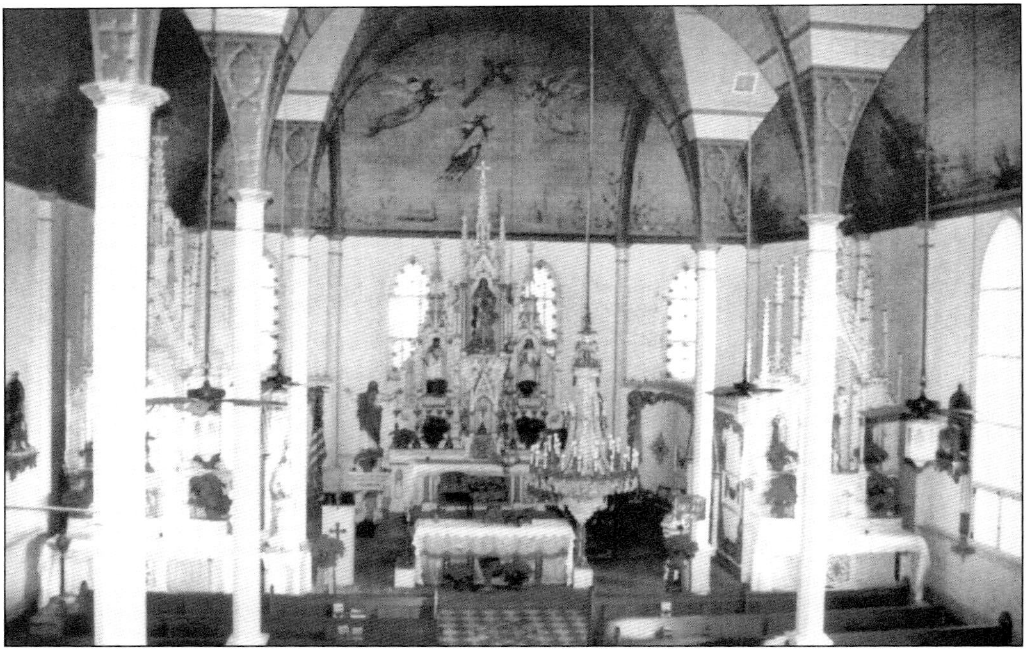

ASSUMPTION OF THE BLESSED VIRGIN MARY CATHOLIC CHURCH, PRAHA. Built in 1895, St. Mary's Catholic Church in Praha is one of the oldest of the Painted Churches. Swiss immigrant Gottfried Flury painted much of St. Mary's interior. Also contributing to St. Mary's beauty was Fr. Louis Petr Netardus, who, after being appointed to St. Mary's in 1902, made additional embellishments to the church's interior. (Gary E. McKee.)

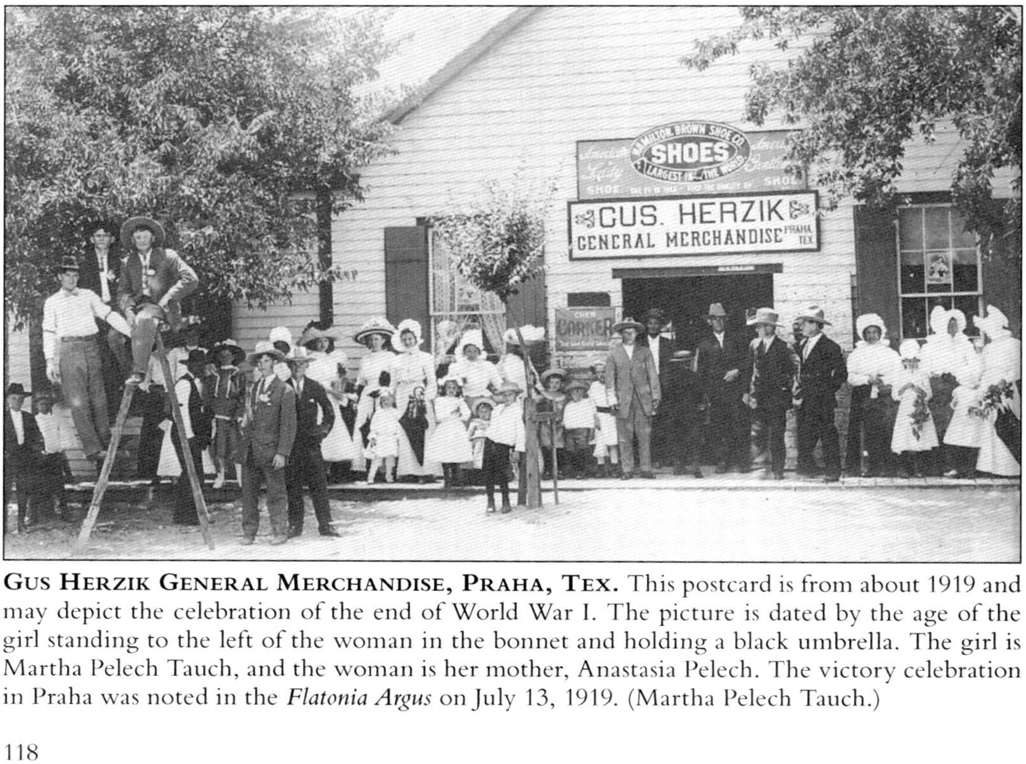

GUS HERZIK GENERAL MERCHANDISE, PRAHA, TEX. This postcard is from about 1919 and may depict the celebration of the end of World War I. The picture is dated by the age of the girl standing to the left of the woman in the bonnet and holding a black umbrella. The girl is Martha Pelech Tauch, and the woman is her mother, Anastasia Pelech. The victory celebration in Praha was noted in the *Flatonia Argus* on July 13, 1919. (Martha Pelech Tauch.)

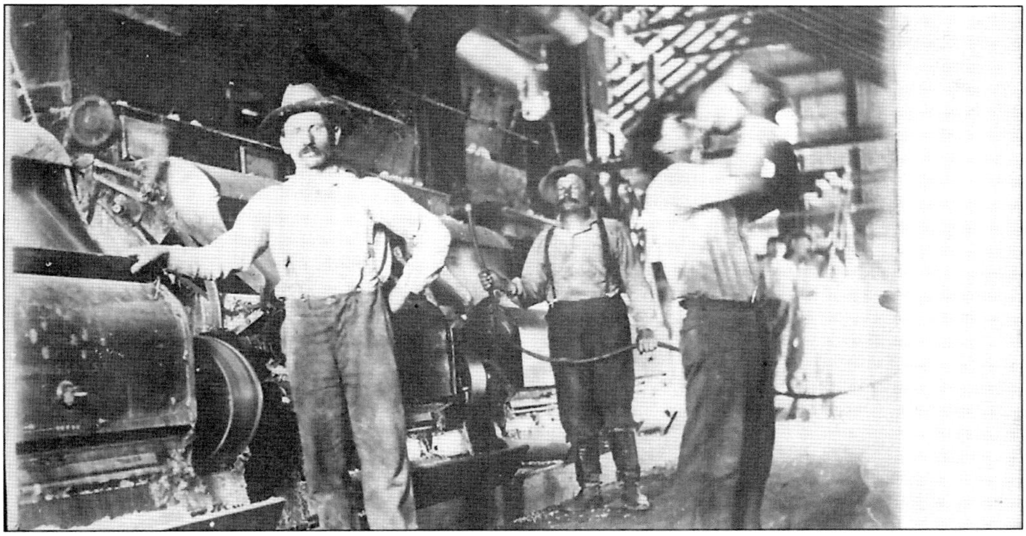

MIGL GIN, NEAR PRAHA. This Migl Gin was located south of Praha. Another Migl Gin was operated by Frank Migl (1866–1946) in Novorhad, Texas, near present-day Praha. The gin shown was run by John Migl (1855–1936), Frank Migl's brother, who emigrated to Texas with his family from Budejovice, Czech Republic. John's parents were Frantisek Migl (1827–1915) and Johanna Jezek Migl (1830–1903), who settled first near Praha, where they rented land from the Jares family. The Migls later acquired a 160-acre homestead through much hard work and sacrifice. (Martha Pelech Tauch.)

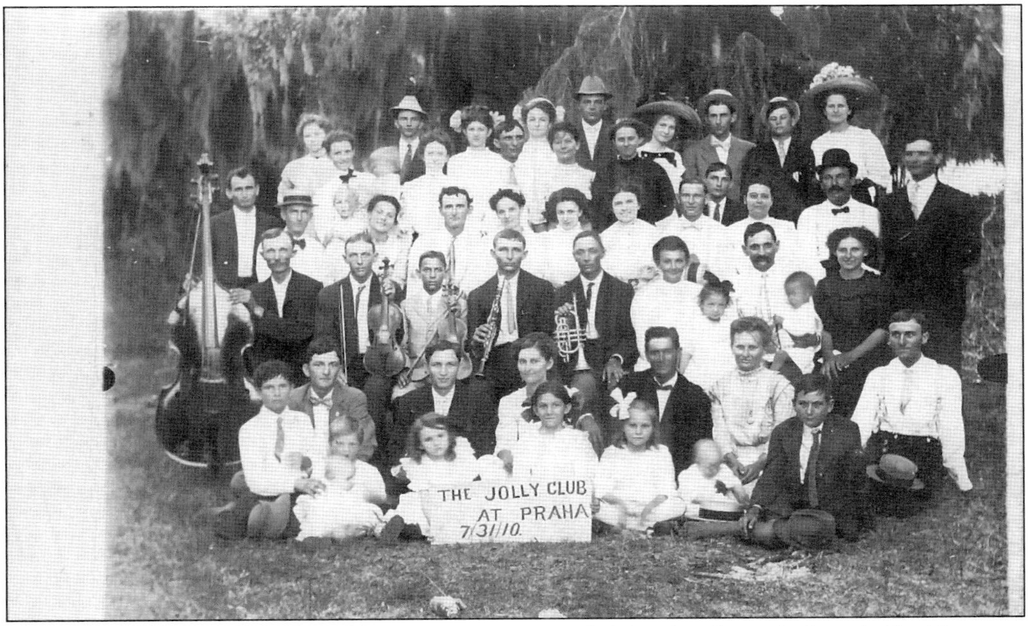

THE JOLLY CLUB AT PRAHA. The Jolly Club, a social club of Praha and Flatonia families, met at Vyvjala's Lake in Praha. This lake was the site of many picnics and parties. In 1915, it was leased and later incorporated as the Flatonia Lake Club, a private social club. The party shown occurred on July 31, 1910, and included members of the Michal, Machac, Bittner, Wotipka, Pechacek, Herzik, Vyvjala, and Starry families, among others. (Vyvjala/Greive family.)

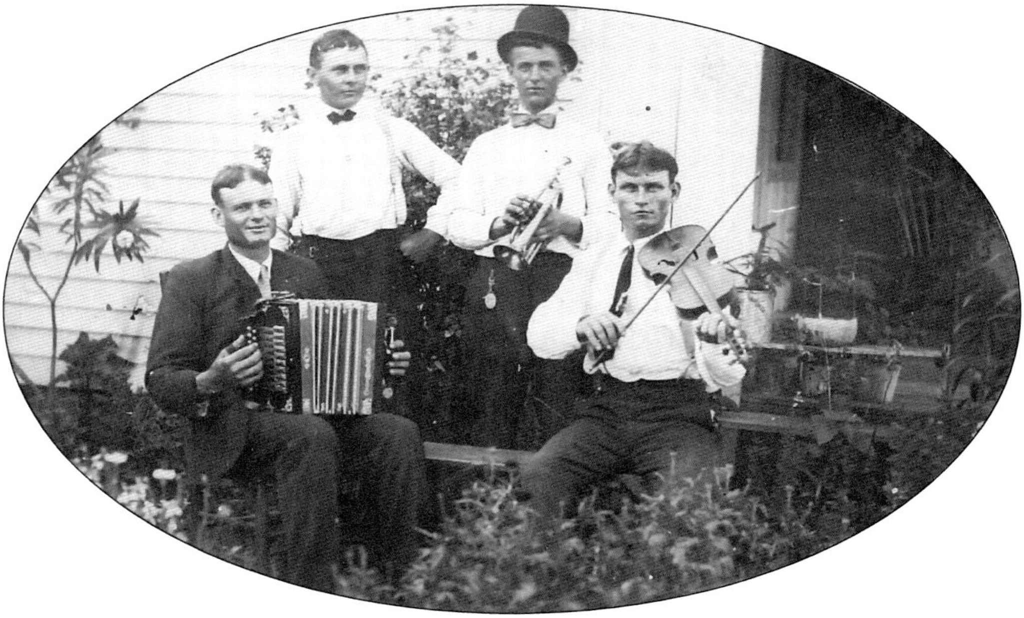

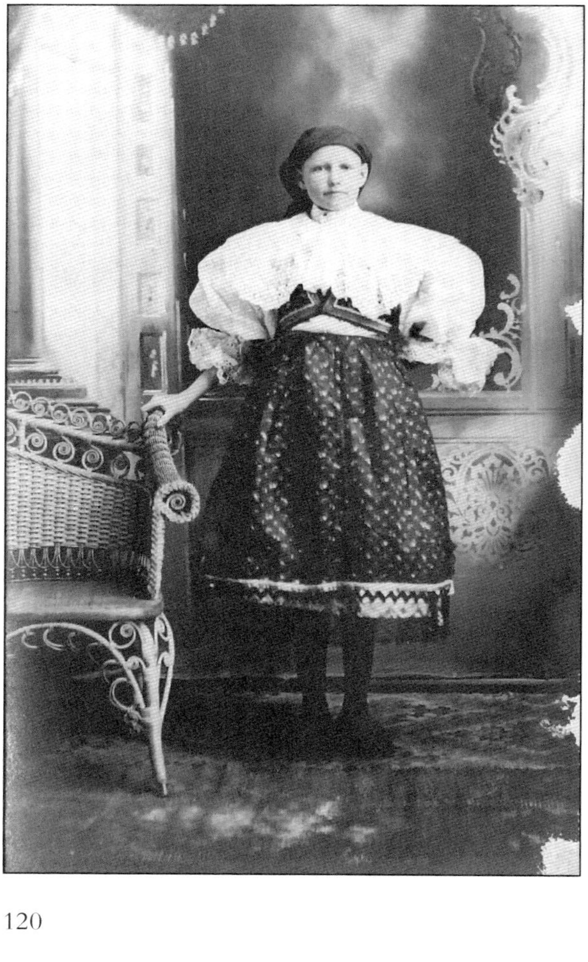

MUSICAL GROUP, PRAHA. This Czech musical group from the Praha community includes Lucas Cerny, Pavel Krejcik, and Rudolf Foitik, among others. Like their German neighbors, Czech immigrants loved music and engaged in concerts and musical entertainments frequently. (Vyvjala/Greive family.)

PRAHA RESIDENT VLASTA VYVJALA. Depicted wearing traditional Czech dress, around 1908, is Vlasta Vyvjala, at about age 14. She married Rudolph Henry Greive and lived in Flatonia, after residing in Moulton for a time. Near Praha, the Vyvjalas owned a spring-fed artesian pool, which had a dancing platform, tables and benches; it was a frequent locale for picnics and social outings. (Vyvjala/Greive family.)

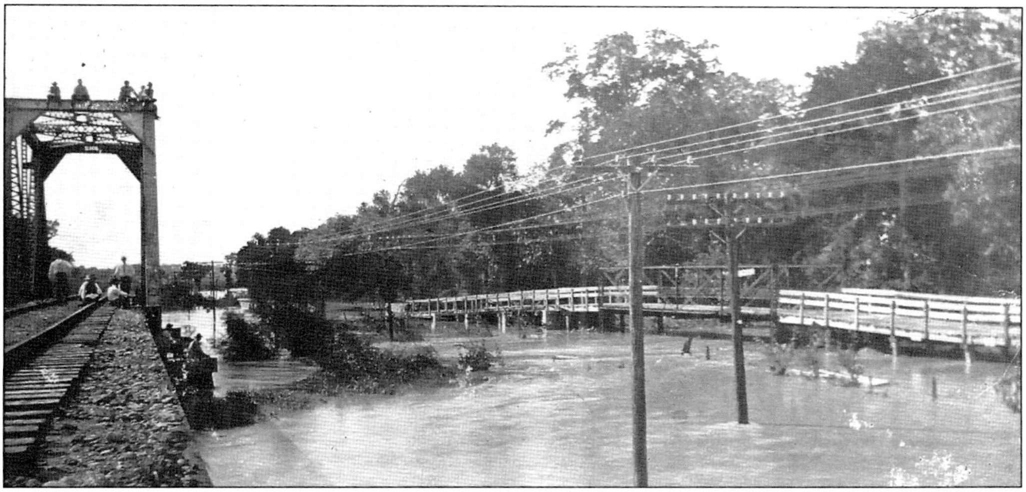

NAVIDAD RIVER OVERFLOW, OCTOBER 3, 1913. On December 5, 1913, Fayette County suffered a devastating flood. The deluge encompassed most of the county's rivers, creeks, and streams, including the Navidad pictured here. Early warnings were given on December 4, 1913, by C.J. von Rosenberg, who then lived upriver in Austin; however, homes and property were lost when the flood reached 56 feet. The floodwaters receded on December 8, 1913. (E.A. Arnim Archives & Museum/Henry and Jeanne Nikel collection.)

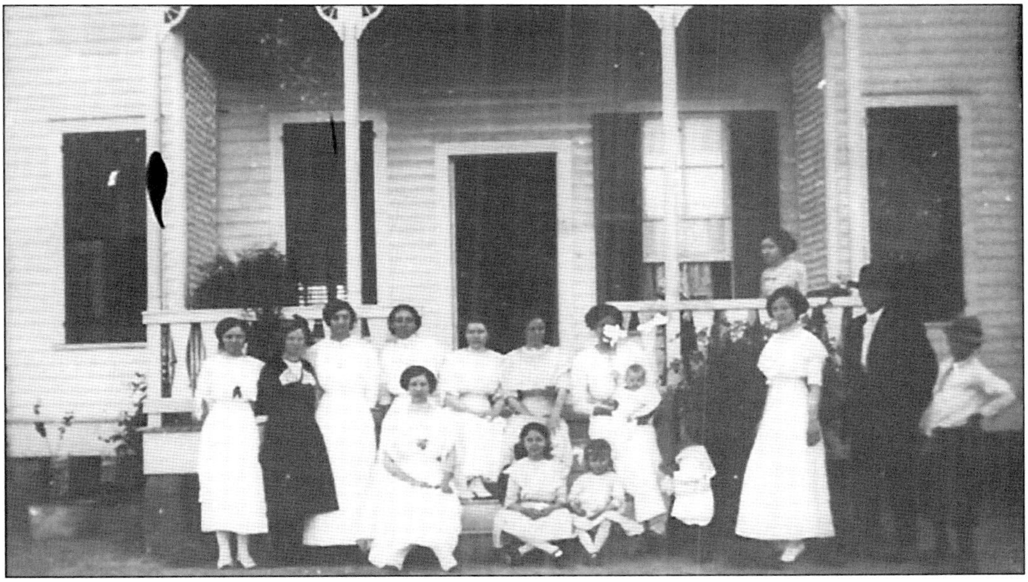

JULIUS OEDING HOME, FREYBURG. Freyburg, seven miles north of Engle, was founded 1868 by Freidrich Thulemeyer and was at first known as Thulemeyer, after his business and home there. Later, it was known as Freyburg, after the German city. The Oeding family, depicted here, immigrated to Texas in 1860 from Schulau, in what was then Denmark; however, they were culturally German, speaking German as their first tongue. Julius Heinrich Oeding (1855–1927), the eldest son of Thomas Hinrich Oeding (1818–1869) and Katharina Kock Oeding (1823–1892), was a farmer who had numerous children, including the author's great-grandfather Paul Edwin Oeding (1882–1938). The home shown was just north of Freyburg but no longer exists. (Author's collection.)

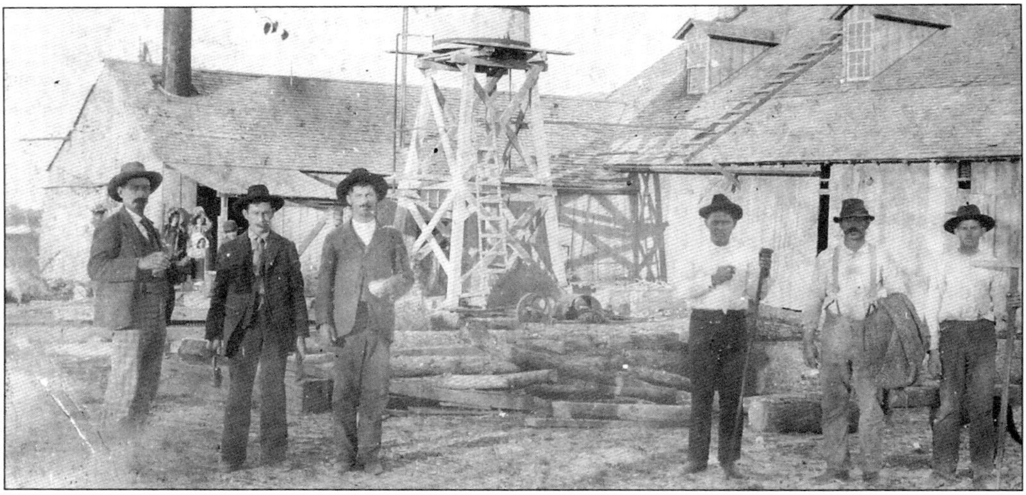

COTTON GIN AND SAWMILL, AMMANSVILLE. Ammansville is located 10 miles southeast of La Grange, off Highway 77. The community was settled by both German and Czech immigrants in the 1870s and represents an example of the comingling of these two prominent cultures that was common to Fayette County. The cotton gin and sawmill shown was run by Joseph Julius "J.J." Munke (1852–1930), the author's great-great grandfather, along with his brother in-law Theophilus R. Heller (1845–1891). Munke's father, Christian Munke (1824–1896), came to Texas in 1846 from Pattensen, Germany, and married Margarethe Pauli-Laux Munke (1824–1912), who came to Texas from Elz, Germany, with her parents in late 1845. (Author's collection.)

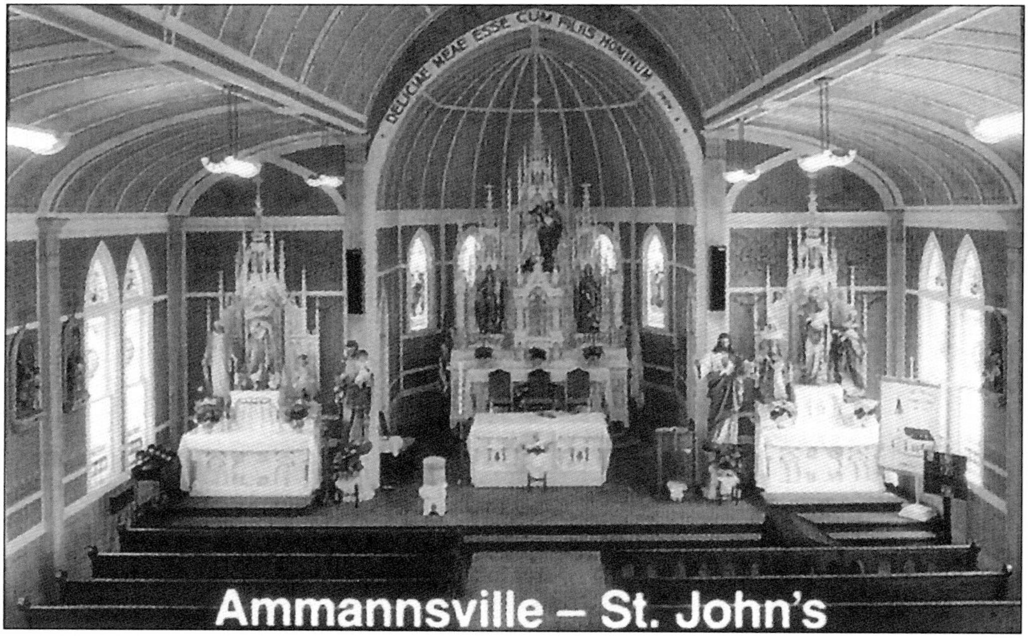

AMMANSVILLE—ST. JOHN'S. Located in Ammansville, St. John the Baptist Catholic Church is beautiful with its pale pink walls that are painted with stencils amidst white millwork. St. John's was founded in 1890; a small frame chapel was built but destroyed by a hurricane in 1909. A second church was built in 1910 and destroyed by fire in 1917. The present church was dedicated on December 22, 1919. (Author's collection.)

ST. MARY'S CATHOLIC CHURCH, HIGH HILL. In 1860, a group of Austrian Moravian families, from the Weiskirchen region of the Sudetenland (in the Czech Republic), arrived in Fayette County, settling in the area of High Hill. In 1861, Rev. Victor Gury came to High Hill, giving Mass in private homes until 1870, when Father Friedochowsky, the first resident pastor, arrived. The redbrick Gothic Revival church pictured here was built in 1906. (Gary E. McKee.)

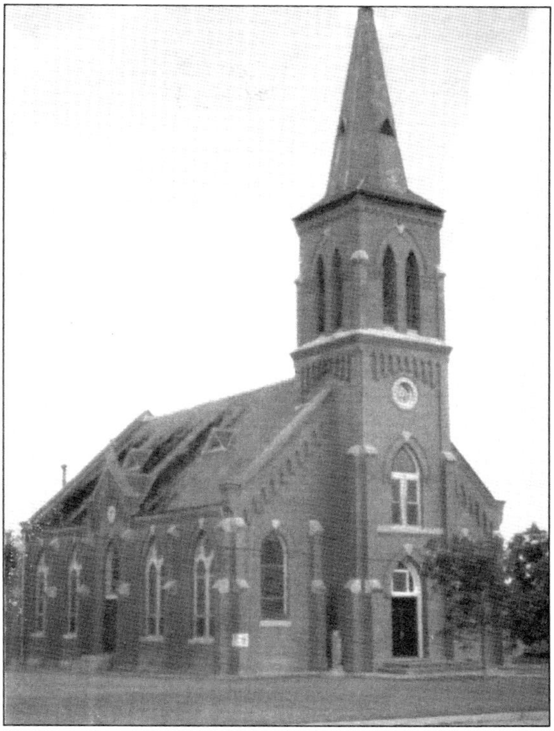

HIGH HILL—ST. MARY'S. In 1899, Father Gerlach came to High Hill to be pastor of the Nativity of Mary, Blessed Virgin Catholic Church. Gerlach built the parish hall in 1900 and the current redbrick church in 1906. In 1912, Ferdinand Stockert and Hermann Kern were employed to paint the interiors, linking St. Mary's Catholic Church of High Hill to Fayette County's other Painted Churches. (Gary E. McKee.)

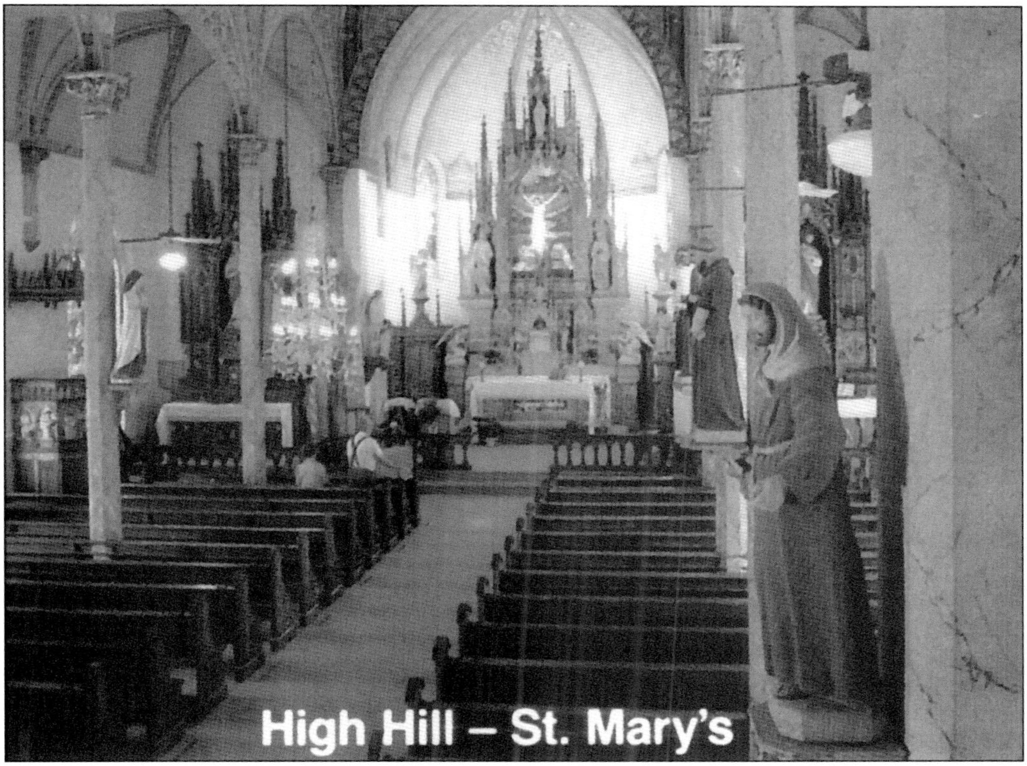

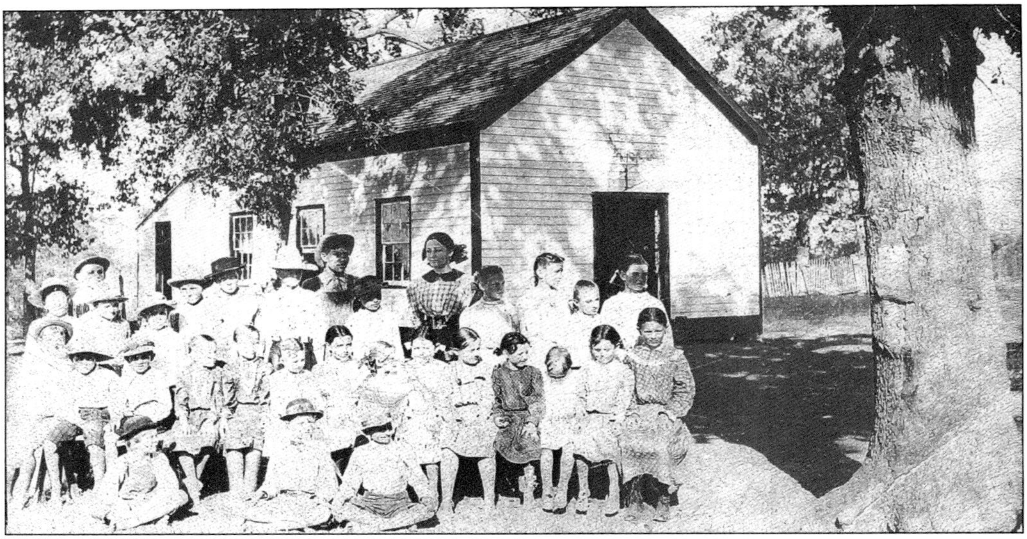

LUCK SCHOOL, O'QUINN, TEX. This school was in O'Quinn, located halfway between La Grange and Flatonia. O'Quinn was initially an Anglo settlement; however, in the 1850s, Germans displaced the original settlers and included among them the Bruns, Melcher, Luck, and Loessin families. The nearby communities of Black Jack Springs and Cedar were closely tied to O'Quinn. Johannes Nathaniel Romberg (1808–1891), the famous poet of Black Jack Springs, had run a prior school, and Louis Luck carried on this work. The author's grandfather John Henry Koenig (1908–1984) attended Luck's School. (E.A. Arnim Archives & Museum.)

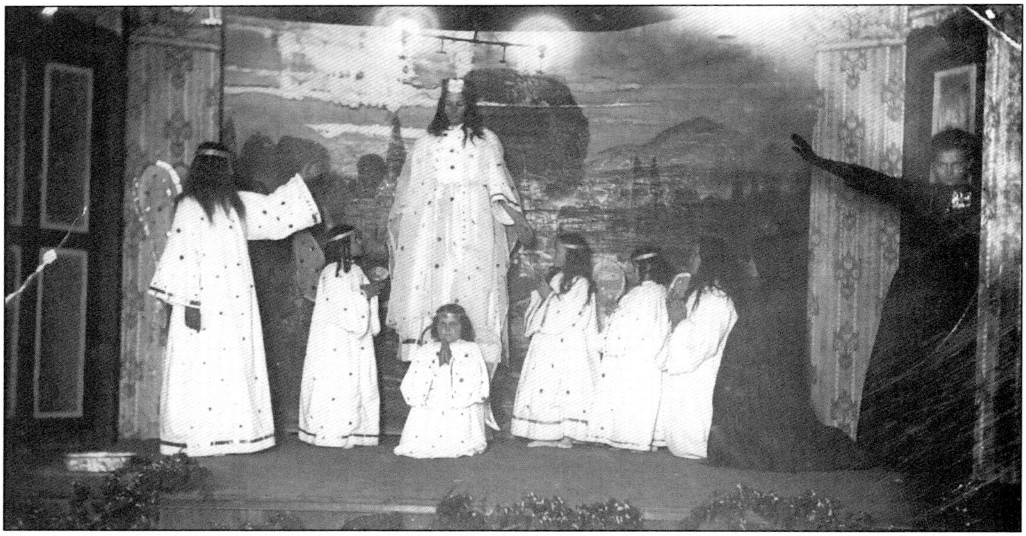

SWISS ALP CHRISTMAS PLAY. The Christmas play shown is associated with either the Swiss Alp School or the Philadelphia Lutheran Church, the local Swiss Alp church. It is most likely associated with the church, given its tradition of holding children's Christmas plays. Founded in 1867, the church was the center of the Swiss Alp community. Its earliest congregants were predominantly of German origin and remain so to this day. The church is now known as the United Evangelical Lutheran Church of Swiss Alp, after merging with the nearby Trinity Lutheran Church of Black Jack Springs (the author was the last infant baptized there) and the Salem Lutheran Church of Freyburg in 1967. (Gary E. McKee.)

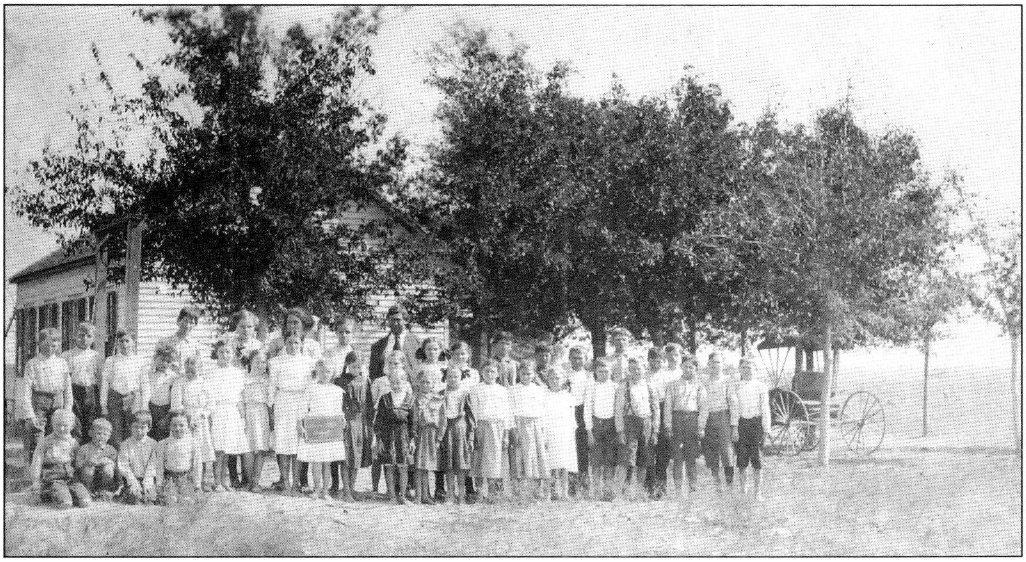

SWISS ALPS SCHOOL. Swiss Alp is located just about halfway between La Grange and Schulenburg. It was first settled in the late 1850s by German immigrants, among them the Carby, Meyer, Foerster, Steinmann, Jochen, Gebert, Koether, Nollkamper, Stoever, Knape, and Bolling families. Some of these families were Wendish and came in 1854 with Pastor Killian's Wendish colonists, aboard the *Ben Nevis*. The school depicted here operated from 1897 until 1947. (Gary E. McKee.)

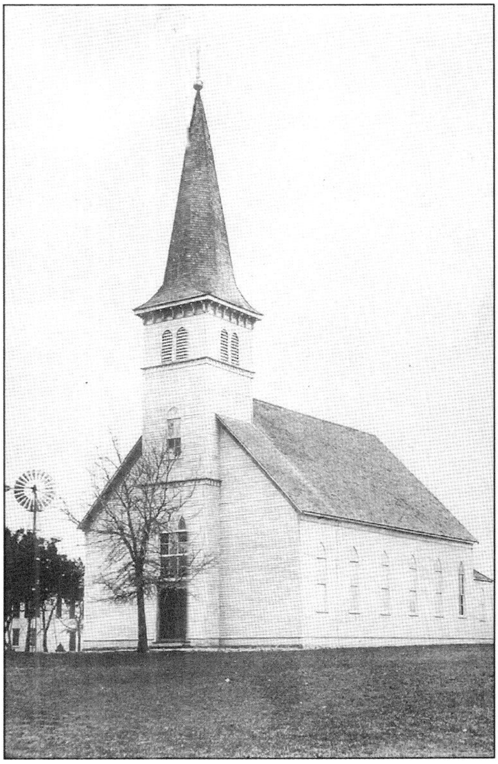

ST. JOHN'S CATHOLIC CHURCH. Located six miles west of Schulenburg is St. John, an early settlement that was home to a number of American pioneer families, among them the Glass, Frazier, May, and Kirk families. By the 1880s, this earlier group had been displaced by German and Czech families, who by 1887 wanted a church. St. John's Catholic Church was erected in 1888 on an elevated location overlooking Schulenburg and southern Fayette County. Some of the later settlers were John Klesel, John Beyer, Anton Sommers, Frank Rohan, Joseph Brossman, and Karl Junger. (Author's collection.)

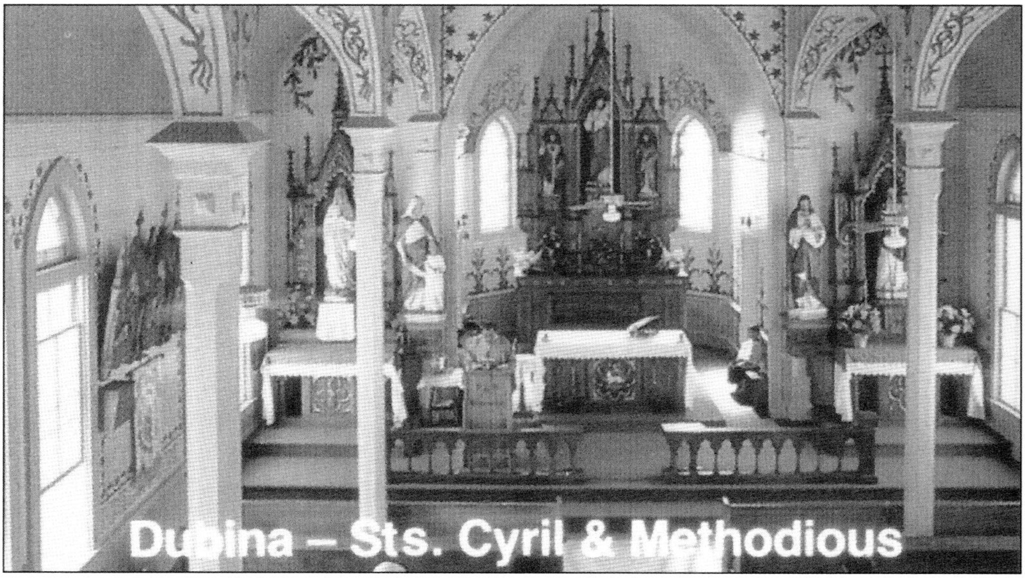

DUBINA—STS. CYRIL & METHODIUS. Dubina is located in south-central Fayette County, between Swiss Alp and Weimar, and is known as the first Czech settlement in Texas. While Dubina's Czech pioneers were not the first Czech immigrants to Texas, they were the first to start a wholly Czech settlement. The community was called Dubina, after the many sheltering oak trees (*dubina* means "oak grove" in Czech). Its first log cabin was built in 1857 by Frances Kossa. The first log meeting hall, where the first Catholic services were held, was erected in 1858 by Joseph Peter. In 1877, a permanent church was built, but in 1909, it was destroyed by a hurricane. In 1912, the pictured SS. Cyril and Methodius Church was erected. (Gary E. McKee.)

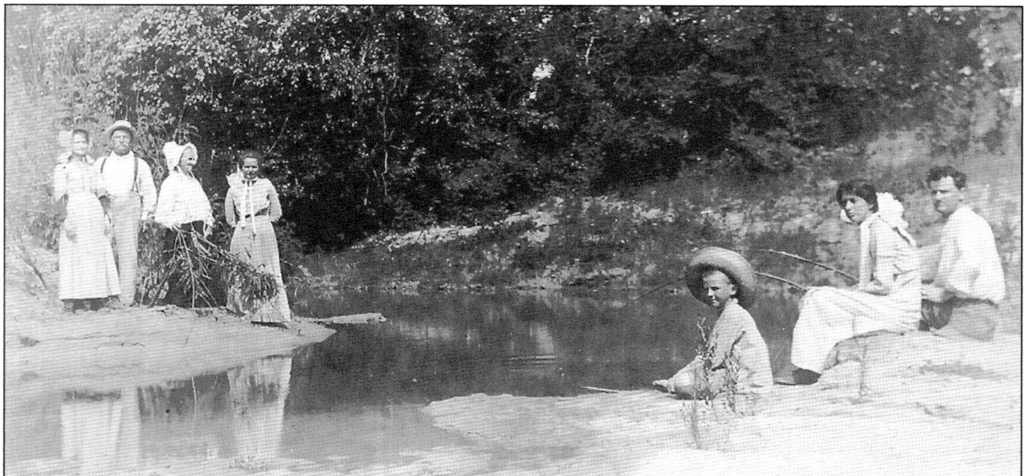

FISHING HOLE, PINE SPRINGS. Pine Springs was so close to Oso that the two names are now synonymous, although both communities no longer exist. Oso was located three miles northeast of Flatonia. When the railroad came to Flatonia in 1873, the community of Oso literally moved its homes, on the back of wagons, to the new town site. The population of Oso was predominantly American and included the Burns, Meneffee, Lane, Cobb, Sullivan, and Harrison families. The Pine Springs Cemetery is all that remains today. (E.A. Arnim Archives & Museum/Henry and Jeanne Nikel collection.)

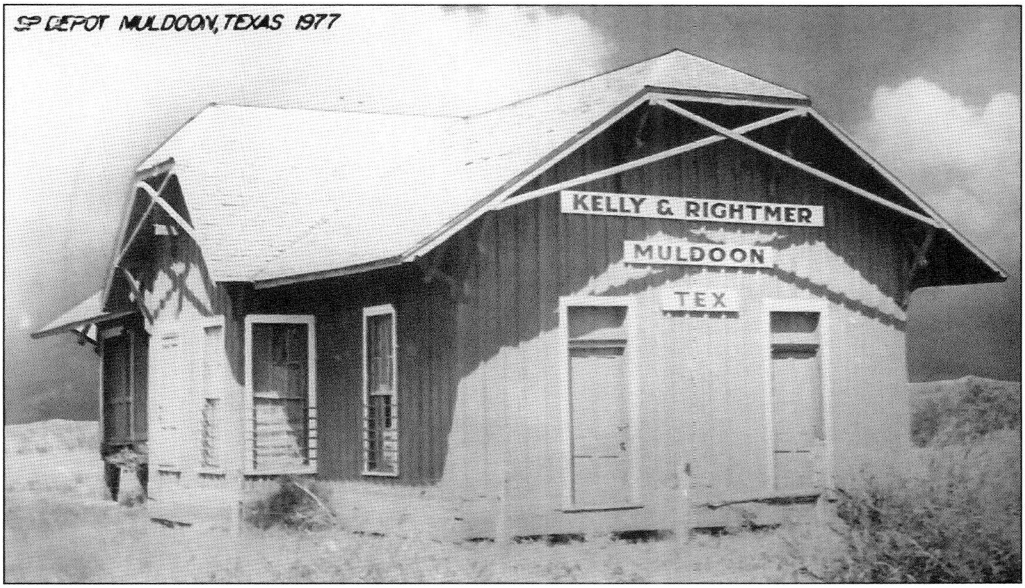

SP DEPOT, MULDOON, TEXAS, 1977. Muldoon, located in southwestern Fayette County, was named after Fr. Miguel Muldoon, who was the spiritual leader of Stephen F. Austin's colony. Muldoon was settled long after its namesake had left the stage; it was platted in 1886, after the Waco branch of the San Antonio & Aransas Pass Railway came through, connecting Flatonia to West Point. The depot pictured was Muldoon's station on that line. (Author's collection.)

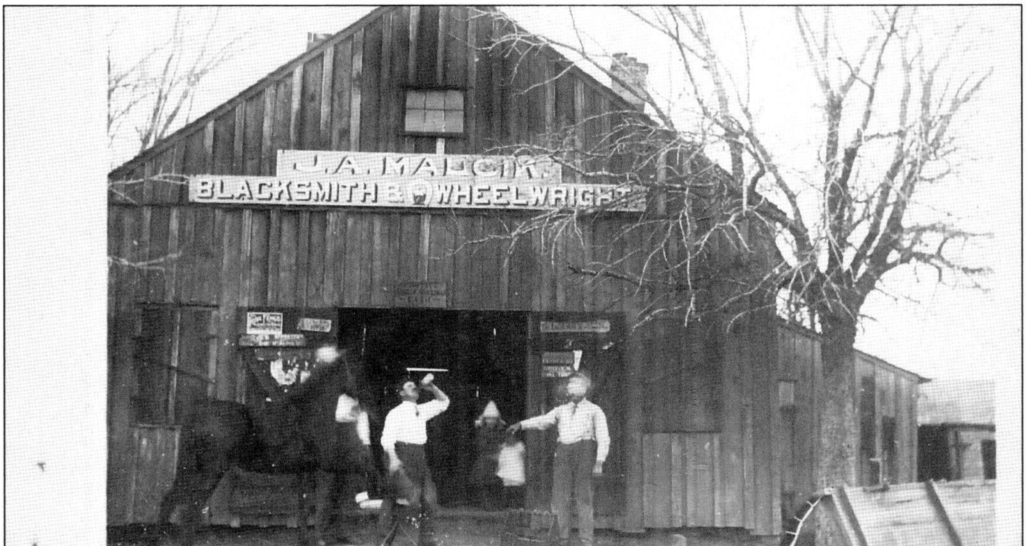

J.A. MALCIK BLACKSMITH & WHEELWRIGHT. Settled in 1852 by Starks and Arthur "Pod" Cockrill, of Missouri, Cistern was once known as Whiteside Prairie and Milton. It was then called Cockrill's Hill, after the Cockrill brothers. It was finally named Cistern in 1857, when a post office name was needed and the large, aboveground cistern at the Cockrill store proved to be it. In the 1880s, Czechs began to supplant the earlier Anglo settlers. John Anton Malcik was one of these Czech settlers; he ran the blacksmith and wheelwright shop shown here. (E.A. Arnim Archives & Museum/Ebelle Malcik Morrill collection.)